THE
Good Housekeeping
BOOK OF
CHILD CARE

INCLUDING PARENTING ADVICE, HEALTH
CARE, AND CHILD DEVELOPMENT
FOR NEWBORNS TO PRETEENS

THE

Good Housekeeping

BOOK OF

CHILD CARE

INCLUDING PARENTING ADVICE,
HEALTH CARE, AND CHILD DEVELOPMENT
FOR NEWBORNS TO PRETEENS

HEARST BOOKS • NEW YORK

GOOD HOUSEKEEPING
Editor-in-Chief Ellen Levine

Medical Editor Gary Edelstein, M.D.; Instructor in Pediatrics, Columbia University College of Physicians and Surgeons; Assistant Attending Pediatrician, Babies' and Children's Hospital

Publisher's Note:
Throughout this book, the pronouns "he" and "she" refer to both sexes,
except where information applies specifically to a boy or a girl.

Produced by ST. REMY PRESS INC.
Publisher Kenneth Winchester
President and CEO Fernand Lecoq
President and COO Pierre Léveillé
Vice-president, Finance Natalie Watanabe

Senior Editor Brian Parsons
Art Director Odette Sévigny
Editorial Contributors Alfred LeMaitre, Elizabeth Lewis,
    Garet Markvoort, Dianne Thomas
Designer Chantal Bilodeau
Managing Editor Carolyn Jackson
Managing Art Director Diane Denoncourt
Production Manager Michelle Turbide

The Library of Congress has cataloged a previous edition of this title.

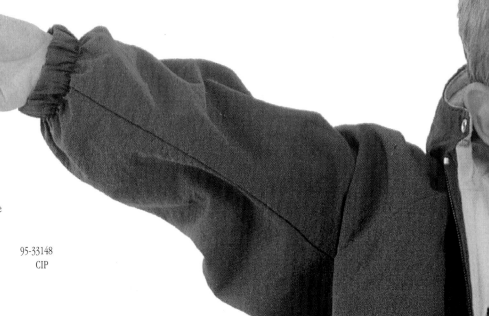

Library of Congress Cataloging-in-Publication Data
The Good Housekeeping illustrated book of child care:
from newborn to preteen—1st ed.
    p.   cm.
Includes index.
ISBN: 0-688-13142-5
1. Child rearing. 2. Parenting. I. Good Housekeeping Institute
(New York, N.Y.)
HQ769.G669   1995
649'.1—dc20
                                        95-33148
                                        CIP

Paperback ISBN 0-688-17547-3
Printed in the United States of America
First Paperback Edition 2000
1 2 3 4 5 6 7 8 9 10

FOREWORD

Taking care of children is one of life's most delightful and challenging experiences; it draws on all our reserves of knowledge and plumbs the depths of our capacity to love. Yet, no matter how much we know or how sound our instincts may be, occasions will arise when more information, a different point of view, or a simple word of reassurance is all we need to feel we are doing the right thing. We hope this book will provide parents with just that extra measure of expertise and encouragement.

Always specific about every stage of your child's development—from infancy to early adolescence—the book encompasses the basics of maintaining wellness and details treatment in the event of illness or medical emergency. It offers a wealth of information that clearly illustrates the relevant issues in your child's physical, psychological, and social development. Regardless of the topic under discussion—whether it is language acquisition, nutrition, toilet training, perception, preparing for puberty, or the formation of identity—the authors have taken special care to emphasize the importance of being in tune with your child's own rhythms and pace. Observing and being sensitive to what your child needs and desires will go a long way toward providing him or her with the very best of care. Ultimately, nothing is more important than simply loving and enjoying our children for all the qualities that make them unique, interesting, and worthy as people.

Ellen Levine,
Editor-in-Chief

CONTENTS

THE HEALTHY CHILD: WELLNESS BASICS 10

FROM BABY TO TODDLER: NEWBORN TO TWO 40

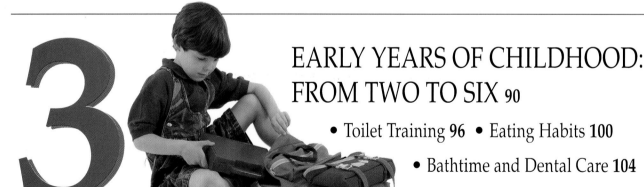

EARLY YEARS OF CHILDHOOD: FROM TWO TO SIX 90

PARENTING
AND TODAY'S FAMILY

Wrinkled, soft, and cuddly, your newborn baby plumbs the very depths of your capacity for love as though signposts pointed the way. Her well-being is paramount to you, and as you wonder how you ever had a full life without her, you also may feel overwhelmed by the awesome responsibility she represents.

Although you're a new parent—which every baby, not just the first, makes you—you'll be amazed at how the knowledge of what to do comes naturally to you most of the time. For all of the helpful, well-meaning advice you may obtain on caring for him, nothing can substitute for the wisdom and insights you gain from being with him. You're the one who knows best his

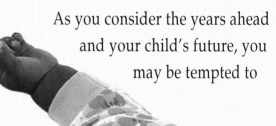

habits, the meaning of his smiles and cries, and what he really needs when he asks for something he wants. This understanding, so vital to his upbringing, evolves automatically out of the patience and imagination that are born of your unconditional love.

As you consider the years ahead and your child's future, you may be tempted to conjure up an image of how you want her to be when she grows up. You might think that by working backwards, you'll be able to figure out ways of making your vision come true for her. But you'll quickly discover that while there are simple steps to follow in teaching her how to care for her teeth, there are no such easy, straightforward paths for you to take to be assured of her growing up into a fulfilled, loving, and responsible adult.

Take comfort in the unpredictability of the future. Let tomorrow's vagaries sharpen the present's adventure and ease the pressure you may feel to be perfect. If you just make the effort to be the best parent to your child that you can be day by day, you won't disappoint him or yourself. Don't be afraid of making mistakes; they're chances to improve your parenting.

Your parenting circumstances may not be the same as the ones you grew up in, but there's no reason to feel you're depriving your child. No matter how different his childhood is from your own, there is at least one constant: He needs to be loved and know he is loved just as you did. No one can convey that message to him better than you. From your loving words, affectionate hugs, and attentive listening to his ideas, he'll develop a strong sense of his self-worth. From your joy at his triumphs and your sympathy with his troubles, he'll acquire an enduring sense of his special value as a unique human being.

1 THE HEALTHY CHILD

WELLNESS BASICS

The healthy child is one who feels good about himself, his family, and his place in the world. While there's no overstating your importance to his physical growth and development, what he also needs from you is infinitely more incalculable. You're his mainstay during these vulnerable years; from you he'll derive his belief in his own worth and his faith in life's myriad possibilities.

Parents, especially first-timers, revel in the uniqueness of their baby and take endless interest in the minute details of his well-being. This fosters feelings of self-worth that are essential to a child's healthy development.

All school-age children compare themselves—seeing how they measure up to peers helps shape their identity. But learning about their own intrinsic worth is just as vital.

The loving relationship between grandparent and child is a pivotal one, strengthening a youngster's sense of belonging.

"Look what I just did!" Her days will be filled with exciting new discoveries and advances, each one—especially during toilet training—deserving its own accolade.

Children learn a variety of skills as they take on everyday projects, such as baking a cake or hemming a doll's dress. The satisfaction she gains from accomplishing it on her own will give her confidence to tackle the next project.

THE ROLE OF PARENT

From the moment you discover that you're going to become a parent, you'll be caught up in a lifelong effort to be the best parent you can be. Over the years, you'll likely find that the process taps into your every known strength and weakness—and several you didn't know you possessed. Sometimes, caring for your child will come naturally; at other times, you'll have to think long and hard about what to do next. You may feel confused at the outset because you don't have all the answers, only to discover as you muddle through that no one else has them either. Parenting is something we all learn by experience, through trial and error. As such, it is likely to be the most consuming and rewarding role you will ever play in your life.

SELF-AWARENESS

Good parenting evolves from a curious alchemy of intuition, instinct, and intelligent awareness. Take time to step back occasionally and examine your approach. It helps to know why you react to certain situations the way you do. A little self-knowledge can help you become a better parent—and to be a bit more forgiving of your imperfections.

Parenting Expectations

If you are like most expectant parents, you'll start out with a preconceived notion of what becoming a parent is all about. Depending on your personal history, your expectations may get in the way of good parenting. Many parents feel inadequate at first. They want so much to be perfect and to raise the perfect child that reality comes as a crushing blow. Give yourself the freedom to make mistakes; it's perfectly normal to get frustrated, angry, or feel at a loss—and not only when raising your first child. Each child is different and will go through a multitude of phases before reaching the age of independence. And while it's up to you to

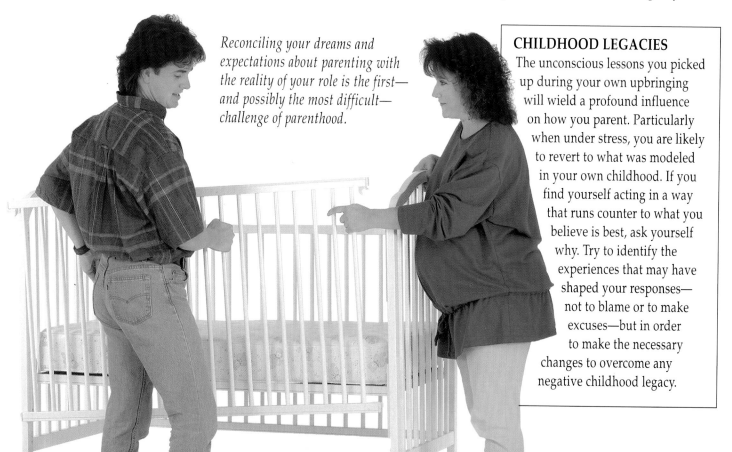

Reconciling your dreams and expectations about parenting with the reality of your role is the first— and possibly the most difficult— challenge of parenthood.

CHILDHOOD LEGACIES

The unconscious lessons you picked up during your own upbringing will wield a profound influence on how you parent. Particularly when under stress, you are likely to revert to what was modeled in your own childhood. If you find yourself acting in a way that runs counter to what you believe is best, ask yourself why. Try to identify the experiences that may have shaped your responses— not to blame or to make excuses—but in order to make the necessary changes to overcome any negative childhood legacy.

Scribbling on walls or furniture can provoke a range of responses. An overly strict parent might spank or yell; an overly permissive parent might hesitate to interfere at all for fear of stifling creativity.

Calmly explain the consequences of scribbling where he shouldn't and direct the child to draw on paper. This way you'll make clear what kind of behavior is inappropriate, while offering an acceptable alternative.

tailor your techniques to the child and to her stage of development, your child is remarkably resilient. The loving spirit of your actions will help temper occasional mistakes in your parenting.

Parenting Styles

It is hardly surprising that today's parents worry about what tack to take in raising their children. Many children live in homes with either one parent or two working parents. And children are exposed to a bewildering—even frightening—array of risks and challenges at an early age. Although by no means a guaranteed formula, a child-centered approach that is loving and nurturing creates an all-embracing context. Treating your child with dignity should be your guiding principle. When you set clearly defined limits and high, yet reasonable, standards of behavior, your child will grow to understand what you expect, will learn self-control, and will absorb your family's moral values. Convey your respect and trust by giving her the freedom to take initiative within those limits. And by making

punishment a logical, reasonable consequence of deliberate wrongdoing, you are likely to gain compliance based on understanding and respect. If you come to a point where intuition and common sense don't seem to be enough, remember that you are not the first parent to

have reached this point. Libraries have books on parenting and child development, community centers, schools, and churches offer parenting workshops, and your pediatrician has had a wide range of experiences; don't hesitate to make the most of the help available.

Youngsters need unconditional love from their parents. This creates an unshakeable bond that allows a child to reconcile his need to be nurtured with his desire to be independent.

If your toddler loves to decorate the floor with his food, you may have to provide an alternative that is at least half as much fun in order to win the battle.

CHILD AWARENESS

Most experts agree that the key to good parenting lies in being able to see the world through a child's eyes. Of course, you should learn all you can about each stage of child development, but it's just as vital to remember how you once perceived the world and your own parents. As long as you keep in mind your child's perspective, you're more likely to develop a greater sensitivity to what may sometimes seem like unreasonable demands and needs.

A Shifting Perspective

Each time you put yourself in your child's shoes, you'll gain a fresh look at her needs. When she's an infant, you can see how she craves your warmth and touch as you feed, change, wash, and lull her to sleep. As a toddler, she needs your reassuring presence and the routines you set to give an essential structure to her life and to enable her to assert her independence. When she's a preschooler, she looks to you, her first teacher, to learn the social skills that will enable her to form meaningful relationships as she grows. And when she reaches school age, her world broadening, her relationships becoming increasingly complex, she needs you to guide her as she reaches outward and to console her when she stumbles. At each stage, your child will need to know where she stands. Clear, firm, and fair limits help a child develop self-control and pave the way for a gradual internalizing of moral values. Your support nourishes her sense of confidence, allowing her to move closer to autonomy. One of the built-in ironies of parenting is that the better you do your job, the less your child needs you. One thing remains constant, however, despite all the changes in your child's perspective over the years: She's always going to need to know that

Respect your child's complex and evolving individuality. Labeling him as "a loner" or "shy" will only lead him into a limited definition of himself.

All children—not just girls—love fussing over their dolls. This kind of play gives them a chance to act out fantasies and fears, as well as to internalize the ways you care for them.

FIRST ROLE MODEL

From the start, your child will do most of her early learning through imitation—and her first model will be you. Be aware that she is picking up more than skills and abilities—important though these will be to her subsequent learning and development. She's also absorbing subtle nuances of expression and attitude that will exert a lasting influence on who she becomes; her ideas about gender and gender roles; her moral values; how she'll deal with feelings such as anger, sadness, and fear; and, of course, how she'll go about raising her own children.

Game-playing develops social skills and may help middle and youngest children to assert themselves with a bossy eldest sibling.

Twins—especially identical twins—may look and sound alike, but each is still a unique individual. Avoid dressing them alike or expecting them to act the same way. Recognize and promote each twin's individuality by organizing opportunities for them to develop their own separate interests.

Raising an only child presents quite a different challenge. An only child tends to miss out on the day-to-day learning of social skills from siblings and may need to be encouraged to play with other children. You might find that you have to take special pains to encourage her to be thoughtful of others. It is easy for an only child to grow overly dependent on parents; you may need to spur her on to try things on her own. Try to avoid letting an only child become the center of the universe—you may create a "spoiled brat" in the process. And be careful not to pin all your hopes and dreams on her—that burden is too heavy for any child to carry.

there's at least one person who will forever be passionately committed to her well-being.

A Place in the Family

Since your child's view of the world is influenced by how you react to her, try to treat each child in your family according to her age and her own needs rather than to her position—the first-born, the middle one, the "baby," one of twins, or an only child. Eldest children, for example, often are saddled with too much responsibility too soon and lose out on what should be carefree early years. Youngest children may be given too little responsibility too late and may remain "babies" all their lives. Middle children, in particular, might need extra reassurance. They need to be reminded that they're just as important as the others. And avoid making comparisons between older and younger children; each child needs to be valued for herself.

Imagining how your child may be perceiving your actions might give you an extra bit of needed patience.

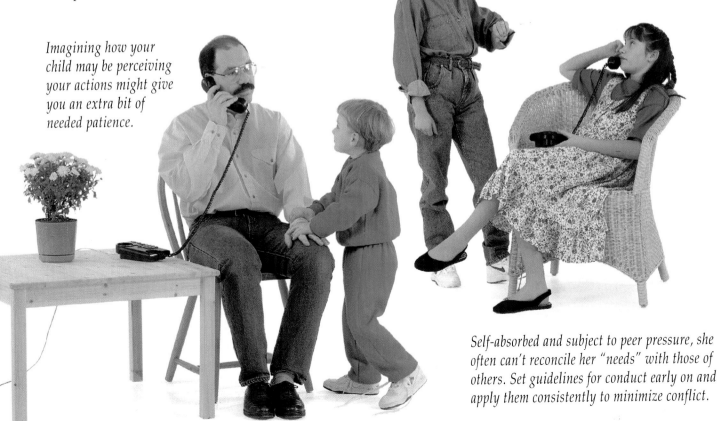

Self-absorbed and subject to peer pressure, she often can't reconcile her "needs" with those of others. Set guidelines for conduct early on and apply them consistently to minimize conflict.

DEVELOPMENT STAGES

One of the chief joys of parenthood is witnessing the transformation of your tiny, helpless infant into a young person with his own thoughts, emotions, and unique personality. Occurring in a continuous series of small, barely noticeable steps—punctuated by major milestones—this seeming miracle encompasses not only his actual physical growth and changing appearance, but also his ever-increasing capacity to think, understand, and communicate ideas. A fascinating psychological portrait is taking shape, too—a complete interweaving of personality, behavior, and emotions that will ultimately affect his self-image and his relationships. Understanding these steps and stages will enhance your pleasure at his emerging individuality.

PHYSICAL GROWTH

Your child will more than double his weight and height over his first two years. Such rapid growth won't be seen again until he hits the growth spurt that accompanies puberty. He'll reach half his adult height by the time he's three and each year from five to 10, he'll probably gain two to three inches and six to seven pounds. At birth, your child's head is almost one quarter the length of his body, and his arms and legs seem small. Because physical development takes place from top to bottom and from the torso to the extremities, his head grows more rapidly than the rest of the body during his first four months. His proportions will adjust until, at 12, his shape is more adult.

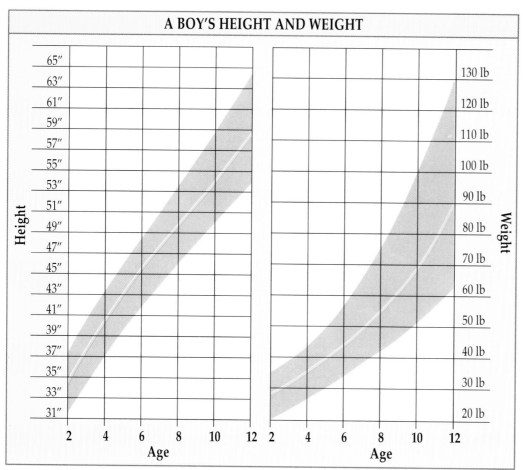

A BOY'S HEIGHT AND WEIGHT

These charts show the "average" and range of normal measurements that you can expect for your child.

Brain, Bones, and Muscles

Your child's physical and mental development follow a predictable sequence of biological steps. Even the simplest feats such as eating or hearing depend on the development of the necessary brain apparatus. Some parts of the brain—those that govern breathing, swallowing, and hunger, for example—are ready to function independently at birth. Others—such as those that control speech and hearing—require more development before they are fully operational. What's still missing at birth are the countless nerve fibers that connect certain brain cells and, in some areas, the insulating coat that sheathes these fibers and keeps the brain impulses from dissipating. As the connections are forged and the process of insulation takes place, he'll master the corresponding skills, from crawling and walking to speech and conceptualizing. By the time your child is 10, his brain growth is 95 percent complete.

Like his brain, your baby's bones and muscles continue to develop long after birth. Soft and malleable, many of the 350 bones are made of tough tissue, or cartilage. Both bone and cartilage grow rapidly, getting longer and heavier as calcium and new bone cells are deposited. Some bones fuse after birth—again the process starts at the head—until at puberty, the child has the 210 bones of the adult skeleton.

Muscle and bone growth contribute greatly to the dramatic weight gains of your child's first years. While the approximately 600 muscles in the human body are already present at birth, they make up only 20 percent of a baby's weight. By adulthood, those muscles account for 40 percent of body weight.

TEETH

Your child's teeth begin to develop before he's born. The crowns of his 20 primary, or "baby," teeth become fully formed in his gums shortly after birth and his 32 permanent teeth are already present as seeds in his jawbone. After birth, the roots of his teeth develop, pushing the crowns up through his gums. While his baby teeth are still coming in, the crowns of his permanent teeth are beginning to develop. The order in which teeth appear follows a set pattern, although when the teeth emerge can vary. His first tooth generally will appear at six to 10 months and his first permanent tooth at six to eight years. By 12, all teeth are in—except wisdom teeth.

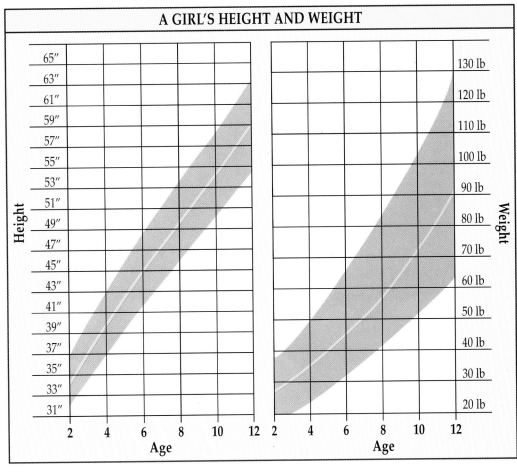

A GIRL'S HEIGHT AND WEIGHT

SKILLS AND ABILITIES

During the first six years of his life, your child will master the basic motor skills that will allow him to do things for himself. However, while his ability to move, eat, wash, use the toilet, and dress by himself will reflect an amazing acquisition of physical skills, his voyage to self-reliance will be only partially complete. He'll need the next six years before he'll be able to consistently combine those abilities with reasoned, mature judgment.

Reflex, Motion, and Movement

When your newborn responds to a slight pressure on his cheek by turning his head and "rooting" for a breast, he's moving reflexively, instinctively responding to stimulation. Over the course of his first few months, such reflex responses will disappear as his maturing brain and developing muscles allow him to take charge of his body and its movements. His control follows the course of his physical development. At first, his movements will be broad and inefficient. But, in time, the flailing arm and jerky leg motions of the infant will gradually evolve into the purposeful grasp and stiff gait of the toddler.

As your child approaches his first birthday, his actions will become more and more purposeful. He'll move with intent when he crawls into your waiting arms. Controlled movements require the use of large muscle groups and reflect an important advance in gross motor skills. Your child's fine motor skills are also developing, which allow him, for instance, to curl his fingers around yours. With time and practice, the precise and dexterous small muscle movements of his hands and fingers will enable him to write and manipulate a pair of scissors.

Keeping Step

Many of his very early motor skills come about as a by-product of his neurophysiological development. But as he

---

A UNIQUE PACE

Your child will develop in a predictable, orderly pattern. However, he will do so at his own pace. You may worry about whether he's normal for his age—especially if the neighbor's daughter is two months younger and already walking while your baby is still exploring the world on all fours. But keep in mind that there is a wide variation within so-called "normal" development, and your child may just naturally proceed at a slower pace.

Pushing him into something before he's ready will do more harm than good. However, once he has acquired a new skill, make sure you give him plenty of encouragement and lots of opportunities to practice.

Occasionally, slow skill development does indicate an underlying problem. If you have any nagging concerns, consult your pediatrician who will assess your child's development according to the norms for his age.

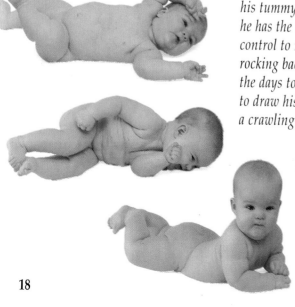

Several weeks ago, this six-month-old managed to roll from his tummy onto his back. Now, he has the necessary muscle control to roll back. He'll enjoy rocking back and forth, and in the days to come may learn to draw his knees up into a crawling position.

At five years of age, most children start to master skipping. Developmentally, this means that they are able to coordinate their large muscle groups. It also means the balancing mechanism in the inner ear has developed.

gets older, skills increasingly will be acquired through learning and practice. Over time, he'll build a sophisticated array of abilities that will allow him to take on full responsibility for himself. All too soon, you'll be hard-pressed to remember how he had to struggle to button up his pajama top when he was three, or how at five, he had trouble tying his shoes.

Show your child how to use his abilities to further his self-reliance, but be careful to match the task to his physical capabilities as well as to his cognitive and emotional levels. Be sensitive to his readiness to take another step toward self-sufficiency—it's critical to both your relationship and your peace of mind. Timing is everything. If you can recognize when your two-year-old is ready to begin toilet training, it'll save you both a lot of grief. If you correctly assess your eight-year-old's maturity and common sense, you'll know when he's ready to be shown how to safely negotiate the route home from school. By helping to ease your child into each new stage, you'll nurture his confidence in his own ability to tackle new challenges.

SELF-SUFFICIENCY	
Age	Characteristic Stages
Newborn to 2 years	Moves from total dependence to needing your help to get most things done; needs supervision at all times. Learns to walk. Shows understanding of language; starts to communicate verbally. Begins to feed self and undress independently. Communicates discomfort when wet or dirty.
2 to 6 years	Learns to eat, wash, brush teeth, get dressed without help. Progresses from minimal control to full control over toilet needs. Imagines the future, remembers the past; chronology still fuzzy. Learns to consider alternatives, understand consequences, and make sensible, simple decisions. Sense of risk distorted; can't be expected to follow safety rules completely or consistently.
6 to 12 years	Hones basic motor skills. Accomplishes all primary self-care tasks. Learns to use money, tell direction and time, and apply such concepts to his activities. Demonstrates good memory skills; can follow complicated instructions. Recognizes danger; can problem-solve in familiar situations, but still needs reminding and guidance.

A seemingly simple task, tying shoes involves dexterity and hand-eye coordination that is usually beyond a child until he's at least four years old.

Your child won't be ready to begin using the toilet properly until the muscles surrounding the bladder and bowels are sufficiently developed in size and strength— usually around the age of two.

As a toddler, she learned to grasp a crayon like a hammer. A year later, she was able to hold a pen more like an adult. By six, her dexterity had increased enough to allow her to print words and begin to define the details of her drawing.

THINKING AND UNDERSTANDING

Even more miraculous than the acquisition of physical skills and abilities is your child's cognitive development—the rapid growth of his ability to think and understand. A complex interaction of his own perceptions of the world, his memory of events and experiences, his ability to reason, and his imagination, cognition begins simply—with the recognition of your face and the sound of your voice. It seems these milestones are barely marked before they're eclipsed.

Caring for a pet can help a child develop a sense of responsibility.

Perceiving the World

Your child's cognition originates in his five senses—in what he sees, hears, tastes, smells, and touches. Although all the senses are present at birth, they are not completely developed. Nor is your newborn able to use his senses in combination or distinguish among them. Very rapidly, however, your child acquires the ability to organize the information constantly being received through his senses.

Playing a pivotal role is memory. Learning is impossible without the ability to retain information and retrieve it for later use. Even when your baby is

And who are you? This six-month-old sees the face of a baby in the mirror, but doesn't yet recognize the face as his own.

just days old, he can recognize sights, sounds, smells, and tastes. Within two or three months, he will be able to remember much of what he has learned—even without the physical stimulus. By the age of two, he may

discover how to enhance his memory through repetition; muttering where he hides a favorite toy helps him remember where it is later. As he's exposed to new experiences, his knowledge base and memory capacity will increase.

Reaching Out to the World

Cooing and babbling mark your baby's first attempts to verbalize his needs, desires, and feelings. These sounds

Last-minute questions before sleep may be more than just a delaying tactic. Bedtime grants a respite to the preschooler, who now has a chance to ponder on some of the exciting things he has seen and done that day.

SELF-PERCEPTION	
Age	**Characteristic Stages**
Newborn to 2 years	Gradually recognizes physical self; begins to see self both as different from and similar to others.
2 to 6 years	Begins to make distinction between public and private self. Learns to describe physical self and feelings. Evaluates own skills and starts comparing self with others. Interprets and is affected by what others think of him.
6 to 12 years	Sees own identity as unchanging and constant. Becomes increasingly aware of personality traits of self and others. Distinguishes multiple aspects of self. Perceives individuality as the result of thoughts and feelings, as well as actions. Realizes that he can keep own thoughts private. Definition of self includes values, beliefs, thoughts, and motivation.

Sorting toys helps a child develop an understanding of categories and classifications.

A PERSONAL WORLD VIEW

Some of the ideas children have about the world seem a long way from reality. Many preschoolers, for instance, respond to inanimate objects as though they were alive, endowing the family car or a toy with human traits. Your child may have an unshakeable faith in the power of ritual and take unusual measures to keep a familiar routine intact. He may tend to interpret your words literally and might be convinced that it's his existence that makes the world go around. Such personal and quirky views may alternately amuse and confound you and are not necessarily a cause for concern. But there are times when your child will need your help to sort things out. Quite often, a child will jump to the wrong conclusions when two things happen almost simultaneously. Try not to make fun of him: Remember, he is just developing connections between cause and effect, so it may seem very logical to him that one thing is caused by the other.

signify an important milestone in the development of language. In fact, he has been learning about language since he first learned to separate your voice from the tumult of sounds around him. Soon after, he discovered his crying could affect your response to him and he began to consciously refine the noises he made. Now, he makes more and more adventurous forays into intelligible communication. Feedback from you gives him the information he needs for continued language development. Partly spontaneous, partly learned, his language skills mirror the astounding advances he is making in cognitive development. When he starts to identify himself as "me," for example, you can see he has discovered that he's separate from you; later, his how and why questions will signal a reasoning mind at work. Don't underestimate your child; he understands far more than he's able to communicate.

Stepping into the World

The school-age child is beginning to make sense of the world beyond the familiar setting of home. Though his view of the world may be incomplete, it nonetheless takes into account concepts as sophisticated as time, money, and work. For several years, he has been refining his understanding of cause and effect—the underpinning of logical thought—and is putting it to work in increasingly subtle and complex ways. Biological maturation, experience, and education all have their place in influencing how early your child will begin to think logically. Certainly by the time he's seven or eight, you will notice evidence that your child can draw conclusions based on his own experiences and then apply them to other situations. He'll find alternative solutions to problems, and be able to assess the possibilities of success or failure—essential life skills.

By the time he's of school age, your child is able to focus his energies and thoughts on tasks that require patience and a delicate touch.

PERSONALITY AND BEHAVIOR

How your child behaves is the result of a complex mix of his personality and life experiences. While your child has an inborn tendency to think and feel in a certain way, these traits will be tempered by the kind of parent you are.

All children, however, go through a similar series of behavioral stages as they grow. Understanding them will help you to modify your expectations and respond to your child appropriately.

Traits and Temperament
Your child is born with a certain genetically programmed set of traits that will determine his innate style of responding to the world around him. Some of these traits—shyness, creativity, and conformity, for instance—have been found to be more genetically influenced than such things as ambition, aggression, and orderliness.

However, personality development does not stop with your child's genes. On the one hand, his inherited traits provide a basic script for his personality. On the other, his environment and his experiences refine, mold, and modify the script, determining how intensely each trait will be expressed. Although his temperament governs how he responds to the world—shyly or exuberantly, for instance—his response, expressed as behavior, will substantially affect the way he is treated by others.

School-age boys may engage in a friendly arm wrestle to see how they stack up against each other—and along the way, further refine their sense of who they are.

And this, in turn, will influence all his subsequent behavior.

Patterns and Stages
As your child grows, you may notice a pattern emerging in his behavior. At times, he may seem completely at odds with his environment and himself as he grapples with his own rapid development. Following such periods, he may appear to consolidate his learning and be much more in harmony with the world around him.

It may seem to you that every "easy" period is followed by a more "difficult" one. When your child is about 10, for

With most of the lessons of learning to share behind her, the well-adjusted five-year-old enjoys being an older sister.

A CHILD'S SELF-ESTEEM
Your child's sense of personal worth begins to take shape from birth, when your influence is paramount. There's no simple formula to follow, and what works with one child may not necessarily work with another. However, keep in mind the following suggestions as you adapt your parenting style to match your child's needs:

• Give your attention generously; talk to him and listen to what he says.
• Let him know that his thoughts and opinions are valued and respected.

• Acknowledge his right to his own feelings; show him ways that he can express them while being considerate of the rights of others.
• Celebrate his unique abilities and personal accomplishments.
• Provide him with opportunities to succeed and praise his successes.
• Give him the freedom to fail—teach him that frustration and disappointment are part of the human condition.
• Establish clear and fair limits of acceptable behavior.
• Love and appreciate him for himself.

Children model their behavior after those who care for them; it's not enough to preach good behavior, adults must practice it, too.

Your child's contrary nature during the so-called "terrible twos"—the peak period of resistance—may frequently result in tears and tantrums.

While his boundless energy may be exhausting at times, you may find yourself admiring—and catching—his infectious enthusiasm for life.

example, you may find yourself enjoying an unrivaled position in his affections and be reassured by the confidence he displays as he tackles the daily challenges of school and friendships. A year later, you may find yourself out of favor with the same child who now is relentless in his criticisms of how you dress, talk, and behave.

Such stages may persist for weeks or even months, and you may have to adjust your parenting style accordingly; what worked with your happy-go-lucky 18-month-old may have no effect six months later, when he's in the full throes of the "terrible twos." As common as some of these behavioral patterns may be, keep in mind that your child has his own personal stamp, shaped by his rate of development and his unique personality. He may go through these stages sooner than most or later than most. He may take longer to emerge from a disruptive stage or he may sail through with no trouble. Your job will be to remain flexible and sensitive to his changing needs.

SELF-IDENTITY	
Age	**Characteristic Stages**
Newborn to 2 years	Thrives on predictability; sensitive to disruptions in routine. Forms intense bonds with parents; anxious when separated from them and wary of strangers. Often takes risks to satisfy curiosity; investigates people and explores objects with great enthusiasm.
2 to 6 years	Asserts independence; may display extreme mood swings. Easily frustrated; may be impulsive and stubborn. Separates more easily from parents; plays more cooperatively. Seeks to conform to please others. May demonstrate strong attachment to parent of opposite sex.
6 to 12 years	Displays increasing signs of self-control; is realistic. Reflects on own thoughts and feelings; brash exterior may contrast with inner sensitivity. Values friends more and more as moves away from family circle. Attachment to parents reflects changing sense of self; progresses from unquestioning devotion to critical appraisal. Develops a sense of community.

NUTRITION AND FITNESS

Your child's physical, psychological, and intellectual well-being, particularly during the critical first 12 years of growth, depends to a great extent on the food she eats and the physical exercise she performs. Meals should be based on foods that supply the proper balance of proteins, carbohydrates, fats, minerals, vitamins, and the most essential nutrient of all—water. She also needs to exercise regularly to maintain and strengthen her muscles, heart, and lungs. By choosing a healthy diet and appropriate exercise for her while she is still dependent on you, you will be instilling a sound attitude toward fitness and food that will last a lifetime.

DIET ESSENTIALS

Children, like adults, need a minimum of 50 different nutrients in their diet in order to grow and stay healthy. When properly combined, these nutrients form a complex web of relationships that function together to give your child the nutrition she needs. Of these, 10 are considered major nutrients: proteins; carbohydrates; fats; the minerals calcium and iron; and vitamins A, C, thiamine, riboflavin, and niacin. When you develop a healthy diet around these nutrients, your child automatically gets the other 40 along with them. Never overlook the importance of water; every cell in her body depends on water to bring it the nutrients it needs to function and to carry wastes away.

Food Basics

Your child needs proteins for growth, normal body functioning, and disease prevention. She relies on carbohydrates to fill her most immediate energy needs: Simple carbohydrates, or sugars, provide a quick boost and complex carbohydrates, or starches, supply more lasting energy. The concentrated energy available in fats is used to keep her immune system functioning properly and to protect vital tissues and organs. It also facilitates the absorption of fat-soluble vitamins A, D, E, and K, which can be stored in body fat and used later—unlike the water-soluble vitamins C and B complex, which need daily replenishment.

Both vitamins and minerals are essential to her growth and development; vitamins produce the chemical reactions that transform food into energy, make cells, and maintain physical systems. Minerals serve a variety of functions, from building bones to aiding the transmission of nerve impulses.

Proteins are found in a wide variety of foods, including cheese, eggs, meat, fish, poultry, potatoes, legumes, grains, and nuts.

Sugars are found in fruits and vegetables, and in foods containing refined sugar such as cookies, cake, and candy.

IMPORTANT VITAMINS AND MINERALS

Type	Some Functions	Good Sources
Vitamin A	Maintains skin, hair, gums; promotes bone growth, night and color vision; helps fight infection.	Citrus fruits; orange and dark green leafy vegetables; low-fat dairy foods; fortified cereals; eggs; liver.
Vitamin C	Maintains gums; fights infection; assists healing; aids in absorption of calcium and iron.	Melons, citrus fruits and juices; broccoli, cabbage, peppers, potatoes; breast milk and formula.
Vitamin B1 (Thiamine)	Aids carbohydrate absorption; promotes functioning of nervous system and a normal appetite.	Lean meats; nuts and seeds; fortified cereals and grains; seafood; brewer's yeast.
Vitamin B2 (Riboflavin)	Contributes to healthy skin and eye tissues; promotes good vision in bright lights.	Dark green leafy vegetables; fortified cereals and grains; meat and poultry; low-fat dairy products.
Niacin	Contributes to use of energy and carbohydrates, and to production of fat cells; aids digestion.	Liver, poultry, and seafood; fortified cereals and grains; peanuts; brewer's yeast.
Calcium	Builds bones and teeth; essential for muscle and nerve functioning, blood clotting.	Milk and milk products; sardines and canned salmon with bones; greens, including kale and collard.
Iron	Vital to hemoglobin formation, fetal growth, and wound healing; prevents iron-deficiency anemia.	Liver, kidneys, and red meats; fortified cereals; egg yolks; dried beans and peas; dried fruits.

Fiber—essential to proper digestion—is found in carbohydrates such as whole-grain breads and cereals, brown rice, fruits with skins, and beans.

Carbohydrates are found in vegetables, fruits, rice, and bread.

Fats are found in oils, nuts, and seeds, and in animal products such as meat, butter, cream, whole milk, and most cheeses.

A BALANCED DIET

To feed your child properly, you need to know which foods she needs and how much is enough. The information here will tell you about the essential food groups, and the accompanying charts will give you an idea of how much to feed her. Start your child on a healthy diet from the time she first takes solids. When you introduce new foods, be patient and offer them a little at a time. Taste and eye appeal may be your child's only concern, but if you have also made her meals nutritionally sound, she'll likely maintain a healthy diet in later years.

AGE-APPROPRIATE PORTIONS

Serve your toddler a portion that is equal to about one quarter of an adult serving.

Serve your preschooler a portion that is about one half of an adult serving.

Serve your school-age child a portion that ranges from three quarters to a full adult portion.

Food Choices

While your child is an infant, all her nutritional needs will be met by either breast milk or formula. However, once she starts eating solid foods, your role in guiding her food choices is crucial. One useful guideline to a balanced diet is the Food Guide Pyramid, shown at right. It divides foods into five essential groups: bread, cereal, rice, and pasta; vegetables; fruits; milk, yogurt, and cheese; and meat, poultry, fish, legumes, eggs, and nuts. The sixth group contains fats, oils, and sweets, which should be eaten only rarely.

Though infants and toddlers need more fat than adults to foster normal growth, children over the age of two should get no more than a third of their calories from fat. However, the food pyramid does not make any distinctions between low-fat and high-fat foods within groups one to five. Whenever possible, opt for a low-fat selection—bread, bagels, or grains rather than croissants or muffins; low-fat yogurt and cheese instead of whole-milk dairy products; lean beef, poultry, or fish rather than sausages and other high-fat meat cuts. This doesn't mean that perennial favorites such as peanut butter, bologna, or ice cream are forbidden. Such foods can be included in her diet, provided that you plan for them and offer lower-fat selections at other meals.

Making Meals

Translating the food pyramid into meals will require a little thought and planning at first. Your job will be easier, though, if you have a few basic cookbooks to work from. Develop a series of weekly menus based on healthy foods to help guide you when you shop for

The Food Guide Pyramid, designed by the U.S. Department of Agriculture, provides the framework for a balanced diet for anyone over the age of two.

Group 2
Vegetables

Group 1
Bread, cereal, rice, and pasta

Group 6
Fats, oils, and sweets, including salad dressings, candy, and butter or margarine

Group 4
Milk, yogurt, and cheese

Group 5
Meat, poultry, fish, legumes, eggs, and nuts

Group 3
Fruits

groceries. Choose fresh ingredients whenever possible; the nutritional value of fruits and vegetables is often lost when they're bottled or canned.

Snacking
Don't forget to include snacks in your child's diet. Children between the ages of two and six need three meals and two or three healthy snacks a day because their stomachs are too small to contain all the food they require in three big meals. Space meals and snacks at least a couple of hours apart so that your child will have a chance to work up a healthy appetite.

Fussy Eaters
The key to a balanced diet is variety—eating as many different foods from the various groups as possible. But children tend to be erratic in their likes and dislikes—falling in and out of love with certain foods, refusing to eat some outright, or wanting to eat one exclusively. Food jags generally don't last very long. And the more strenuously you oppose your child, the more stubborn she will become. Try substituting a food from the same group for the one she hates so that she is offered choices. The more control she has over what she eats, the less likely she is to resist.

DAILY FOOD SERVINGS	
Age	**Recommendations**
2 to 6 years	Group 1: 4 servings Group 2: 3 servings Group 3: 3 servings Group 4: 2 servings for 2- to 4-year-olds; 3 servings for 4- to 6-year-olds Group 5: 2 servings Group 6: sparingly
6 to 12 years	Group 1: at least 6 servings Group 2: 3 to 5 servings Group 3: 2 to 4 servings Group 4: 2 to 3 servings Group 5: 2 to 3 servings Group 6: sparingly

PHYSICAL ACTIVITY

At three, your child seems to have boundless energy and you may think she is active enough. But this is the time to instill a lifelong habit of physical exercise. Studies show that 50 percent of North American children between the ages of five and eight are not getting the exercise they need to develop healthy lungs and hearts and to ward off obesity. Set a good example yourself; show her that exercise is fun, then let her decide which activities she'd enjoy.

Timely Activities

Even before she starts walking, you can encourage exercise by playing actively with her; move and stretch her arms and legs as you are bathing and dressing her. Once she's walking, encourage her to stretch, run, jump, and climb. Fancy equipment isn't necessary. Swimming is an excellent conditioning exercise for all age groups—even babies, as long as they like it. Make sure the water is warm and that your child is never left alone. Avoid introducing skills that are too advanced for her age; three-year-olds can throw a ball, for instance, but not catch or bat it.

Until she's about six, she probably won't be ready for the stress and control required in organized sports. But she can start learning some skills—throwing, catching, and kicking a ball, and skipping. Teach her to do stretching exercises—touching her toes and reaching for the sky—before beginning strenuous play to reduce the risk of injury.

When she begins to move into a more structured physical fitness program, be alert to boredom, frustration, or stress. Many children aren't ready to handle the pressure that accompanies competitive sports until they're at least eight. This doesn't mean that she can't play in a children's baseball or soccer league—just make sure that you choose a team where participation is more important than winning.

Your six- to 12-year-old needs to get 20 minutes to one hour of aerobic exercise three to five days a week to develop a strong, efficient cardiovascular system. Aerobic activities are those that use the body's large muscle groups, raise body temperature, increase heart and breathing rates, and are maintained continuously for several minutes. Strength training, or weight lifting, should be put off until she's 12, unless the program is specifically designed and monitored closely to prevent injury.

COMPETITION

One of the easiest ways to spoil a child's enjoyment of a sport is to push her into serious competition before she's ready. Competitive stress can result in low self-esteem, high anxiety, and may even cause aggressive behavior.

You can reduce the effects of competitive stress by emphasizing her enjoyment of the sport and by giving her plenty of positive encouragement and praise no matter what the result. Teach her that winning or losing is less important than how hard she tried and how much fun she had.

Whether he chooses team sports or prefers activities he can do on his own, the important thing is to stay active year round.

You don't have to be a star athlete to help your child develop good habits. A family frisbee game, a bike ride, or a cross-country hike are all easy and fun ways to exercise.

AGE-APPROPRIATE ACTIVITIES

Start-up Age	Activity	Physical Benefits	Safety
2 to 4 years	Tricycling	Balance and leg strength.	Helmet; supervision required.
	Swimming	Conditioning and coordination.	Constant supervision required.
	Cycling	Overall aerobic conditioning, balance, and leg strength.	Helmet; training wheels until balance and strength assured.
4 to 6 years	Roller-blading	Coordination, endurance, and balance.	Helmet and protective guards for knees, elbows, and wrists.
	Ice skating	Coordination, endurance, and balance.	Helmet.
	Cross-country skiing	Cardiovascular conditioning, endurance, and leg and arm strength.	Warm clothing, and protection for eyes and skin.
	Downhill skiing	Coordination, perceptual skills, balance, and leg and arm strength.	Helmet, warm clothing, and protection for eyes and skin.
6 to 8 years	Soccer	Cardiovascular conditioning, eye-foot and body coordination, endurance, and agility.	Shin guards and shoes with soccer cleats.
	Martial arts	Balance, strength, self-discipline, and body control.	Proper floor surface; loose clothing; headgear may be necessary.
	Gymnastics	Aerobic conditioning, coordination, strength, flexibility, body control, and self-discipline.	Crash pads and careful spotting techniques required; equipment must be well maintained.
	Tee-ball/soft-ball/hardball	Hand-eye coordination, balance, and basic motor skills.	Helmet and face guard when batting and running bases.
	Raquet sports	Cardiovascular conditioning, hand-eye coordination, and body control and conditioning.	Child-size raquets; eye protection for squash or racquetball.
	Basketball	Cardiovascular conditioning, hand-eye and body coordination, and endurance.	Shoes with good traction.
	Ice hockey	Cardiovascular conditioning, coordination, balance, and endurance.	Helmet, mouth guard, face mask, and pads.
	Volleyball	Hand-eye coordination, and upper body and leg strength.	Knee and elbow pads.

MEDICAL CARE

Most of the medical care your child will need for the first dozen years of his life can be handled at home under the guidance of a trusted family doctor or in your pediatrician's office. Make sure you take your child for regular checkups and familiarize yourself with the common childhood illnesses and ailments. Being able to recognize and identify symptoms means that treatment can be started promptly and your child will get well sooner. You may decide to take a first aid and CPR course, but at the very least you should learn simple techniques of at-home nursing care, such as aspirating a clogged nose and taking a temperature. Despite all your care, your child will get sick, but rest assured that most childhood ailments are relatively mild.

HEALTH PROFESSIONALS

Your relationships with the people who care for your child will depend on your trust in their knowledge and expertise. You'll also want to be absolutely sure that they like and respect children, otherwise it'll be difficult for your child to talk freely with them. In turn, you'll need to educate yourself about any special needs your child may have; to do their job well, these health care professionals will require your informed contributions.

Choosing a Doctor
First decide whether you'd prefer a pediatrician, whose specialty is children's medicine, or a family doctor—someone trained in family medicine who can treat both you and your child. If possible, start looking for the right person while you are still pregnant. Compile a list of potential candidates: Consult family, friends, and neighbors for recommendations, or ask your obstetrician. Your childbirth teacher or local hospital also may have suggestions. When narrowing down the list, consider the location of the doctor's office, the doctor's fees, office hours, availability after hours, and group practice support during vacation time. Interview each candidate on your list until you find one that best suits your needs. Go prepared to ask questions about checkup schedules, and find out whether the doctor is willing to answer questions over the phone.

Respect and trust are essential to a good working relationship with your child's doctor. If possible, begin developing this vital rapport before your child is born.

CHECKUP SCHEDULE

Your child's first medical exam should occur within 24 hours of his birth. Have his weight checked two to three weeks later. Further checkups should follow at two, four, six, nine, 12, 15, 18, and 24 months. After the age of two, take him for a checkup at least once a year.

Begin taking him to the dentist to have his teeth examined sometime between two and three years of age. After that, his teeth should be checked every six months or so.

Try to get a sense of whether the doctor's philosophy of child-rearing and health care practices—whether to immunize or not, for instance—is in harmony with your own. Above all, be sure that the doctor you choose inspires your confidence and your trust.

Routine Checkups

At each checkup, the pediatrician will weigh and measure your child. Until he's two, this will include taking the circumference of his head, which provides a rough idea of how the brain is developing. His measurements will be plotted on charts that continue through adolescence so that his growth can be evaluated over a long period of time. Your child's heart, lungs, ears, mouth, internal organs, skin, genitalia, and rectum also will be checked. By observing how your child moves, the pediatrician will assess his nervous system and muscle development. Questions will be asked to assess his behavioral development as well. When your child is about three or four, he will start having his blood pressure taken. Vision and hearing should be assessed at each visit. Be sure to report any concerns you have.

Child-Doctor Rapport

From early on, encourage your child to feel comfortable asking questions and telling the pediatrician how he feels. Use his regular checkups as an opportunity for him to become more aware of his body and the processes of change that are affecting it as it matures; the more he knows about what it takes to stay healthy, the more likely he'll be to make healthy choices. Soon he'll reach an age when he'll want to be examined without having you present. If you are confident that he'll be open and cooperative, he should be able to handle the examination on his own—a list of questions, prepared beforehand, may help.

SPECIAL NEEDS

If you have a child who has special needs due to a disability or chronic condition, your pediatrician can help you get assistance. Together, you'll be able to plot a strategy for seeing that his physical, medical, and educational needs are addressed. When it comes to meeting his day-to-day emotional needs, however, your influence will be vitally important. Let your child know that you and the rest of the family members accept him for who he is. Encourage him to make the best of his talents and abilities, and show him how to adopt a realistic but positive outlook on life. Always treat him as you would any beloved child.

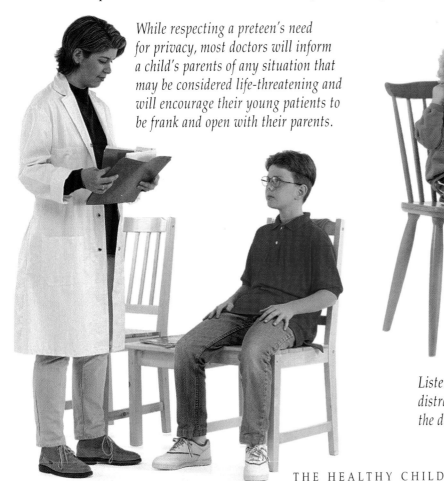

While respecting a preteen's need for privacy, most doctors will inform a child's parents of any situation that may be considered life-threatening and will encourage their young patients to be frank and open with their parents.

Listening to her own heartbeat with a stethoscope distracts her from feeling shy or intimidated while the doctor examines her.

HEALTH RECORDS

Good medicine is characterized by prevention and early detection. The more information you provide about your child's personal and family medical history, the better equipped your pediatrician will be to help you handle your child's inevitable ailments and accidents. Knowing that your child is prone to ear infections, for example, or that a close blood relative developed a genetically linked illness in mid-life will help the doctor prescribe drugs appropriately or order timely diagnostic tests. If your child is adopted, tell the doctor so that any gaps in his genetic history can be taken into account when ordering tests or prescribing medication.

Keeping Track

Take the time to maintain a record of your child's medical history as he grows up. It's a useful document to have on hand when it's time to fill out forms for daycare or school, or if you have to switch doctors, or take your child to a hospital emergency room. Your personal file should contain anything you think is relevant to his med-ical history; for example, the names and addresses of any doctors or dentists who have treated him; his allergies; his medications; the dates and results of any specialized examinations, such as those for hearing or eyesight; any lab tests or X-rays he may have undergone; any surgery or hospitalization; any serious illnesses or injuries; and, of course, his history of childhood diseases, such as chicken pox. If you and your pediatrician have made the decision to immunize your child, file the vaccination records for safekeeping (pediatricians usually record the vaccines in their own medical files as well as in a separate booklet for parents).

Tracing your family's medical history will help the pediatrician determine whether your child is at risk for developing a disabling condition, disorder, or illness.

FAMILY MEDICAL TREE

A family medical tree is a useful way to organize information about your child's genetic heritage. Include all immediate blood relatives, such as his parents, brothers and sisters, both sets of grandparents, and aunts, uncles, and cousins. For each person, try to include their dates (birth and death), blood type, and allergies. Also list any history of heart disease, mental illness, alcoholism or other substance abuse, and any incidence of birth defects, cancer, or genetic disorders—for example, cystic fibrosis or muscular dystrophy. Because certain health problems can be attributed to old age rather than to genetics, note the age of onset of any such illnesses or disorders when you can.

Immunizing

Vaccines are made from tiny amounts of the virus or bacteria that cause a specific illness. The virus or bacteria is altered so that instead of causing the disease, it stimulates the body to produce antibodies that protect against the illness.

There are two kinds of vaccines: killed vaccines (DTP, for example), which are made from inactive viruses or bacteria; and live vaccines (MMR is an example), which are made from active viruses or bacteria. Some vaccines require booster shots because the effect of artificial immunity wears off with time and the body needs to be reminded to keep producing the protective antibodies. It's important, therefore, that you have your child follow the recommended schedule.

Although many potentially fatal diseases have been almost eradicated in the United States thanks to the immunization program, these illnesses still do exist—and can be life-threatening.

If you have any concerns regarding vaccines, discuss them with your child's doctor. No vaccination is completely safe or effective, though the possibilities of a serious reaction are small. Studies show that vaccines provide protection for some 95 percent of those who receive them. And in most cases, any side effects are mild and short term. There are parents and pediatricians, however, who prefer to take a more holistic approach and do not subscribe to immunization.

IMMUNIZATION SCHEDULE		
Age	**Vaccine**	**Comments**
Birth	HBV (1st dose)	• **HBV**, the vaccine against the Hepatitis B virus, is now more widely recommended. The timing of each dose may vary depending on the mother's medical history. • **DTP**, the vaccine against diptheria, tetanus, and pertussis, is currently given along with Hib. DTP side effects include swelling or redness at the injection site, mild fever, and slight irritability. Contact your pediatrician immediately if: your child cries constantly for more than three hours and cannot be comforted; your child's crying is unusually high-pitched; your child is excessively sleepy or difficult to wake up; your child is limp or pale; your child gets a high fever; or your child has a convulsion. • **Hib**, the Hemophilus b conjugate vaccine, grants immunity to a group of bacterial illnesses that includes types of meningitis and epiglottis; it is often conjugated with DTP so your child will receive one injection. Side effects include mild swelling and redness at the injection site. • **OPV**, the oral polio vaccine, grants immunity to poliomyelitis. Because OPV is a live vaccine, it is not recommended if your child has a lowered immune system response or he is living with someone with an immune deficiency. In these cases, the inactivated poliovirus vaccine (IPV), a killed vaccine, will be given. • **MMR** grants immunity to measles, mumps, and rubella (German measles). Some states require a booster at five years of age (school entry). Side effects include a rash and a fever seven to 12 days after vaccination. The MMR vaccine should not be given if your child has a severe allergy to eggs and, in some cases, is not recommended if he has an immune deficiency.
1 to 2 months	HBV (2nd dose)	
2 months	DTP (1st dose) Hib (1st dose) OPV (1st dose)	
4 months	DTP (2nd dose) Hib (2nd dose) OPV (2nd dose)	
6 months	DTP (3rd dose) Hib (3rd dose, depending on vaccine)	
6 to 18 months	HBV (3rd dose) OPV (3rd dose)	
12 to 15 months	Hib (3rd or 4th dose, depending on whether dose was given at 6 months) MMR (1st dose)	
15 to 18 months	DTP (4th dose)	
4 to 6 years	DTP (5th dose) OPV (4th dose)	
11 to 12 years	MMR (2nd dose)	

AT-HOME ATTENDING

No one likes to be sick, but for a child the experience can be even more distressing because he may not realize that his illness is a temporary state. From time to time, you may need to reassure him that his sickness will pass and that soon he'll feel much better. Find ways of keeping his spirits up and taking his mind off his discomfort; a "sick" box filled with special books, toys, and games may soothe anxiety and stave off boredom—for a while at least.

FAMILY MEDICINE CABINET
Even if your child is rarely ill, you should keep a well-stocked medicine cabinet that includes these basic products as well as any specialized medications that your child may require:
- Children's analgesics—acetaminophen for fever, ibuprofen for pain. Don't use aspirin, unless specified by the doctor, since it has been found to be dangerous for children under certain conditions.
- Cough drops or corn syrup to relieve coughs and a scratchy throat; administer only to older children.
- Saline nose drops for a stuffy nose.
- Antihistamines if your child is prone to hay fever; these should be used only under the direction of your doctor.
- Thermometer—may be a traditional glass and mercury thermometer or new digital thermometer that registers a temperature in less than 30 seconds.
- Dosage spoon or dosage dropper for liquid medicines.
- Plastic eye cup for bathing injured or infected eyes.
- Nasal aspirator for unplugging a clogged nose.
- Cotton balls and swabs for cleaning cuts and scrapes.
- Sunscreen and lip balm for protection against sun and wind.
- Bandaids in assorted sizes and shapes.
- Hydrogen peroxide three percent solution for cleaning wounds.
- Rubbing alcohol for sterilizing needles and skin.
- Petroleum jelly for skin and lubricating rectal thermometers.
- Calamine lotion to soothe and relieve itchy skin rashes.

Parenting a Sick Child
Whenever your infant gets sick, it's a good idea to get in touch with his pediatrician. As he grows older, you will probably learn to recognize the signs of a simple cold or stomach flu and know how to proceed without calling the doctor each time. To help you decide when extra advice or medical care is needed, consult Chapter 5, The Sick Child (page 190).

Keep your sick child as comfortable as possible. For most minor illnesses, such as colds, he should increase his intake of fluids. But don't worry if he isn't interested in eating much food; his appetite will pick up again once he's feeling better. And there's no need to insist he stay in bed whenever he's sick, although he may want to if he has a fever. Just make sure he doesn't play too strenuously. Dressed comfortably in pajamas, slippers,

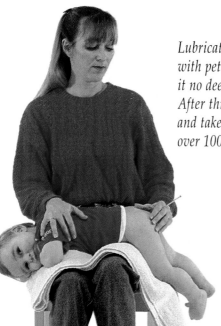

Lubricate the bulb of a rectal thermometer with petroleum jelly before gently inserting it no deeper than one inch into the rectum. After three minutes, remove it, wipe it clean, and take the reading. A rectal temperature over 100.4°F is a fever.

By the time she's five, she probably won't mind holding a thermometer under her tongue for about three minutes; a fever is present if the reading is over 99.5°F. It may be easier to take a toddler's temperature by holding the thermometer in her armpit for five minutes or so; in that case, 98.6°F or over means a fever.

and bathrobe, let him play quietly with his favorite toys or watch TV. Spend as much time with him as possible; reading to him or playing cards or a board game will not only help him to pass the time, but also will nourish the special bond you share. If you can't stay with him because of work or other obligations, take the time to telephone during the day to check on him and speak to him—and spend time with him as soon as you arrive home.

When taking your child's temperature, keep in mind that mild elevations up to 101.2°F may sometimes be caused by such simple things as overdressing, strenuous exercise, or a hot bath. If you suspect that something like this may be the cause of your child's temperature, wait a half hour and take it again.

If your child is prescribed medication, make sure that both the doctor and the pharmacist know about any other medicine your child may be taking. Before giving medicine to your child, read the directions carefully. And never give it to anyone but the person for whom it was prescribed.

> HOSPITAL PROTOCOL
> At some point, you may have to have your child admitted to the hospital. If you can manage to be reassuring and optimistic, your child will cope with the experience amazingly well. You may be able to room in with him if you want; check with the hospital. Make sure that all procedures or treatments are clearly explained to you and your child. Knowing what to expect alleviates the fear of the unknown. And don't hesitate to ask questions or voice your concerns. Once he's out of the hospital, expect a period of adjustment. Without spoiling him, let him know how happy you are that he's back home. Try to resume his usual activities as soon as feasible so that family life returns to normal.

Once you've given a young child her liquid medicine, you may have to hold her mouth shut until she swallows it. If she dislikes the taste, mix the medicine into a small quantity of juice, or have a favorite drink on hand to take away the aftertaste.

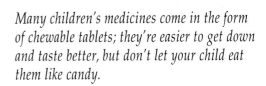

Many children's medicines come in the form of chewable tablets; they're easier to get down and taste better, but don't let your child eat them like candy.

When using a dosage dropper, be careful not to squirt the medicine into her cheek; instead drip it slowly onto the back of her tongue using a side-to-side motion.

STRESS AND RESILIENCE

Your natural instinct as a parent is to protect your child at all costs—to shield her from pain and unhappiness and to provide her with a carefree childhood. Not only is this next to impossible, it is not necessarily even desirable. Stress—a person's emotional response to life-changing events and situations—is a natural part of life and of growing up, and much of her ability to cope with the inevitable stresses of adult life should be learned in childhood. You'll deprive her of the chance to learn how to deal with life if you are overprotective. Instead, help her weather life's storms—big and small—by teaching her coping strategies, by fostering resistance to stress, and by teaching her to reach out for support when she needs it.

FAMILY IN CRISIS

Nothing will affect your child as much as a crisis within your own family. In such circumstances, old routines collapse, familiar roles are often switched, and powerful—frequently conflicting—emotions are expressed. And that's just the beginning. For a young child who will recast the experience in light of her own self-centered view of the world, the stress may be compounded further by feelings of abandonment, personal responsibility, and insecurity.

A Child's Perspective
Children are often ignored—and sometimes manipulated—during periods of family stress. Ironically, the times when a child most needs help to understand what's happening to her once secure world are often the very times she is least likely to receive it. If your family undergoes a particularly difficult stage, take time to ease some of the turbulence for your child by trying to put yourself in her place so that you can see things from her perspective. Such insights will give you the sensitivity to say and do the things that will help her cope.

From your child's point of view, there is one thing that all family crises have in common; they occur for reasons

Creating a memory book of photographs and stories can help children come to terms with the death of a loved one.

Color-coding a calender with "Mommy days" and "Daddy days" helps set a comforting routine as she struggles to adapt to the unsettling arrangements following a divorce.

beyond her control, emphasizing her powerlessness. Paradoxically, it's not unusual for a child to assume responsibility for the event. If, for example, she was angry with her grandfather last week and this week he dies, her egocentric view of the world and her still maturing sense of logic may lead her to see a direct causal relationship between her anger and his death.

Another common reaction to upheaval may be the resurgence of her fears of abandonment. Once again, her interpretation of events can have its own slant. If one parent moves away from home, what's to stop the other parent from leaving, too? If a loved one dies, what's to keep the other people she loves—or she herself—from dying?

A Child's Preparedness

When you know that the stable rhythm of her day-to-day life is going to be radically disrupted—even when you think that the change will be for the better—take the time to prepare your child. In the process, you will be reassuring her

and establishing a pattern of open communication. This can only strengthen your relationship and lays the groundwork for the support you can give your child during the aftermath of the upcoming changes.

Tell her as clearly and concretely as possible what is going to happen and—most importantly—how it will affect her. Keep your explanation short and simple, and gear it to her level of understanding. Don't take refuge in euphemisms; they may confuse her even more. Information, relayed in a straightforward and loving manner, will act as a bulwark against any future misunderstandings and feelings of betrayal. Invite her to ask questions; you may be able to clear up misconceptions or squelch feelings of responsibility or guilt before they take root. And encourage her to express her own feelings—this may require some gentle prompting since children are often reticent about articulating negative emotions such as anger or sadness.

Your child may need repeated reassurance that a new addition to the family will never displace her in your affections.

As he sorts and packs his own books and toys for a move, he is asserting some control over an event that will change his life.

FAMILY TURNING POINTS

The measure of a resilient family is its ability to cope with a crisis—those decisive moments in a family's life when its members are under pressure to respond to change. Such crises are usually caused by one of the following:

• Loss: when parents divorce, for instance, or a relative or close family friend dies.

• Dislocation: when a family member is seriously ill, when a breadwinner in the family loses a job, or when the family moves.

• Addition: the birth or adoption of a new sibling, parental remarriage, or amalgamation with a step-family.

• Dysfunction: when a parent is a substance abuser, or when a parent abuses the children or partner physically, sexually, or emotionally.

SUPPORT SYSTEMS

While your child's first and primary support will be you, the network of relationships that help give her strength will widen as she grows and, you hope, flourish. Studies show that people with strong support networks cope better with the stressful events in their lives. A beloved grandparent, a loyal sibling, an intimate friend, or a sympathetic teacher—any of these people may make that extra bit of difference to your child at a critical time.

Fostering Resilience

Some children seem to be resilient from birth; others need to learn it along the way. Nurture whatever inborn capacity your child seems to have and you will see it grow. Begin by setting daily examples for her to follow; each time you respond positively and with flexibility to unexpected changes, you'll be demonstrating effective ways of dealing with potentially stressful situations.

As your child matures, find ways to enhance her sense of autonomy. She needs to know that her own actions can make her feel better. If she learns, for instance, that creating a memory book of a beloved aunt helped her to say good-bye after her aunt died, then she has discovered one way to reconcile the pain of loss. But she also needs to learn to distinguish between stressful situations over which she has some control and those over which she has none. When she can have some influence or effect, direct her energies toward finding useful strategies or solutions. When the event is beyond her control, she'll benefit from your support as she tries to come to terms with what she cannot change. And when bad things do happen, reassure your child that they were not caused by some fatal flaw in her character. You want her to learn to accept some things without blaming herself inappropriately.

Coping Strategies

Your child is a creature of habit; her world is defined by the routines and rituals of daily life. When a crisis disrupts that routine, she may feel that her entire universe is collapsing around her, threatening her sense of belonging and adding to her uncertainty. By returning her to the familiarity of old routines or setting up new ones for a new situation as soon as possible, you will help restore her sense of equilibrium.

If your family is going through a bad time, you may feel that your reservoir of energy and patience is being exhausted just by coping with your day-to-day responsibilities. Even so, try to make time for the ordinary activities that have traditionally brought you close to your child. She may need your nonjudgmental support before she can tell you how she truly feels. In return, you can share your feelings with her, although you may need to be careful

A story that duplicates the unsettling events in your child's life can furnish a timely opening for the two of you to have a heart-to-heart.

Crisis has a way of drawing siblings closer; don't underestimate the support and comfort they may be able to provide each other.

A teacher may be the one to inspire your child to make that extra push, reinforcing her growing understanding that her personal efforts will produce positive results.

SIGNALS OF DISTRESS

Persistent regressive behavior—thumb-sucking, clinginess, bed-wetting, tantrums—may signal distress in young children. Signs of unhappiness may be revealed by a child of any age in the following areas:

• Emotions—becoming a worrier; constantly demanding reassurance; frowning or complaining a lot.

• Health—developing frequent headaches, abdominal pains, or asthma attacks; appetite loss or overeating; insomnia or repeated nightmares.

• School—dropping grades; neglected homework or decreasing attention span.

• Behavior—withdrawing from family and friends, skipping classes, stealing, becoming increasingly aggressive or irritable.

If your child exhibits these or any other behaviors that disturb you in their intensity or persistence, consult her pediatrician or school guidance counselor for advice.

not to make her your confidante; she needs to feel that no matter what happens, she can count on your strength to cope with the situation.

But don't think that you have to cope without help. Seek professional help if you think you or your child will benefit. A mental health counselor, a member of the clergy, grandparents, siblings, and, of course, friends, are all potential allies in helping you and your child get through a difficult period.

Don't feel that her need for the support of others reflects badly on you; the stronger the circle of support around her, the better able she'll be to deal with life's challenges, and the more she will learn how and when to ask for help.

Spending a night at a friend's house may bring him the reassurance he needs and help take his mind off his troubles.

When his world is topsy-turvy, he may draw untold comfort from the familiar warmth of his grandmother's love.

2 FROM BABY TO TODDLER

NEWBORN TO TWO

The months seem to fly by; no sooner is your baby home than she's sitting up, feeding herself, and taking her first tentative steps. Her development is tremendously exciting, with each "demand" announcing another advance toward independence. Some days you may be dizzy with exhaustion, but just her unexpected smile is enough to remind you that there really is no other experience like having a baby.

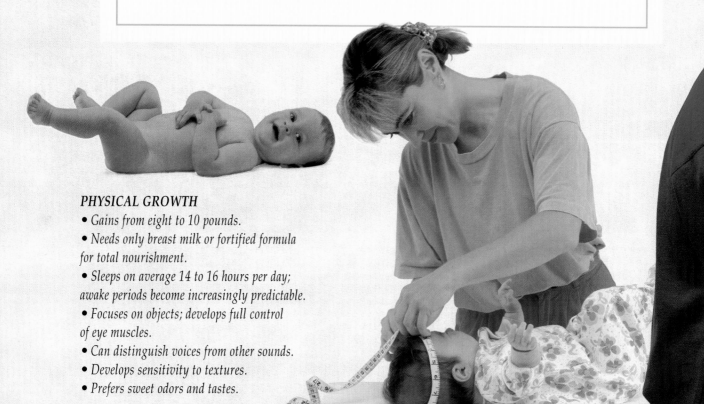

PHYSICAL GROWTH
- *Gains from eight to 10 pounds.*
- *Needs only breast milk or fortified formula for total nourishment.*
- *Sleeps on average 14 to 16 hours per day; awake periods become increasingly predictable.*
- *Focuses on objects; develops full control of eye muscles.*
- *Can distinguish voices from other sounds.*
- *Develops sensitivity to textures.*
- *Prefers sweet odors and tastes.*

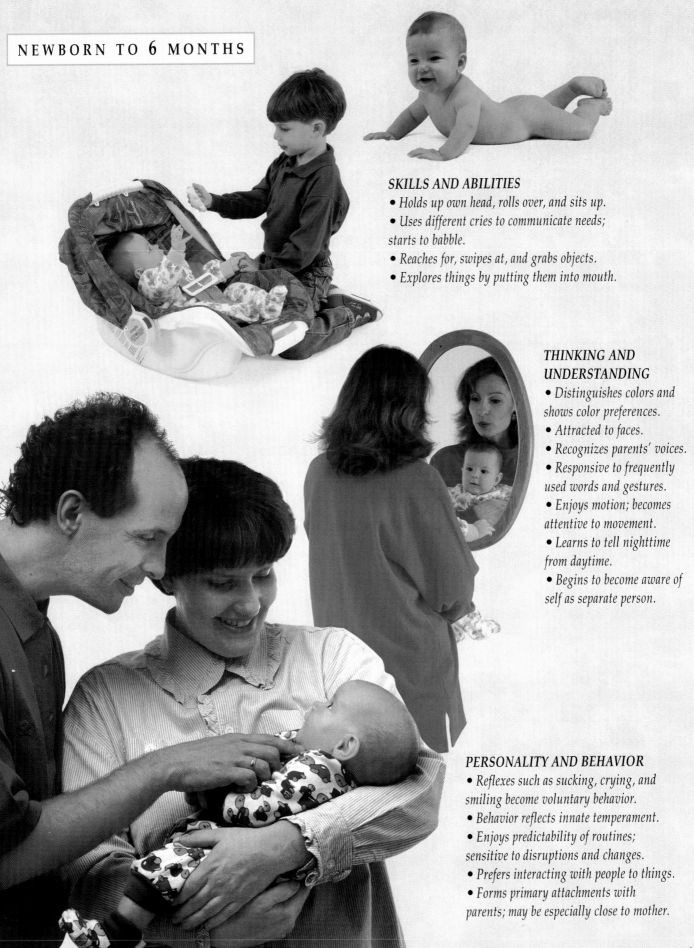

SKILLS AND ABILITIES

- *Holds up own head, rolls over, and sits up.*
- *Uses different cries to communicate needs; starts to babble.*
- *Reaches for, swipes at, and grabs objects.*
- *Explores things by putting them into mouth.*

THINKING AND UNDERSTANDING

- *Distinguishes colors and shows color preferences.*
- *Attracted to faces.*
- *Recognizes parents' voices.*
- *Responsive to frequently used words and gestures.*
- *Enjoys motion; becomes attentive to movement.*
- *Learns to tell nighttime from daytime.*
- *Begins to become aware of self as separate person.*

PERSONALITY AND BEHAVIOR

- *Reflexes such as sucking, crying, and smiling become voluntary behavior.*
- *Behavior reflects innate temperament.*
- *Enjoys predictability of routines; sensitive to disruptions and changes.*
- *Prefers interacting with people to things.*
- *Forms primary attachments with parents; may be especially close to mother.*

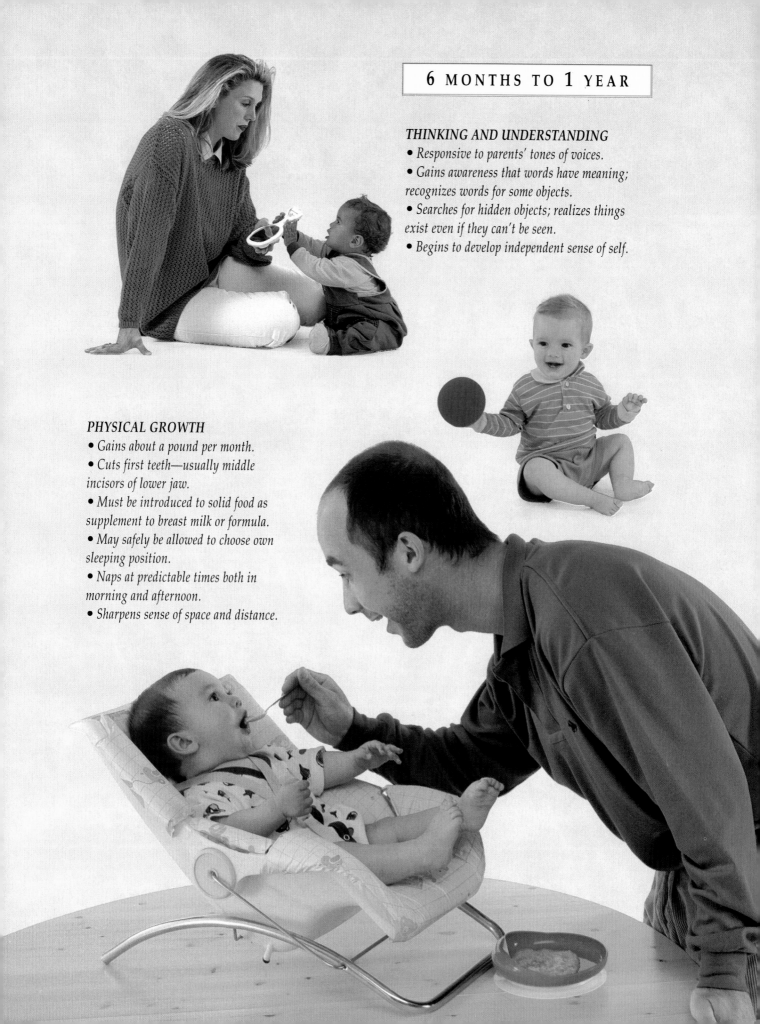

THINKING AND UNDERSTANDING
- *Responsive to parents' tones of voices.*
- *Gains awareness that words have meaning; recognizes words for some objects.*
- *Searches for hidden objects; realizes things exist even if they can't be seen.*
- *Begins to develop independent sense of self.*

PHYSICAL GROWTH
- *Gains about a pound per month.*
- *Cuts first teeth—usually middle incisors of lower jaw.*
- *Must be introduced to solid food as supplement to breast milk or formula.*
- *May safely be allowed to choose own sleeping position.*
- *Naps at predictable times both in morning and afternoon.*
- *Sharpens sense of space and distance.*

PERSONALITY AND BEHAVIOR

- *May cry up to an hour per day.*
- *Initiates talking sounds and body gestures to get attention.*
- *Instigates as well as responds to displays of affection.*
- *Anxious at being apart from parents and wary of strangers.*
- *May comfort self using security object such as a pacifier or blanket.*
- *Fascinated with objects; keen on testing effects of own actions on them.*
- *Often takes risks to satisfy curiosity.*
- *Develops attachments to siblings.*

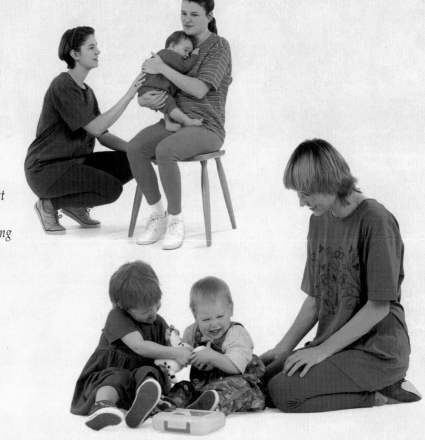

SKILLS AND ABILITIES

- *Gets into and out of sitting position.*
- *Practices own style of crawling; can stand and take steps with support.*
- *Babbles in speechlike manner; makes sounds that can be understood as words.*
- *Responds to simple commands.*
- *Develops control of hands; can hold an object in each hand and transfer an object from one hand to the other.*
- *Drinks from own cup and feeds self using spoon.*

THINKING AND UNDERSTANDING

- *Enjoys repetition of stories and songs.*
- *Identifies details in pictures.*
- *Comprehends simple instructions.*
- *Masters concepts such as full and empty.*
- *Begins to sort things by color and shape.*
- *Gains confidence and self-esteem; refers to self by name.*

PHYSICAL GROWTH

- *Gains from three to five pounds.*
- *Stands 34 inches tall on average.*
- *Size of head reaches about 90 percent of eventual adult size.*
- *Starts cutting molars.*
- *May begin to display tendency toward right- or left-handedness.*

PERSONALITY AND BEHAVIOR

- *Often contradictory; vacillates between "me do it" and "you do it."*
- *Capable of negativism; may respond to almost anything with "no."*
- *Frustrates easily; susceptible to mood swings and temper tantrums.*
- *Imitates behavior of parents and older siblings.*
- *Initiates humor; enjoys making others laugh.*
- *Begins to show preferences for people and things.*
- *Engages in make-believe play.*

DEVELOPMENT WATCH

Milestones don't predict development; they're only a guide to the general changes that you can expect. Alert your pediatrician to signs of delay such as:

- *can't sit with support at six months*
- *doesn't respond to or initiate soft sounds at six months*
- *can't stand with support at one year*
- *doesn't use gestures with finger or head to communicate at one year*
- *can't walk heel-toe at two years*
- *doesn't follow simple instructions or speak two-word sentences at two years*
- *doesn't understand normal function of common objects at two years*
- *doesn't imitate others at two years*

SKILLS AND ABILITIES

- *Stands and walks on own; climbs and descends stairs same-foot first.*
- *Can seat self on child-size chair or stool.*
- *Speaks words; uses two-word sentences.*
- *Capable of rolling and throwing a ball.*
- *Grips with finger and thumb; can pick up tiny things.*
- *Controls conventional cup and spoon.*
- *Manages simple riding toys.*

LEARNING TO WALK

Your baby learns to coordinate and move his body in a sequence: He can't walk until he can stand; he can't sit up before he's able to hold up his head. The pace at which your baby develops control over his body, though, isn't as predictable. He may crawl early and walk late, or he may crawl hardly at all before beginning to walk. While your baby is dependent on you to get around, you may find him a handful. But once he can sit up and crawl around on his own, you'll be just as busy keeping all hazards out of his way.

HANDLING WITH CARE

Babies aren't as fragile as they may seem. However, your newborn's head is floppy and requires constant support. Toward the end of his first month, your baby may be able to hold up his head for a short time. At six weeks, he probably has just enough strength in the muscles of his neck to lift his head to turn it from side to side. Not until about three months is your baby likely to have the ability to hold up his head to look around while he lies on his stomach.

Getting Comfortable
The urge to hold and carry a baby is instinctive. But the ability to handle a newborn properly often doesn't come as naturally. Don't worry; in the usual course of getting adjusted to your baby, you'll have plenty of opportunities to practice and build up confidence.

You and your baby need time to gain an understanding of each other.

As in any relationship, comfort goes two ways: Your feelings about holding and carrying him affect his feelings about being in your arms, and vice versa. If you're nervous and handle him awkwardly, he may get upset and cry, making your handling of him all the more difficult. If you relax, chances are he will, too. Be patient; together you'll soon find what works best.

Holding and Carrying
Sudden movement and loud noise startle babies, especially during the early months. Approach your baby calmly and warn him before you pick him up; let him see you, and tell him what's about to happen. Pick him up and put him down in smooth, flowing motions. Hold him firmly, bending over him to keep him close to your body; the sensa-

PICKING UP YOUR BABY

1 Slide one hand under his lower back and bottom to support his weight. With your other hand, prop his head to keep it from lolling back.

2 Supporting his body and neck, lift him gently and slowly. Keep your arms positioned on opposite sides of his body to prevent him from rolling.

3 Prop his head up against your shoulder with one hand and shift your other hand down under his bottom to take his weight.

tion of free-fall may alarm him. Until he can sit up on his own, be sure to support his neck to prevent his head from lolling back.

Your baby needs to be held in a way suited to his stage of development as well as the activity at hand. For his first two months, you may carry him and keep one hand free using the so-called football hold: your forearm under his back and your hand supporting his head, his body pressed against your side, his head facing you and his feet tucked under your elbow. By three months, he may wriggle out of all but a sure two-handed hold. At six months, he may be carried one-handed with his legs straddling your hip, your forearm supporting his back and your hand gripping his body; by then, he'll hold onto you if he feels insecure.

Using Carriers and Packs
Babies love rhythmic motion and visual distraction. If your baby is like most, he'll enjoy safe, warm rides in an infant carrier—and you'll have both hands free. When you lean forward, though, prop his head to be sure his neck gets adequate support. By three months, he's likely to be big enough for a front- or back-worn pack.

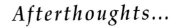

To cradle your baby against you, support her back with one hand and prop her head in the bend of the elbow. Use your other arm to support her lower body and take her weight.

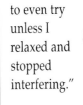

When you hold your baby facedown, straddle her arms and legs on opposite sides of your arms to balance her weight. Rest her head against your upper arm.

Getting your baby into an infant carrier is easiest if you sit down on a chair and lean back so his weight is supported on your chest and stomach.

SITTING UP AND CRAWLING

Most babies can sit unsupported for brief moments by six months and for 10 to 15 minutes a few months later. At 10 months, the average baby controls his sitting and can turn to one side. A month later, he's able to shift from lying down to sitting up—and back again. Crawling on hands and knees—which some normal babies may never do well, if at all—takes an ability to bear weight on extended arms and bring the knees up under the body.

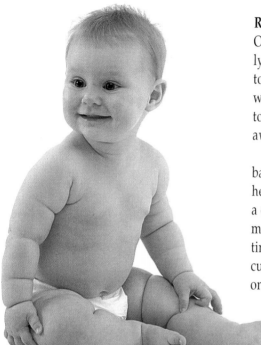

Once an infant can sit up on her own, she's better able to look around and to use her hands—and can more easily amuse herself.

Rolling Over

Once a baby can hold up his head while lying on his stomach, he's in a position to satisfy his curiosity. Better able to see what's going on around him, he's free to turn toward things of interest and away from things he doesn't like.

Between four and five months, your baby is likely to use the weight of his head to propel himself onto his back— a discovery so shocking to him that he may burst out crying. Within a short time, he'll next master the more difficult task of turning over from his back onto his stomach. This first event, too, may come accidentally.

Once your baby can turn over, he's at risk of rolling off any surface on which he's placed. Since his first roll is difficult to predict, keep an especially close watch on him as soon as he first shows that he can hold up his head.

Getting Up and Around

Through exercises such as lifting his head and turning himself over, a baby develops control of his body. Gaining strength and coordination, he learns to sit up without support for increasingly longer periods of time.

Your baby's ability to sit up on his own brings him new perspective. Better positioned to look around, he's also freer to reach for, pick up, and manipulate things of interest. Struggling less to maintain his balance, he can begin to concentrate on his surroundings and on keeping himself entertained.

Crawling comes next, but both the timing and the technique itself vary. Your baby may never get around well on hands and knees, instead adopting a bottom-shuffling "crab walk," a pull-by-the-arms "commando crawl," or a straight-legged "bear walk."

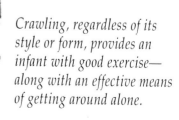

Crawling, regardless of its style or form, provides an infant with good exercise— along with an effective means of getting around alone.

FIRST STEPS

Walking usually is mastered by 15 months, but may begin as early as nine months or as late as two years. While you needn't worry if your baby hasn't started walking by 18 months, you should consult your pediatrician.

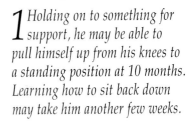

Standing and Walking

To stand or walk on his own, a baby needs to develop his sense of balance. Months after he can bear his weight on his feet, he may still need to hold on to something to stand up and sit back down.

Your baby may walk with support as soon as he can pull himself up to a stand. Arms held out and feet wide apart for stability, he's likely to walk on his own by the end of his first year.

By 18 months, your baby probably won't be as tottery when he walks. More confident, he'll step forward and backward with arms at his sides and feet close together. For a while yet, though, he may find sitting down an easier thing to do than trying to stand still.

1 Holding on to something for support, he may be able to pull himself up from his knees to a standing position at 10 months. Learning how to sit back down may take him another few weeks.

2 More confident of his ability to stand up and sit down toward the end of his first year, he may begin to "cruise." As he shuffles along on his feet, he'll hold on to something for balance—initially with both hands, then just one.

3 His discovery that he can walk may come by accident: Forgetting to support himself, he lets go and takes a few steps. Even if he walks on his own early, he may not be very steady on his feet until well into his second year.

House Call

My one-year-old son has flat feet. Could they be interfering with his ability to walk?

Every baby is born with flat feet. An absence of visible arches in your son's feet is normal, and not a particular reason for you to be concerned about their structure. Only in rare instances are flat feet a disabling condition that require treatment. And awkward walking at 12 months, in itself, isn't necessarily the sign of a problem.

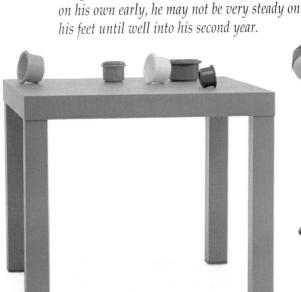

LANGUAGE BEGINNINGS

With your baby's first cry at birth, she's already learning about language. But not until the end of her first year is she likely to speak her first word—a sound understood by those closest to her. By the end of her second year, her speech probably will consist of only simple two-word sentences, made from combinations of a few hundred nouns, verbs, and adjectives.

Your baby's language development, though, involves more than just learning to speak words: She first needs to learn that words have meaning. And even as she develops her ability to understand and speak words, she has other ways of communicating—initially, through different cries and nonverbal signals; later, also through cooing, babbling, and more complex gestures.

THE CRYING CODE

All healthy babies cry. Initially, crying is your baby's chief way of communicating her physical and emotional needs. Don't be discouraged if at first you have trouble interpreting her cries; recognizing differences in them may take a month or two. Even once you can tell her cries apart, there probably will be times when nothing you do seems enough to comfort her. Be patient and keep trying; your efforts won't spoil her.

Signaling Need
Anticipate bouts of crying throughout your baby's first year. On average, she can be expected to cry for between 30 minutes and two or more hours per day during her first week, slightly more from then until she's six months old.

On some days, your baby may cry for up to 20 minutes or more as many as four or five times. By her sixth month, though, she'll be further along in her development and gradually will cry less often.

Initially, your baby's crying is a reflexive reaction to discomfort—caused by pain, hunger, or irritability at being too hot, too cold, or trapped in a messy diaper. From her third or fourth week until her third or fourth month, she may suffer prolonged, intense periods of crying that are commonly known as colic, a condition thought to be the result of normal development of the central nervous system.

After your baby's third month, she'll begin to cry as well to signal loneliness or boredom, or overstimulation or tiredness. By about six

Interpreting cries can be a worrying, trial-and-error process, but your efforts to respond help to strengthen the bond between you and your baby—even if the crying doesn't stop right away.

months, she'll cry not only to express needs, but also to convey emotions—especially fear and frustration.

Hearing the Message

Your baby's cries at first may all sound alike, but don't be overwhelmed. You'll soon discover that there's a pattern to her crying and recognize distinct differences in her cries. The piercing shriek that is a cry of pain, for example, isn't one you're likely to mistake—even if its cause doesn't always seem obvious. Also easy to identify is a cry of hunger: a rhythmic complaining, with a series of short outbursts interrupted by brief pauses. Eventually, you'll even hear her whining and fussing as different, distinct cries of irritability, loneliness, over-stimulation, and frustration.

Learning your baby's repertory of cries helps you to understand and respond to her needs. Comforting her may take time and sometimes seem impossible, but your immediate and patient efforts add to her sense of control and security. Lengthy bouts of unexplained crying, however, can be troubling. Be alert to crying that is accompanied by symptoms of illness—fever, diarrhea, or constipation, for instance. If ever her prolonged crying seems to be from pain, for no apparent reason, or severely straining your ability to cope, contact your pediatrician as soon as possible.

COOING AND BABBLING

By three months, your baby is likely to begin making coos—delightful sounds that are her first vocal expressions of happiness. A couple of months later, her cooing may suddenly stop as she gains the ability to experiment with other sounds: gurgles, growls, and trills. By six months, she'll probably have started to babble and be gradually developing enough control of the sounds she makes to repeat them over and over again.

Vocal Play

A baby's coos, vowel sounds such as "aah" and "ooh," emerge first singly and then in series; they may seem like words and sentences, but they lack both timing and meaning. Babbling starts with the adding of consonant sounds, and usually consists of repetitive syllables such as "bababa" or "dadada."

As your baby learns to string together different sounds, she's likely to begin varying the pitch of her voice in speech-like patterns. She may become so adept at babbling that she can sometimes convey exactly what she wants. But even if she doesn't, she'll always enjoy and benefit from having you imitate her babbling so that she can repeat it back to you.

Entertaining exchanges of cooing and babbling sounds help your baby learn how to converse.

BODY MESSAGES

From the moment your baby is born, she's giving you messages with her body. And even after she can speak with words, she uses her body to help communicate her emotions. Her unspoken language at times may seem complicated, but you can gain a lot of insight into her basic nonverbal patterns just by being observant.

He expresses distaste by squinting his eyes and lowering his bottom lip; when disgusted, he also sticks out his tongue and spits.

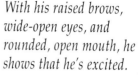

With his raised brows, wide-open eyes, and rounded, open mouth, he shows that he's excited.

Silent Signaling

Your newborn tells you more about herself with her body than she probably ever could with words. Until she's about 18 months old, most of what her body reveals is basic:

• Breathing. Slow, deep breathing shows she's relaxed, possibly about to fall asleep. Rapid, shallow breathing indicates she's troubled or upset.

• Facial expression. By two months, her smiles have meaning: She's contented. Her curiosity is shown by raised eyebrows. A furrowed forehead signals her displeasure.

• Hand motion. Open, relaxed hands are signs that she's calm; with slow, rhythmic arm movements, she express-es playfulness. Clenched hands held close to her face usually mean discomfort; her agitation will be shown by rapid, forceful arm movements.

By 18 months, your infant's emotions are becoming complex; so, too, are her body's messages. She may at times be

His intent, focused eyes, pursed lips, and purposeful, exploring hands mean something has caught his interest.

able to give you an idea of how she feels using words, but you'll probably get a better—and more reliable—sense of her moods from her unspoken language:

• Eye contact. Inability to make eye contact suggests that she feels tense, nervous, or guilty. If pleased, she makes direct eye contact while speaking.

• Posture. With her shoulders held back and her head upright, she signals confidence. Drooping shoulders and a bowed head are signs of unhappiness, possibly self-pity or shame. When sitting with her arms and legs crossed, she's express-ing defensiveness.

• Hand gestures. If she tucks her hands into her back pockets, she's showing aggressiveness. When she rubs her hands together, she's excited. Hands clenched together suggest that she's worried or anxious. One hand tightly holding the opposite upper arm means that she's angry.

Interpreting the Unspoken

Keep building your understanding of your toddler by taking readings of her body's messages in different situations. As she gets older, look for variations in her body talk with you and among her friends. Observe her body's movements in context as a whole; single, isolated gestures can be misleading. To confirm your readings, ask friends or relatives who can be objective.

Mirror your toddler's body when you have difficulty interpreting its messages; copying her gestures can give you clues about their meaning. Be aware of your own body talk and watch for nonverbal signals of yours that she adopts. You'll probably find that many of her gestures are like your own—and carry similar meanings.

WORDS AND SENTENCES

Most babies master the use of a word by their first birthday. At two years, toddlers usually command a vocabulary of about 300 words and speak in telegraphic two-word sentences. Don't be concerned, though, if your infant seems slow to develop her ability to speak. As long as she shows an interest in language and appears to understand what's said to her, you needn't worry if she begins to speak in words only toward the end of her second year.

Understood Vocabulary

Your baby is already developing an understanding of words at birth. During her first weeks, she reacts more to speech than to any other sound. By three months, she may turn her head toward the sound of a voice.

As your baby learns to make vocal sounds of her own, she's better able to distinguish differences in words spoken to her. By six months, she's likely to recognize that frequently repeated words with gestures have meaning—for example, "bye-bye" and a waving hand, "up" and open arms, and "come" and an outstretched hand.

Spoken Vocabulary

Your baby's spoken vocabulary is always more limited than the number of words she understands. Months before she speaks her first word, she may respond to her own name and understand enough vocabulary to answer simple questions with gestures such as finger pointing.

As your baby begins to develop her spoken vocabulary, she might use the same word with varying intonations and gestures to attempt different statements. By the time she has a spoken vocabulary of 10 words, she may understand as many as 50.

Encouraging Words

Speaking isn't something your baby needs to be taught, but you can promote her understanding of words by giving her a rich verbal environment from the start. Take the opportunity for relaxed talk and verbal play with her during everyday routines such as feeding, bathing, and getting dressed.

Read or recite rhymes to your baby; hearing them again and again helps her to anticipate familiar sounds. Speak slowly and clearly, facing her so she can see your mouth. Use facial expressions and gestures to help her understand the meaning of your words.

Saying the word for an object of interest to your infant helps him to learn that things have names.

SPEAKING	
Do use words to identify objects and actions for your child. **Do** respond in words to your child's sounds and gestures. **Do** listen patiently when your child talks. Make eye contact with her and wait until she has finished speaking to respond. **Do** repeat what your child says using proper words. **Do** seek out opportunities for your child to practice new words. **Do** engage your child in conversation on subjects of her choice.	**Don't** underestimate how many words your child can understand. **Don't** ignore your child or insist that she communicate using words. **Don't** interrupt or hurry your child when she talks. Avoid jumping in while she's speaking to complete her sentences. **Don't** point out and correct your child's mistakes. **Don't** assume your child has forgotten a word that she stops using. **Don't** force your child into conversation on subjects of no interest to her.

FEEDING AND NUTRITION

Breast-feeding or bottle-feeding provides your baby with all the nourishment he needs to thrive for his first six months. Settling into a regular, four-hour schedule of feedings—four or five during the day, one or two at night—may take a few months; until then, your baby will want to be fed on demand, probably at least every two or three hours.

By six months, most babies are ready to start eating solid foods, which can be phased gradually into their diet. Slowly, with practice, a baby learns to take food into his mouth, then chew and swallow it. By the age of two, your toddler will probably have mastered the use of a cup and spoon, skills that—along with the use of his fingers—he applies efficiently to feeding himself.

BREAST-FEEDING

Always fresh and instantly available, breast milk provides your baby with valuable antibodies against infections and is easy for him to digest. Expressed into a sterilized container, breast milk can be frozen and stored for up to one month—so your baby doesn't always have to be fed by his mother. Don't be deterred by a little uncertainty, especially in the early days; you'll find lots of professionals, relatives, and friends keen on offering helpful advice.

Giving Breast Milk
Mastering the art of relaxed breast-feeding may take a few weeks, so be patient. Before each feeding, make sure that your back and arms are well supported. To stimulate your baby's rooting reflex, you may need to stroke the cheek nearest to your breast. As he takes the breast, make sure his mouth covers a large area of the areola; if he sucks on only the nipple, he won't get milk. Offer him the second breast only after he empties the first, and start the next feeding with the breast he had last.

Expressing Breast Milk
You can express breast milk by hand or with a breast pump. Expressing by hand requires no special equipment, but can be difficult and time-consuming. Before opting for a breast pump, though, talk with your physician.

NURSING BASICS

1 Get into a comfortable position with your baby cradled close to you. Gently guide his open mouth onto your breast, his chin up against it and his tongue under the nipple.

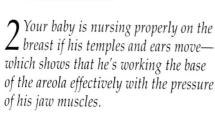

2 Your baby is nursing properly on the breast if his temples and ears move—which shows that he's working the base of the areola effectively with the pressure of his jaw muscles.

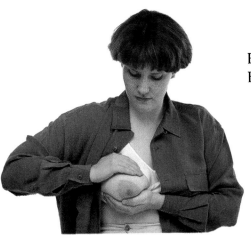

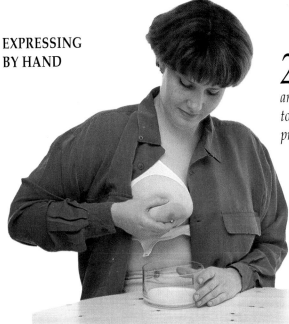

1 *To stimulate the flow of milk, support the breast in one hand and massage it using the other. Press gently from your chest toward the areola, working around the breast at least 10 times.*

2 *Place your thumb and forefinger just behind the areola, then squeeze them together and at the same time press back toward your chest; milk should spurt out of the nipple. Continue this way, alternating between breasts every two minutes until milk stops flowing.*

BOTTLE-FEEDING

Ask your pediatrician to help you choose the best formula for your baby. Powdered or liquid concentrate is less costly than ready-to-serve, but needs careful mixing with water following instructions. Prepared bottles of concentrate must be refrigerated and used within 24 hours; if refrigerated, unused ready-to-serve can be kept for 48 hours.

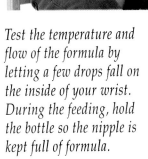

Test the temperature and flow of the formula by letting a few drops fall on the inside of your wrist. During the feeding, hold the bottle so the nipple is kept full of formula.

Afterthoughts...

"Breast-feeding made traveling easy: no worry about keeping formula cool, and no bottle to warm."

"With bottle-feeding, I could relax; seeing how much formula he'd taken was reassuring. And his total dependence on me to be breast-fed would have been exhausting."

"Breast-feeding was quite time-consuming at first, but the comfort of sucking always helped to soothe him. Within a few weeks I was grateful for being spared the chore of sterilizing and preparing bottles."

Giving Bottles

The formula your baby gets must be no more than tepid; cold is safe, but he may not like it. Warm the bottle in a bowl of hot water—not in a microwave oven, which can overheat portions of the formula. The nipple should provide your baby with a few drops of formula per second. If the formula flows too quickly, replace the nipple; if the flow is too slow, enlarge the opening with a sterilized needle. If the nipple collapses while your baby is feeding, let air into the bottle by moving the nipple around in his mouth; or, take away the bottle to loosen and retighten the cap.

BURPING AND DIGESTION

Whether breast-fed or bottle-fed, your baby swallows air along with his milk or formula. Distending his stomach, the air makes him uncomfortable until it's expelled. Along with a burp to bring up air, your baby may sometimes spit up a little milk or formula—a normal occurrence that's likely to happen less frequently as he reaches nine months of age. To protect your clothing while burping him, keep a cloth diaper or receiving blanket on hand.

Aiding Digestion

Calm, unhurried feedings help your baby's digestion. Until he's a month old, burp him every five minutes or so if he's breast-feeding; after every two or three ounces if he's bottle-feeding. By three months, he may not need to bring up air until he finishes feeding.

As long as your baby is feeding happily, there's no need to interrupt him. Wait for a pause in his sucking, then burp him. If he fusses, though, he might need to bring up air. If he was hungry and cried to be fed, he probably swallowed air and will need burping early in the feeding.

Encourage your baby to burp by gently patting or rubbing his back. Don't keep trying for longer than a few minutes at a time; if he doesn't burp, wait for a while before repeating your efforts. Unless he complains, he can be put down after his feeding and left to burp on his own.

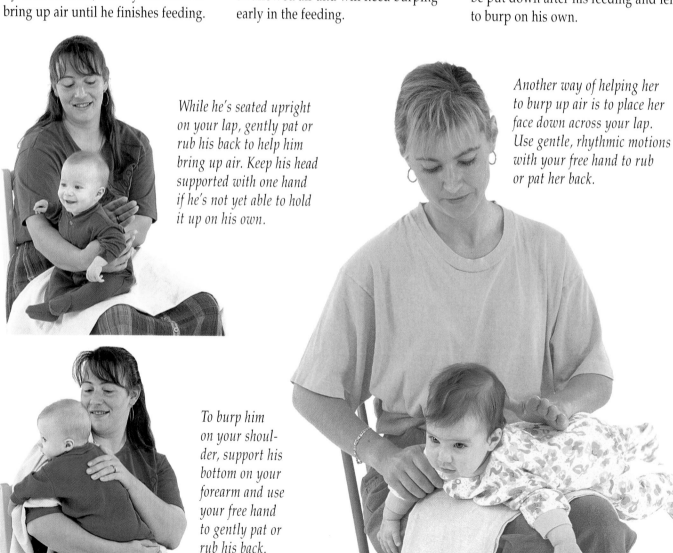

While he's seated upright on your lap, gently pat or rub his back to help him bring up air. Keep his head supported with one hand if he's not yet able to hold it up on his own.

Another way of helping her to burp up air is to place her face down across your lap. Use gentle, rhythmic motions with your free hand to rub or pat her back.

To burp him on your shoulder, support his bottom on your forearm and use your free hand to gently pat or rub his back.

INTRODUCING SOLID FOODS

By your baby's sixth month, your pediatrician will probably recommend that he start eating solid foods. At first only a supplement to—not a substitute for—breast milk or formula, solids should be introduced one at a time. Wait a few days after your baby starts each new food and consult your pediatrician if he shows signs of intolerance—such as vomiting, skin rash, diarrhea, or wheezing.

A milestone at which parents like to be celebrants, the first solid food tasted by an infant is usually a bland cereal mixed with breast milk or formula.

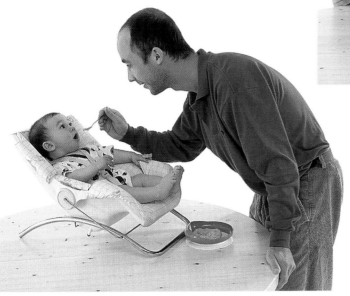

An infant needs practice just to bring in and swallow a tiny, baby-sized spoonful of solid food.

First Solids

Your baby's first solid food should be a bland, easy-to-digest cereal such as rice. Wait until later on to try feeding him oat or barley cereals. Because wheat and mixed cereals sometimes cause an allergic reaction, they're best introduced last.

Mix a teaspoon of cereal with breast milk or formula and put a tiny bit on the tip of a baby spoon. Place the spoon just inside your baby's lips and let him suck at the cereal; if you go too far back in his mouth, he'll gag. If he spits out the cereal—a natural first reflex—try again.

As your baby gets accustomed to eating cereal, you may gradually increase his portion at each feeding. Don't serve him more than four to six tablespoons at a time, though, unless you've decided that he's ready to start being fully weaned.

Adding Foods

Once your baby has accepted a cereal, you may introduce him to other grains, as well as to strained vegetables, fruits, and meats. Within a month of starting solids, his daily diet can include all of them—in addition to breast milk or formula.

Introduce your baby to as many foods as possible, but let him decide the amounts he wants to eat. The order in which you start foods isn't important, but he may not take to vegetables as easily if he has already started fruits; he needs meats least and will probably like them least. Wait until his second year to try hard-to-digest foods such as corn, spinach, tomatoes, citrus fruits, and fish.

READY FOR SOLIDS	
✓	Controls his head and can hold it up on his own; allows an open, clear passage for food to go down his throat.
✓	Begins chewing motions and shows an ability to swallow; can use his tongue to bring food into his mouth rather than only to push it out.
✓	Starts to drool; the saliva that he secretes helps him to swallow food.

Weaning and Self-feeding

Only you and your baby can decide the best time to begin weaning and when he should give up the breast or bottle entirely. However, your pediatrician may advise that he not be fully weaned off a nipple until he's a year old.

Your baby's ability to feed himself at first isn't as strong as his desire. But by the time he's two—an age at which he may not yet be totally weaned—he'll likely have mastered the use of a conventional cup and spoon.

Giving Up Breast or Bottle
Weaning your baby is best done gradually over a period of at least two or three months. To switch him from breast to bottle, start by offering a bottle every third day in place of a midday breast-feeding. Progress slowly, dropping no more than one breast-feeding every three or four days. Nighttime breast-feeding is usually given up last.

Dropping bottle-feedings may go quickly once your baby reaches six months of age and can use a trainer cup. But whole cow's milk is hard to digest and shouldn't be substituted for formula before he's at least nine months old; your pediatrician may recommend waiting until the end of his first year. And while at two years he may be able to handle a conventional cup, he may still insist on having a bottle before bedtime.

Taking Up Cup and Spoon
Your baby's self-feeding skills develop through many months of practice—with inevitable spills and messes. Along with a bib and washcloth for him, you also may want to keep an apron on hand for yourself.

Sanity Saver

Your baby's insistence on feeding himself needn't leave you short on time and patience. Minimize the mess that needs to be cleaned up by placing a washable plastic tablecloth under his high chair. While you use one spoon to feed him, give him one or even two spoons so he can also help himself.

As long as your baby doesn't get frustrated by trying to feed himself, give him control of the bowl and allow him to practice.

When your baby is very hungry at the start of a meal, you may want to feed her the first few spoonfuls of food.

Introduce your baby to a cup when he's calm and not too hungry—perhaps midway in a feeding. Don't force him to drink; if he rejects the cup, simply try again another time. Once he accepts breast milk or formula from a cup, you may try offering him water or natural fruit juices in a cup as well.

Encourage your baby's eagerness to feed himself, letting him try to handle his cup and spoon as well as eat with his fingers. As he cuts teeth, he's ready for foods with coarser texture—such as diced, well-cooked vegetables, sliced fruits, and chopped meats—that also are easier for him to manage.

Your baby's control of a cup isn't always reliable at first, so you may want to fill it only halfway.

LIKES, DISLIKES, AND INCONSISTENCY

When he turns away from a food, he may dislike it or have eaten enough. Never coerce him to eat food he refuses.

Finger foods, which he controls on his own, provide natural health benefits: He eats what he likes and stops when he's full.

Erratic eating habits and unpredictable food preferences are likely to be the norm for your baby during his first two years—maybe longer. As his growth rate slows at the end of his first year, his appetite may diminish. At the same time, he may be a lot more finicky about what he eats.

Tackling New Foods
Getting accustomed to the consistency, texture, and taste of foods is a gradual process for your baby. He may be eager to try new foods; more likely, he'll be indifferent or suspicious. Sensitivity to the odor or flavor may cause him to refuse something new. Or, he simply may be in the mood for something familiar.

The best way of ensuring that your baby's nutritional requirements are met is to serve him a balanced diet of healthy foods in a form he likes. Offer him a wide range of different foods, both uncooked and cooked various ways. Don't worry if he rejects a food; try it again another time.

Your baby's most apt to accept new foods if they're introduced gradually and in small amounts. Never try to make foods more appealing to him by adding salt or sugar; too much salt can strain his kidneys and sugar promotes tooth decay. If you offer him a broad choice of healthy foods, he'll eventually pick enough of them to get all the nutrients he needs.

WASHING AND DRESSING

Life with your baby, especially in the early months, may seem like an exhausting, never-ending round of repeated activities: putting on and taking off clothes, changing diapers, and giving baths. But at no other point in her life are you as physically close to her, so you needn't feel that entire days go by without any-

thing to show for them. If everything necessary is on hand at the start, seemingly mundane bathing, changing, and dressing routines can be stimulating, fun-filled opportunities for you and your baby to get to know each other: What better times are there for a little face-to-face conversation and spontaneous play?

BATH RITUALS

During the first weeks after your baby's birth, a sponge bath every so often is enough to keep her clean. She's ready for tub baths after the stump of her umbilical cord has fallen off and her navel has healed completely. Fit her bath time into

your routine, planning it for a time that's convenient and can be interruption-free. Once she's able to sit up unsupported, line the tub with a slip-proof rubber mat. Watch her closely in the tub; don't ever turn your back—not even for an instant.

Skin Care
Bathing your baby two or three times a week is suffi-cient until she begins to crawl and feed herself, when she may need a bath daily. Fill the tub no more than a few inches deep with luke-warm water. Use mild infant shampoo and soap to wash her—only water for her face. Don't try to clean inside her ears or nose; their sensitive membranes may be harmed.

Likewise, there's no need to clean inside her genitals—nor under an infant boy's foreskin. Rinse the folds and creases behind her ears and at her neck, armpits, and groin especially well. Use a soft towel to pat her dry; rubbing may chafe. Powders

can be irritating and are harmful if inhaled, so don't powder her after a bath unless your pediatri-cian advises it.

1 If his hair needs washing, apply water from the tub carefully using your hand or a clean cloth. Avoid splashing water into his face.

2 Clean his body with a soapy cloth, then rinse him well. Even if he's in a tub that supports him, you must be careful he doesn't slip.

3 Once he can sit up on his own, bath toys provide him with endless opportunities for water play. Even at two years of age, though, he can't be left in the tub unattended.

TEETH AND NAILS

Routine dental care should begin with the arrival of your baby's first tooth—an event that may be preceded by a lengthy period of general discomfort in which she drools incessantly and constantly needs to bite. Her fingernails must be kept short and smooth to prevent her from scratching herself, and trimming them as often as every few days may be necessary throughout her early infancy.

Clean your baby's first teeth and gums with a wet washcloth or gauze pad.

Tooth Care

Clean your baby's teeth and gums at least twice daily, after breakfast and before bedtime. Use a washcloth or gauze pad until the end of her first year, then introduce her to a soft toothbrush; before she's two years old, toothpaste isn't necessary. While she needs to have her teeth brushed for her, also encourage her to use the toothbrush herself.

Limit both your baby's intake of sugar and the amount of time it stays in her mouth. Letting her go to sleep with a bottle of juice or milk promotes so-called "nursing bottle mouth," serious tooth decay caused by prolonged contact with sugary liquids. If she insists on taking a bottle to bed, fill it only with water.

Unless you suspect a problem, there's no need to schedule dental checkups during your baby's first two years. You may wish to consult your dentist or pediatrician, however, for advice on providing her with supplemental fluoride.

Nail Care

The best time to trim your baby's fingernails and toenails is right after her bath, when they're soft, or during her sleep, while she's still. Cut her fingernails to the shape of her fingertips; her toenails, which grow slowly and need trimming less often, should be cut straight across to keep them from becoming ingrown.

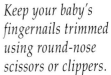

Keep your baby's fingernails trimmed using round-nose scissors or clippers.

TEETHING

Do give her firm objects such as teething rings to bite on.	**Don't** give her objects from which she could bite off a piece and choke.
Do chill objects in the refrigerator that she can bite on. Coldness helps to soothe her gums.	**Don't** completely freeze objects for her to bite on. Her gums are susceptible to frostbite.
Do give her whole teething biscuits and carrots up until the time she cuts teeth.	**Don't** give her whole solid foods that she can't properly chew and swallow once her teeth erupt.
Do massage her gums for brief periods at a time using an ice cube tied up in gauze.	**Don't** apply teething medications to her gums unless advised by your pediatrician.
Do try giving her acetaminophen to help ease her pain when other options fail to bring her relief.	**Don't** massage her gums with more than a finger's touch of fruit-flavored brandy or other alcohol.

DIAPERING AND CLOTHES

Changing diapers seldom is as distasteful as anticipated. But even if you don't adjust easily to the routine, you should try not to make your baby feel that there's anything dirty or disgusting about her bodily functions.

Your baby's clothing should be designed to make diaper changing as easy as possible. As she learns to get around and do things for herself, the clothes she wears will also need to fit comfortably and provide freedom of movement.

Diapering Basics

Changing diapers is nobody's favorite task, but it's simple and quickly becomes second nature. And when you take the time to chat or play with your baby while changing her diaper, her bottom gets a chance to air—which helps to prevent diaper rash. Cover a boy's penis with a cloth, though, to avoid being squirted.

As long as your baby's diaper is clean and fits comfortably, she's unlikely to care if it's cloth or a disposable. Stools reacting with urine provoke diaper rash, so change her promptly after each bowel movement. Changing only wet diapers is most practical at routine intervals—such as after feedings and before naps—but at the first sign of diaper rash, change her right away.

Clothing Basics

Choose your baby's clothes for comfort, convenience, and durability. Soft, absorbent fabrics that breathe—cottons and knits—are best. Judge design by efficiency, not just appearance: How easy is the item to put on and take off, and does it facilitate diaper changing? Look for sturdy necks and waistbands, seams that are strong without being

CHANGING YOUR BABY'S DIAPER

1 Clean as best you can with unsoiled parts of the old diaper, then use a moist washcloth or disposable wipe. Wipe gently back and forth across his body to clean his stomach.

2 Using a fresh washcloth or disposable wipe, clean the folds and creases of his thighs. Wipe gently downward, away from his body.

3 Lift up his legs to clean his genitals and anus. Use a fresh washcloth or disposable wipe to wipe gently from front to back, without trying to clean under the foreskin—or inside a girl's vaginal lips.

scratchy, tape-reinforced snaps, and stitching-bound buttonholes. Be sure that sleepwear meets federal requirements for being flame resistant.

By six months, your baby may have more than doubled her birth weight, so get items one or two sizes too large, or that feature elasticized waists, adjustable straps, or grow tucks. By then, she needs clothes that also provide her with the greatest freedom of movement. Unlike T-shirts and overalls, dresses—however adorable—can interfere with her ability to crawl.

Outfits with separate tops and bottoms simplify diaper changes, and can be mixed and matched to suit the weather—as well as what's in and out of the laundry. Clothing for outdoors must be large enough to fit comfortably over indoor clothes. Until your baby begins to walk, her footwear should consist of only socks and fabric booties or sneakers; hard-soled shoes aren't recommended before then because they can inhibit proper growth of her feet.

Giving her a choice of what to wear at an early age enlists her cooperation in getting dressed—and may help to prevent issues about clothes as she gets older.

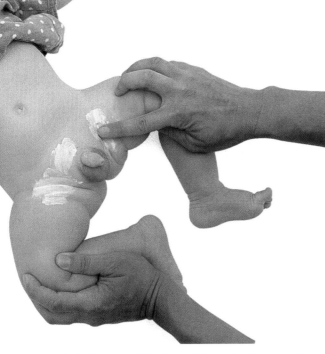

4 *Once he's clean, pat him dry with a soft, clean towel or tissues. If recommended by your pediatrician, apply cream or ointment to the skin around his genitals and anus before putting him into a fresh diaper.*

FIRST ESSENTIALS

- ✓ Four to six undershirts—if they feature front snaps, they don't have to be pulled over the head
- ✓ Two or three bodysuits—crotch snaps give access for diaper changing
- ✓ Six to eight stretchsuits—front and crotch snaps make them easy to get on and off
- ✓ Three or four nightgowns
- ✓ One or two sleepers
- ✓ Two or three sweaters—if they're finely woven or knitted, fingers won't get tangled
- ✓ Two or three pairs of socks
- ✓ One or two pairs of fabric booties
- ✓ Two tie-on hats—a broad-brimmed, cotton sun hat for summer; a warm, knitted hat that covers head and ears for winter
- ✓ One or two pairs of tie-on mittens
- ✓ One padded windsuit—a lined jacket and pair of pants that block out wind
- ✓ One hooded snowsuit—a two-piece outfit is easiest to get on and off, and the top can be worn without the bottom

SLEEPING PATTERNS

Your newborn baby will get all the sleep he needs; it just won't always happen at the times best suited to you. Until he settles into a normal sleeping and waking cycle, you can expect many nights of interrupted sleep—and sometimes no sleep. Take heart; by the end of his first year, he'll probably be getting through the night without needing a feeding or diaper change.

By then, though, your baby is also old enough to feel anxious about being apart from you; consequently, he may start having difficulty falling asleep and staying asleep in his own bed. Nighttime battles of wills can be avoided if you establish a bedtime routine for him early on, but don't be discouraged if at times he needs your encouragement to keep to his sleep schedule.

EIGHT HOURS UNINTERRUPTED

Most babies sleep randomly day and night at first, but as they get older their sleep habits become more predictable. By your baby's third month, his waking hours may occur primarily during the day. At six months, he may wake up only once or twice at night for a quick feeding and diaper change. Until he's at least two—probably older—he'll need to take naps in order to get through the day without becoming tired and irritable.

Telling Night from Day
Your baby is born with his own internal clock, so don't worry if he seems to sleep more or less than others. During his early months, your primary concern should be responding to his cries and attending to his needs. You'll find his sleeping patterns gradually begin to conform to yours as the weeks go by and he becomes more responsive to you.

Until your baby is about six months old, he isn't capable of consistently sleeping for up to eight hours without waking up to be fed and have his diaper changed. But you can begin as early as you want to encourage him to get most of his sleep at night by helping him to distinguish it from the day.

Save your baby's stimulating playtime activities for the hours that he's awake during the day. Establish a quiet bedtime routine to help him anticipate night's approach and get ready for going to sleep. Keep his awake periods at night as subdued as possible, helping him to fall back to sleep right after he's been fed and had his diaper changed.

PUTTING YOUR BABY TO BED AT NIGHT

1 Keep bedtime routines calm right from the start to help her learn that nighttime is for sleeping.

2 Get her accustomed to falling asleep on her own by putting her into her bed while she's still awake.

SLEEP SCHEDULE		
Age	Day and Night Cycle	Issues and Strategies
Newborn	From 14 to 16 hours: periods of one to four hours at night and during day	Limit socializing during nighttime feedings to help him distinguish night from day
6 months	From 14 to 16 hours: 10 to 12 hours at night with one or more interruptions; naps of one to two hours mid-morning and mid-afternoon	Place a few toys in his crib at night to occupy him when he awakens; he may then be encouraged to fall back asleep all on his own
1 year	From 12 to 14 hours: 10 to 12 hours at night without interruption; naps of one to two hours mid-morning and mid-afternoon	Wake him after he's napped for two hours, but give him time to adjust before introducing an activity
2 years	From 12 to 14 hours: 10 to 12 hours at night without interruption; nap of one to two hours early afternoon	Shorten or abandon his afternoon nap as needed to be sure that he's ready for sleep by his designated bedtime at night

Night and day are easier for your baby to tell apart if she naps routinely somewhere other than in her bed.

House Call

If I keep my three-month-old up later at night, will he sleep later into the morning?

Postponing your baby's bedtime so he'll sleep in may seem like a good idea logically, but it isn't biologically. When he's put to bed overtired, his body's natural response is to fight being tired, causing him difficulties in both getting to sleep and staying asleep.

3 Tuck a blanket snugly around her so she feels safe and secure. Keep her from being able to roll onto her stomach until she's three months old.

NIGHTTIME ROUTINES

By six months, most babies are beginning to develop consistent sleeping patterns. Try not to feel frustrated, though, if your baby isn't always sleeping through the night by the end of his first year. You'll find that getting him to sleep and stay asleep at night is easiest if you stick to a predictable bedtime routine. But be patient if you encounter setbacks; even the slightest advance in his development can disrupt his sleeping and waking cycle.

Getting to Sleep

You can help your baby to prepare for sleep at night by following the same bedtime routine every evening. Set a time for him to go to bed that best suits your household and is easy for you to always accommodate. Some time between 6 and 8 p.m. is usually convenient—late enough for you to be at home, early enough for you to have some of the evening for yourself.

Giving your baby a bath is an ideal start to his routine; fun and relaxing, it's also a natural way around resistance he may have to getting out of his clothes and into pajamas. If he dislikes being bathed, a quiet game or other activity in his room—once he's dressed for bed—is a good substitute.

Spending time together in your baby's room helps him to make the transition to his sleep environment. Away from stimulating distractions elsewhere in the home, he gets rewarded with your special attention. Reading a story is a settling ritual—the beginning of a worthwhile lifetime habit.

After tucking your baby into bed, leave the room while he's still awake; you don't want him depending on your presence to go to sleep. Let him fall asleep with his favorite playthings in bed beside him; they'll help calm and comfort him. Soft music also may help lull him to sleep. Let him decide if the room is left dimly lit or totally dark, and whether the door is kept open or closed.

Staying Asleep

Your baby's bedtime routine adds to his sense of security, but it won't work all the time. Don't despair if he sometimes has difficulty getting to sleep and staying asleep. Whenever his fussing and crying is uncharacteristic, be sure to check him first for signs of possible illness.

After you've ruled out sickness as the cause of your baby's inability to sleep, offer him a little reassurance. But unless he needs to be fed or have his diaper changed, leave him in his bed. Talk soothingly to him while rubbing his back or stroking his cheek or neck, then leave the room to encourage him to fall asleep on his own.

If your baby fusses or cries again or reawakens later during the night, don't rush to him right away. Give him a few minutes to try calming himself, then call out to him reassuringly, encouraging him to quiet down himself. Tolerate thumb-sucking, bed-rocking, chanting, or other habits he uses to help lull himself to sleep.

1 Reading her a story after she's bathed and in pajamas is the type of routine that helps her to make the transition from day to night.

2 Settle her into her bed at the designated time. If she's not ready to fall asleep, give her something she can play with alone.

Whenever your baby's fussing or crying persists, though, you should go to him and try to help him to settle back down in his bed for sleep. Resist the temptation to take him into your bed to sleep, or to comfort him with a snack; he may soon learn to expect these responses and eventually become unable to sleep without them.

Even after your baby starts sleeping through the night, he may at times awaken and call out—normal episodes following a change in routine or advance in development. But if he consistently awakens more than once or twice at night beyond six months, consult your pediatrician about a possible medical problem.

BEDTIME	
Do establish a nighttime routine that includes a set time for him to go to bed. **Do** settle him into his bed while he's drowsy to get him used to falling asleep and waking on his own. **Do** encourage him to comfort himself when he awakens by leaving a few of his favorite playthings in his bed. **Do** allow him to include a light snack and a drink before bed as part of his nighttime routine. **Do** go to him and offer reassurance when he awakens during the night and cries for more than a few minutes.	**Don't** vary the hour of his bedtime or unnecessarily disrupt his routine. **Don't** wait until he falls asleep to put him in bed; he may wake up feeling disoriented and be upset. **Don't** encourage him to be dependent on only you for comfort at night by always letting him fall asleep on or with you. **Don't** give him sleep-inducing medications or offer him food or drinks as comfort. **Don't** run to him the instant he awakens and fusses during the night or take him out of his bed to reassure him.

3 *Sleep may come to her more easily with music and a few of her favorite toys—which also may keep her amused for a while when she awakens.*

4 *Go to her if she fusses for more than a few minutes after you have left the room, but do your best to settle her down in her own bed.*

FORMATIVE PERSONALITY

A baby is a unique individual with a character of her own at birth. Not until she's about six months old, however, does she begin to become aware of herself as a separate person. Right at the time she's developing secure attachments to both her mother and father, she's likely to seem suddenly anxious about being apart from them—and wary of others.

While dependent on you, your baby also pursues her independence. For comfort during the transition, she may turn to a security object such as a pacifier or stuffed animal. As she learns to master her body and control her environment, she develops a sense of herself and her own worth. She gains a lot of autonomy by the end of her second year, but she doesn't need you any less.

TEMPERAMENT

Your baby is born with personality traits all her own that influence her behavior. Because she's so greatly affected by her environment, her inborn disposition isn't always a reliable guide to what her personality will be as she gets older. But your baby's temperament can play a big role in her early relationships and pace of development. By tuning in to her innate disposition, you can get a head start in adapting your parenting to best suit her character.

Gradual Bonding
The attachment of parent and child may be magical, but it's neither instantaneous nor automatic. The bonds between you and your baby evolve over time through your interactions, so don't worry about every little detail of your relationship.

The general ways in which a baby responds to her environment—such as her energy level, degree of movement, and crying patterns—are all clues to her temperament. Your baby's early behavior may seem to be random and unpredictable, but you'll find that it gradually conforms to a pattern—possibly within a few days of her birth. If her temperament is difficult for you to gauge, your understanding of her behavior may come more slowly, but don't worry; eventually you'll begin to figure her out.

Although a baby inherits traits from her parents, her temperament

A baby's intent exploring of his parent's face helps to strengthen the bond between them.

Imitating stimulates learning, and a baby's powerful, first role models are her parents.

A baby who reaches out delightedly for new playthings displays traits of an easy temperament.

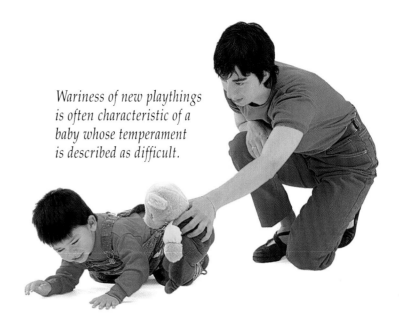

Wariness of new playthings is often characteristic of a baby whose temperament is described as difficult.

can't be either credited to or blamed on them. Your baby's nature isn't caused by you, so you shouldn't feel guilty if getting along takes a little time and requires some compromise. Since how compatible you are with each other depends greatly on your expectations, you should try to keep them within reason; don't demand too much from her or yourself.

Nature Nurturing

A baby's temperament isn't the only factor in her development; the environment in which she's raised is another big influence. Recognizing and accepting your baby's nature doesn't mean that there's no role for you to play in shaping her personality. On the contrary, you're sure to have some of the most profound effects on her character—intended and not.

How well suited a baby's environment is to her temperament can affect when and how comfortably she gets through each stage in her development. Just by responding in ways that are appreciative of your baby's nature, you can encourage her along at her own pace. If yours is the average "easy" baby, she'll probably be in a good mood most of the time and adapt quickly to change. Try not to feel overwhelmed, though, if she has difficulty adjusting; she won't suffer if her growth is a little slower.

A parent's biggest influence on a baby's personality is often the least deliberate: the results of normal, everyday interactions. Your baby naturally learns to do things in the ways they're done by those closest to her. And since she's also integrating attitudes and values along the way, her personality can be shaped by almost anything that happens in a day. So just remember that she's an individual, with a right to be herself—regardless of who you may have wanted her to be.

SEPARATION ANXIETY

Until your baby is six months old, she won't really care who comforts her. As she becomes aware of herself as a separate person, though, she'll probably feel insecure unless you're with her. Don't be alarmed by her anxiety at being apart from you or approached by strangers; it's a normal, healthy sign of her firm attachment to you. She isn't likely to be as apprehensive by the end of her second year, but may still be shy and clingy when stressed.

First Fears

A baby's separation anxiety isn't a sign of regression; it's positive proof she's developing an awareness of herself and forming secure attachments to her parents. So when your sunny and friendly baby suddenly turns fearful if you're not always with her, don't think you've done something wrong. Having identified and attached herself to you as her caregiver, she naturally seeks to stay in your protective company and not venture too close to someone who isn't as familiar to her.

However, a baby's separation anxiety can be difficult at times for a parent to handle—perhaps most awkward when triggered by a grandparent or other relative. Since your baby's degree of fearfulness is influenced in part by her own temperament, you should try not to feel embarrassed or guilty. You can't stop her anxiety by arguing, so be patient with her. Keep in mind that she looks to you in out-of-the-ordinary situations for cues on how to behave. Simply by staying calm, you can avoid reinforcing and prolonging her fearfulness.

If a baby is prepared for her parents' absence or a newcomer's arrival, her separation anxiety often isn't as intense. Rehearse departure and greeting scenarios with your baby as much as possible in advance of the event; make sure they always end with your return. When greeting a newcomer, let her keep a distance and observe you interacting in a friendly way. Don't insist on her involvement or leave her alone with someone unfamiliar. If the right tone is set, her wariness will eventually give way to her curiosity.

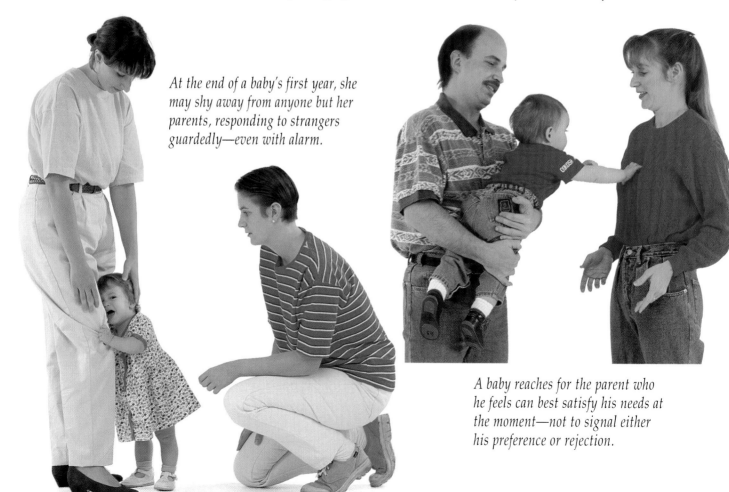

At the end of a baby's first year, she may shy away from anyone but her parents, responding to strangers guardedly—even with alarm.

A baby reaches for the parent who he feels can best satisfy his needs at the moment—not to signal either his preference or rejection.

SECURITY OBJECTS

As your baby begins to sense that she's a separate person, she must cope with the conflict between her desire for autonomy and her fear of losing closeness with you. To help relieve the tension, she may seek security in an object—something that she can use to comfort herself. Until she understands that your absence is only temporary and gains confidence in her ability to get by on her own, she probably will turn to her security object whenever she feels anxious.

Your baby may comfort himself by sucking, reaching for a pacifier to satisfy a powerful, natural urge.

Transitional Comfort
Before the end of a baby's first year, she usually finds some way of comforting herself—such as sucking on her thumb, fingers, or a pacifier, rocking back and forth, or clinging to a certain stuffed animal or blanket. Whatever method your baby adopts to cope with her feelings of anxiety, you should try not to interfere; the habit isn't likely to last long enough to become a problem. If you respond patiently to the behavior, she's more likely to outgrow the need for it at an early age.

In most instances, a baby's need for a comfort object is short-lived and she gives it up on her own. But don't worry if your baby becomes attached to her security object: She may talk to it or invest it with special powers, or refuse to have it washed or repaired. Don't be concerned by the behavior or try to stop it; she's not likely to be ready to give it up and you may simply add to the stress that's prompting it. If you're worried that her need for comfort is affecting her development, though, you should consult your pediatrician.

HIGH-NEED BABY

- ✓ Even with frequent feedings, seeks additional sucking—on a pacifier, thumb, or other object
- ✓ Sleeps only lightly for short intervals; rarely sleeps long or deeply
- ✓ Mindful of activity and easily distracted; difficult to calm or settle down
- ✓ Insists on always being held or carried; requires frequent rocking
- ✓ Sensitive to noise and easily startled
- ✓ Reacts strongly to stimulus: fusses and cries before bowel movements; easily irritated by external sources of discomfort

Carried around from place to place, a stuffed animal, blanket, or other object can help your baby to cope with the stress of transition.

AUTONOMY AND SELF-ESTEEM

Your baby's awareness of herself as a person starts her on the long road to autonomy. Well beyond the end of her second year, she'll still be veering between dependence and independence in her drive toward self-control. But from the time she begins turning the first corner, she's already developing a sense of her own worth—which is key to her ability to adapt. Out of increasing independence, she gains a sense of self—and with it, self-esteem.

Sense of Self

A baby's sense of self develops as she learns to control her environment. Even while your baby is dependent on you to meet all her basic needs, she's gaining awareness of her independence through mastery of her body. Once she can walk, she's able to go away from you. Once she can talk, she's able to start a conversation with you. And reflected in every aspect of her behavior as she acquires new skills, you'll soon discover clues to how she feels about herself.

Out of the responses a baby gets from her environment, she begins forming attitudes about herself. Not surprisingly, therefore, your baby's first notions of her self-worth are shaped by you—her biggest influence and the one with whom she interacts most during her early years. From the time she first smiles and you smile back, she's developing a sense of achievement; through every little way you show her that she's valued, she learns to value herself.

The environment a baby needs for a positive sense of herself is one that allows her to gain personal competence. Your bonds of unconditional love are essential to your baby's self-worth, but so, too, is a home where she can explore and learn, try and succeed. Her experience starts with basics such as feeling hungry and beginning to cry. When you respond right away, she gets more than just the comfort of a nourishing feeding; she

Being able to take off and put on clothes gives him a sense of achievement. Congratulate him on his efforts— even when he gets his head stuck or puts an item on backward.

Autonomy brings her the power to satisfy her own curiosity. She may take risks in her quest for discovery, so watch her closely.

Accidents are an inevitable part of his learning to take care of his own needs. Instead of criticizing him for a spill, encourage his cleanup efforts.

learns that she matters to you and that she can have some control of her surroundings. As she gets older, she needs playthings that she can master herself with a little effort and a play area where she can safely satisfy her own curiosity.

Sense of Confidence

Walking and talking are abilities that provide a toddler with the opportunity to become an ever more active participant in her environment, especially in interactions with her parents. As your toddler begins to more forcefully project her needs for independence and self-expression, your responsiveness is important to her sense of confidence. You may find her behavior difficult to deal with at times, but remember that she's trying

to test her own limits—not your patience.

A toddler builds her self-confidence as she develops her ability to do things on her own; and as soon as she's sure that she's capable of doing something, she usually feels ready to start doing something else. When your toddler begins wanting to do things herself, her insistence may sometimes seem like a challenge to your authority. However, you should try not to take her behavior personally; what she's rejecting isn't you, but a sense of being helpless.

Even when a toddler isn't entirely certain that she's capable of something she wants to do, she may be prepared to test all limits for the chance to try anyway. Rather than engage in battles with your toddler over minor

issues just to show that you're in charge, you should try getting her to test herself on doing things at which she's likely to be successful without too much help from you. Set realistic standards for her performance of a task, then give her lots of praise as she works to improve her skills.

Two of the things that a toddler eventually wants to try on her own are feeding

and dressing herself. Set your toddler up to feed herself in a place where a little mess doesn't matter. Give her utensils that she can handle and cut her food into pieces small enough for her to manage. Get clothes that are easy for her to put on and take off. Encourage her sense of ownership and responsibility by putting labels with her name on some of her favorite items.

Being separate at first may mean the right to possess. Before he can be expected to share, he needs to fully experience ownership.

A sense of independence makes possible the taking of initiative. She learns that she can show affection—not just respond to it.

EARLY DISCIPLINE

A baby doesn't need a lot of discipline. But as your baby begins to get around on his own and communicate verbally, he needs your guidance to help him learn to control his behavior. Your goal shouldn't be to restrict him or keep him in line by doling out punishments; what he requires is the freedom to develop in his own way within limits that he can manage.

A baby's struggle for independence doesn't make discipline an easy job for his parents. Even if you're prepared for your baby's rebelliousness, you may find his unpredictability and negativism to be exasperating at times. Don't be discouraged if his defiant moods and tantrums sometimes try your patience; these experiences are a natural part of his development.

LIMITS AND OUTER CONTROLS

Developing an awareness of self is both exciting and frightening for your toddler. At one extreme, he wants total freedom from you; at the other, he wants to depend absolutely on you. Trying to achieve a balance is likely to be a turbulent period for both of you. By the time he turns two, there may be slightly less swinging back and forth, but the striving for perfect equilibrium will last for many years beyond—possibly his entire lifetime.

Trials of Independence
Your toddler's development requires him to assert his independence from you. But he can't gain autonomy without your help. While encouraging his efforts to be less dependent, you must keep in mind what he's able to handle. If his environment is adapted to his capabilities, his attempts to control it are more likely to be successful.

You can tailor your toddler's environment to his abilities by eliminating sources of frustration. Give him a stool to stand on so he can reach the sink to wash his hands. Get T-shirts and pants with elasticized waists so he doesn't have to fumble with buttons and zippers to get dressed. When he wants to do up his coat, join the bottom of the zipper to give him a head start.

Your toddler gains self-confidence every time he accomplishes something new. For each success, though, there are likely to be many frustrated efforts. And his alternately insisting "Me do it myself" and "You do it" adds to the potential for conflict. He may be contrary and demanding, but be patient; he needs your help to handle disappointment and not be discouraged by failure.

SELF-CONTROL	
Do set behavior limits. **Do** communicate the reasons for rules. **Do** apply consequences for ignoring limits. **Do** reward good behavior. **Do** stay patient and maintain a sense of humor. **Do** discipline respectfully. **Do** be sympathetic and understanding when applying consequences.	**Don't** expect too much. **Don't** justify limits using simple authority. **Don't** enforce rules harshly or inconsistently. **Don't** ignore misbehavior. **Don't** turn every little thing into a crisis. **Don't** shame or humiliate. **Don't** withhold love or affection as a way of applying punishment.

Before you take away something he can't have, offer him something he can have in exchange.

She's learning self-control when she overcomes her frustration at not getting what she wants and turns to something else.

Codes of Conduct

Your toddler needs to gain control of his behavior as much as he needs to develop a sense of accomplishment. Firm, consistent discipline on your part is critical. Discipline isn't the same as punishment; it's guidance, and you should try to strike a balance between extremes. If you're too rigid, he won't have enough freedom to experiment and make his own decisions. If you're too permissive, he'll have too much control and not enough opportunity to discover what's expected of him. Don't agonize too much; as long as you're clear and consistent in your expectations, he'll learn the value that you place on standards of behavior.

Setting reasonable rules for your toddler promotes his autonomy; if he's sure of his limits, he can maintain the sense of security that's so vital to his efforts to gain greater independence.

But while he needs to learn what he may and may not do, he also needs to understand the reasons for your rules. If your reasons are not explained or are justified by "Because I say so," he'll have difficulty internalizing the rules into his own sense of self. Remember, too, that some rules should change as he develops; you'll need to rethink your reasons from time to time.

You'll find that your toddler learns to discipline himself most readily the more he is praised for good behavior and the less he is criticized or punished for misbehavior. Your praise motivates him in the positive ways he knows; if you simply find fault, he's given a lesson only in what not to do. When he breaks a rule, though, you shouldn't overlook it or be lax about applying the consequences. Whenever you're offering praise or correcting mistakes, be sure that you keep the focus of your attention on his behavior—not him. If he misbehaves, you want him to know that his action is wrong, not that he's bad. If you praise him rather than his action, he's likely to worry that you may love him less if ever he behaves differently. He won't develop positive, self-confident behavior overnight; but as long as you keep letting him know that he's capable of it, he'll succeed eventually.

Until he develops enough self-control to accept delayed gratification, even a promise of something he likes better may not get him to stop what he's doing.

Independence and Defiance

Your toddler will assert himself in negative ways, so don't be shocked if he starts saying no to everything. He may be so relentlessly negative that he says no even when he sometimes means yes. Be patient; once he starts to develop control of himself, he won't seem as defiant.

Negative Assertiveness

When your toddler ignores your questions or does the opposite of what you request, he doesn't really mean to defy you. Saying no and disagreeing are simply his ways of trying to assert his separateness from you. By being negative, he's trying to prevent you from taking him for granted and make you deal with him as an individual.

Your toddler's negativism may be intense, but he'll soon outgrow it. Just try to reduce the chance for conflict in your interactions with him. Rather than forbid him to do something, suggest options he may do. Ask questions that offer choice and don't beg refusal: "What toys do you want in your bath?" instead of "Do you want a bath now?"

1 Restraint isn't easy if temptation is in reach. Don't expect her to comply just because you forbid her to touch something.

2 Don't discourage inquisitiveness by being too strict. Showing her how to handle something allows her to satisfy her curiosity.

Temper Tantrums

When your toddler has difficulty mastering a task or makes a demand you won't meet, he may feel frustrated by his helplessness. Sometimes his frustration may surge into uncontrollable anger and erupt in a tantrum. In a venting of overwhelming emotion that is as alarming to him as to you, he may scream, kick, or throw things. Take heart; his displays of temper will ease as he gets better able to express himself verbally and control his behavior.

Warning Clouds

Your toddler's first tantrum might occur early in his second year, but may happen sooner. By the time he's two years old, he may have tantrums regularly once or twice a week—more often if he's very active, energetic, and determined. Don't panic too much, though; once you figure out how to anticipate and handle his tantrums, they won't seem so extraordinarily stressful.

If your toddler could give you the reasons for his tantrums he wouldn't need to have them, so don't expect him to help you avoid them. Since the frustration that sets him off into a tantrum can be due to simple hunger, overtiredness, or overstimulation, you shouldn't overlook the obvious. Other flashpoints for his tantrums that are the natural products of his temperament may take you time to recognize.

Weathering Storms

Your toddler's tantrums can't all be prevented, so you shouldn't berate yourself when you fail to see one coming. When his inevitable tantrum occurs, you need to stay calm. His loss of control is frightening for him—much more so if you lose control, too. He's beyond reason, so don't argue with him; screaming back or threatening punishment isn't helpful or effective.

1 *Reasoning isn't likely to overcome a toddler's opposition. But if you beg melodramatically, she just may think you're silly enough to put on her coat.*

House Call

I'm terrified when my daughter gets frustrated; she sometimes holds her breath so long that her face turns blue. What should I do?

Check with your pediatrician to be sure that her breath holding doesn't have a medical cause and isn't harmful. Then, simply ignore her whenever she starts this type of tantrum. She may get to the point that she faints, but her breathing will then be automatic and she'll recover quickly. After an episode, act like nothing has happened. Her tantrums may become both more frequent and dramatic at first, but if you persevere with the strategy, they'll eventually stop. Attention is what she wants most; and if she gets attention when she holds her breath, she's naturally encouraged to continue doing it.

2 *Imitating a toddler's resistance can sometimes enlist her cooperation. Take her part and cast her in the role of getting you to wear your coat.*

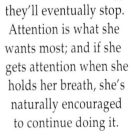

If you allow your toddler's tantrum to run its course, he'll probably end it within a few minutes and return to his normal self. By simply turning your back, leaving the room, or in some other way ignoring the tantrum, you're letting him know that it has no effect on you. In time, he'll learn that a tantrum isn't the way to get what he wants.

However, when your toddler's tantrum is so extreme that you fear he may hurt himself or someone else, you should pick him up as gently as you can and remove him to a quiet place. A violent tantrum is usually best handled by staying with him; let his need for support and comfort come before concern about discouraging the behavior.

You should try not to feel embarrassed if your toddler throws a tantrum in public; even more than at other times, he needs your control. Don't give him special treatment because of worry about what others might think. If you can't pick him up and take him off somewhere else, you should at least stand your ground and hold him until the tantrum ends.

Under no circumstances should you respond in a way that your toddler might interpret as a reward for having tantrums. For example, don't try to divert a tantrum by offering him candy or other treats. And you shouldn't ever let him know that a tantrum upsets you. If he learns to get satisfaction out of having tantrums, he's likely to throw more—not fewer.

TOYS AND PLAYTIME

Play is a baby's work, a self-motivated way of learning with its own reward: If it isn't fun, it isn't play. Even though you can't play for your baby, the best plaything she can have is you. Playing together is a great way to build your understanding of each other: Nothing can match the joy of it; nor is anything as rich with chances to promote her confidence and self-esteem.

A baby needs her parents to enable her to play. Your role, though, is to provide your baby with the right environment for play—the things, the example, and the encouragement. Don't go overboard; if her play is too structured and too much like work for you, it won't be fun for her. And until she develops her ability to concentrate, she won't find anything fun for long.

MOBILES, MUSIC, AND MIRRORS

Your baby's ability to figure out her environment develops so naturally that you may not even notice. But the process doesn't happen automatically; she needs to have lots of opportunity to experiment with her vision, hearing, and other senses before she can learn to interpret using them. Your daily interactions help her along the road to understanding; every time you draw her attention to something, you're encouraging her to sharpen her perceptions.

Sights and Sounds
Your baby's eyes and ears are important tools for exploring, and she won't need encouragement to use them. The ordinary is enough to fascinate her, so you needn't go out of your way to introduce her to new experiences; on the contrary, too much stimulation can overwhelm her.

During your baby's early months, she'll be especially captivated by your face and voice. Just holding her and singing or changing expressions is the best play you can offer her. Smile and talk to her as you go about everyday routines. Repeat things for as long as she seems attentive, but stop when she loses interest and turns away.

Your baby's vision and hearing also benefit from playthings such as mobiles and music boxes. Magazine cutouts and voice recordings are sufficient; you needn't be elaborate. Encourage her to watch herself by hanging an unbreakable mirror in her crib. Give her a rattle or other noise-making toy so she can make sounds.

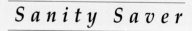

A brightly colored musical mobile is good sensory stimulation for your baby. The sound of a noise-making toy motivates him to practice handling it.

TOUCH AND TEXTURE

During your baby's early months, she'll make increasing use of her sense of touch to explore her environment. By moving her mouth or hands over something, she's able to experience both its texture and shape.

Touching things is good exercise for your baby, too. As she learns about an object using her lips and tongue or fingers and thumbs, she's putting to work and learning to coordinate her muscles, tendons, and joints.

Tactile Learning

As your baby starts moving around on her own, her mouth and hands become added tools for discovery. You'll need to watch her closely to make sure that she doesn't get into anything dangerous, but try not to interfere otherwise with her exploring. Let her seek out and go after things at her own pace and in her own way. She'll want to know that you can see her, and probably will check every so often for your response. Support her natural curiosity by complimenting her exploring and commenting positively on all her discoveries.

Your baby doesn't need expensive playthings to develop her sense of touch. Balls, blocks, rings, and cups of different materials and sizes are among the many worthwhile toys that she can learn from, but don't be surprised by her interest in exploring everyday items in your cupboards and purse. And there are many ways she can use her sense of touch to be creative—with anything from fingerpaints or play dough to a pile of sand or container of water. Just be sure she doesn't get her hands on anything sharp or with small pieces that may come off in her mouth.

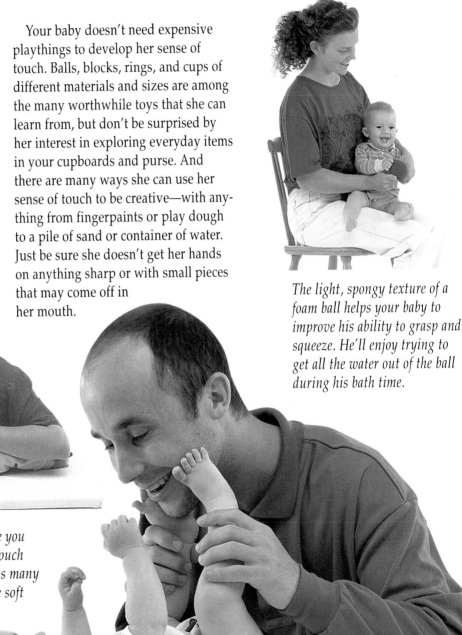

The light, spongy texture of a foam ball helps your baby to improve his ability to grasp and squeeze. He'll enjoy trying to get all the water out of the ball during his bath time.

Your baby's change table is a place where you spend a lot of time together and a little touch play comes naturally. Introduce him to as many sensations as you can think of—from the soft and soothing to the prickly and ticklish.

MOTION AND PERSPECTIVE

Being able to move around doesn't just give your baby greater opportunity to explore; it brings her perspective and a better vantage on her environment. As her physical skills improve, she's less challenged by the need to control her body and freer to investigate using all her senses. And once she's capable of purposeful actions such as reaching and grasping, changes occur in her play.

Space and Distance

Your baby won't pay much attention to inanimate things during her early months; her biggest interest will be people—especially you. But as she gets better able to use her hands for picking up and grasping, and can move around steadily on her feet, you'll find that she develops a greater fascination with objects of all shapes and sizes. And being capable of holding things, she'll naturally start to explore what happens when she lets go of them.

Your toddler's investigation of objects helps her to improve her perceptions of space and distance. She becomes better at judging if something is close or far and at adjusting her grasp to its shape, size, and other features. You'll probably observe her deliberately dropping things one after another and following the motion with her eyes. If you give her a container of things that she can dump out and put back in, she'll also gain an understanding of in and out as well as full and empty.

Your toddler can learn a lot about the motion and momentum of things from toys that have wheels.

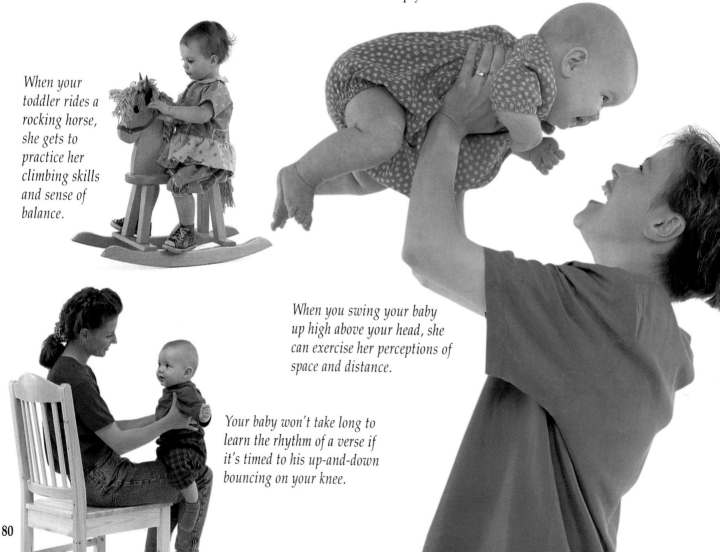

When your toddler rides a rocking horse, she gets to practice her climbing skills and sense of balance.

When you swing your baby up high above your head, she can exercise her perceptions of space and distance.

Your baby won't take long to learn the rhythm of a verse if it's timed to his up-and-down bouncing on your knee.

PEEKABOO AND PAT-A-CAKE

Your baby's developing fascination with objects won't diminish her need for social play. But her interest in both people and things is a sign that she's beginning to recognize she's separate from them, so you'll have to be careful not to discourage her sense of independence. Encourage play that belongs to her by letting her make the decisions and following her directions; save your suggestions for when she's frustrated or can't think of what to do next.

Memory and Coordination

Your baby's memory and coordination aren't things that you should worry too much about; their development doesn't normally require special attention. But there are many fun-filled ways you can interact with her in the course of a day that allow her to practice using her skills. You'll soon discover that the best exercises evolve naturally out of ordinary routines and simple repetition—and don't call for a lot of equipment.

Peekaboo is one universal game your baby is sure to enjoy by the time she's six months old. Copying you, she'll quickly learn to cover her face with her hands and pull them away—and soon invent her own variations of the game. Initiating peekaboo is apt to be her first act of humor, a trick that shows she's capable of forethought and intent. The game also indicates that she has a memory of you and is secure enough to try a short period of separation under her control.

Other types of basic hiding games provide your baby with the same opportunity to practice her memory and coordination. Until she's at least six months old, she probably won't search for an object, even if it's only partially out of sight. A few months later, though, she'll go after something you've hidden; because she now understands that it exists even when she can't see it, she'll find the game amusing. You may not always be as entertained by her games of "come and get me" and "pick up what I drop," but try to be patient; she'll soon outgrow them.

Clap-and-rhyme games such as pat-a-cake are other enjoyable ways that your toddler can practice her skills. You'll quickly discover that there are many, many more games, too; and you're bound to make up some of your own together. Don't insist on doing any game a certain way and never put the focus on getting results; as long as you're both having fun, whatever game you're playing is working.

The simple repetition of a game like pat-a-cake is good for your toddler's developing memory and coordination.

Peekaboo and other kinds of hiding games help to promote your baby's self-awareness and confidence.

WiNNiNg WaYS

PLAYMATES

• Provide her with lots of opportunities to play alongside others, but don't pressure her to interact. She probably won't be ready to engage with others for any length of time until she's at least two years old.

• Supervise her play alongside others constantly, but don't intervene unless there's a risk that someone may get hurt. If she loses control or can't handle the situation for any reason, simply take her out of it.

• Be a good role model, but don't expect her to catch on right away. Even with the best of training in etiquette, she'll need time to practice and figure out the reasons for it.

TOPPLING TOWERS

Playthings help your toddler to improve her dexterity and sharpen her conceptual thinking. She needs good visual ability to reach for small things, fine motor coordination to pick them up, and perceptual skills to understand what her eyes are seeing and hands are doing. Her playthings—whether they're toys or everyday objects—also give her a means to both express herself and interact with others.

Before your toddler is capable of building things, he needs to practice knocking them down.

Cause and Effect

By the end of your baby's first year, she's likely to be a lot better at using her hands and beginning to show an ability to concentrate. Instead of having to let go of one object in order to get another, she'll be able to hold an object in each hand. She'll also be capable of transferring an object from one hand to the other and have mastered the pincer grasp, which allows her to pick up even the tiniest of crumbs.

As your toddler gains greater control of her hands, you will find that her interest in things is backed by much more purpose. No longer simply curious about an object, she wants to know what happens when she does something to it. Her exploring of cause and effect may try your patience at times, but don't take her behavior personally.

Emptying a pail onto the floor can lead her to discover that the water changes shape; her action may be deliberate, but her motive isn't just to anger you.

The best environment for your exploring toddler is one that's safe and free of restrictions. She'll need an open space for play where she can reach her playthings—which needn't all be expensive toys. Simple, everyday objects that she can stack, sort, push and pull, and fit together and take apart will do. Don't forget things she can fill and empty for use in the bathtub and sandbox—two other excellent places where she can do a lot of exploring.

As your toddler tries putting things together, he's learning about their qualities and characteristics.

PLAYTHINGS		
Age	**Suggestions**	
Newborn to 6 months	Mobile Pictures of faces Music box or voice recordings Unbreakable mirror Rattles	Toys that squeak Balls of various sizes Blocks of different shapes Rings of various colors Cups and containers
6 months to 1 year	Soft fabric toys Durable wooden or plastic toys Activity center Nesting cups Stacking rings	Large building blocks Toy telephone Unbreakable kitchen toys Stuffed animals Toys with wheels
1 year to 2 years	Play dough, paints, and crayons Sandbox toys Bath and water toys Large interlocking blocks Simple puzzles	Cars, trucks, trains, and planes Push-pull and riding toys Dolls that can be dressed Dress-up clothes Simple picture- and storybooks

PRETEND PLAY

Your toddler's ability to pretend is a natural result of her developing physical and intellectual skills. Not only does she become more capable of imitative behavior, but she starts to think in symbolic terms—for example, using a chair to represent a car. She can't drive a car, but by copying someone's behavior she can begin to make sense out of it. In similar ways, she gains greater freedom to explore relationships as well as concepts and ideas.

Early Imagination

Your baby isn't born with a developed sense of imagination. Her understanding of her environment at first is limited to her interactions with the people and things around her. But as she becomes able to form mental images and develops vocabulary to give them names, she can begin to think with symbols and explore both objects and ideas in creative ways. A stuffed bear, for example, she'll imagine is hungry and needs to be fed.

Sometime into your toddler's second year, she'll probably make her first attempts at pretending—most likely just simple imitations of actual experiences. She'll pretend to drink from a cup that's empty, for example. However, her pretending may evolve quickly beyond the bounds of her own direct experience. For instance, she may pretend to be the mommy and put you in the role of being the baby who has to go to sleep.

Your toddler's pretending is her way of trying to figure out her environment and her place in it, so you shouldn't interfere. Be supportive of her pretending by setting aside a dress-up box of old grown-up clothes and things that she can incorporate into kitchen, bedroom, and other scenes. Her imagination can't harm her, so don't worry about her behavior.

> **GOOD TOYS**
>
> ✓ How safe is it? Check that there are no sharp edges and no long strings or cords. Be on the lookout for breakable parts and small pieces that can be easily pulled off.
>
> ✓ Is it durable? Inspect the workmanship closely to be sure that it's well made. Consider whether it's washable as well as if repairs are likely to be needed and would be easy to do.
>
> ✓ How suitable is it? Something that doesn't correspond to her interests and stage of development is apt to either bore or frustrate her. It probably won't get much use.
>
> ✓ Can it be used in different ways? Consider its versatility. If it isn't relatively unlimited in its applications and doesn't challenge or stimulate, she's likely to outgrow it quickly.

When your toddler pretends that she's you, her behavior says a lot about how she perceives you.

Your toddler's make-believe dinnertimes are likely to approximate some of the real ones he's had.

HOME ENVIRONMENT

You'll naturally want your baby to be raised in a home that's safe and comfortable. He will require the security of an environment that accommodates his developing skills and abilities, one that's neither restrictive nor arranged with only grown-ups in mind. Your goal isn't to limit his freedom, but to give him a safe place in which to satisfy his curiosity.

Remember, too, that ensuring your baby's well-being means more than just providing the right equipment and toys. As important as you are to his physical safety, you're even more important to his sense of emotional security. And whenever you're apart from him, you'll want to know that he's getting competent care from someone responsible.

CHILD EQUIPMENT

Although there's a great deal of useful equipment available for babies, most of it isn't usable for longer than a few months. Before giving in to expensive buying impulses, you should first consider what baby equipment you really need, how it's going to fit into your home, and whether you can borrow it or adapt furniture you already own. Providing the best for your baby doesn't mean shouldering an unnecessary financial burden.

Early Basics
Once you've decided on a safe, quiet, and convenient location for the nursery, you'll need to figure out the space available for three essentials: a crib, a change table, and storage. Another basic item that you'll have to get is a car seat; even if you don't own a car, you'll require one at least for the ride home after the baby is born.

Your baby's crib is the biggest item and needed the longest time, so arrange other furnishings around it. The crib must meet minimum safety standards:
• Rails—at least 22 inches high above the mattress in its lowest position.

• Slats—at most 2⅜ inches apart.
• Side latches—baby-proof; safest require two separate actions for release.
• Mattress—firm support and tight fit; a space of no more than two fingers between it and the frame.
Bumper pads must be tied to the slats in at least six places and

A restraining strap or bar is required to keep your baby from slipping down between the tray and seat of his high chair.

Your baby may still be sleeping in a crib at the age of two, so invest in one that's sturdy and meets all minimum safety standards.

the loose ends cut off; they should be removed once the baby can pull himself upright. If you obtain a secondhand crib, make sure that the teething guards and finish are in good condition; if you refinish it, use a high-quality, nontoxic enamel product.

Your baby's change table can be simply a wide, padded dresser, but you'll need a space nearby to keep diapers and clothes. For storage, you can use anything from drawers to shelves or baskets. Just be sure that whatever equipment you get is well constructed and sturdy, with no sharp edges.

Later Options
Decisions about equipment extras such as infant seats, playpens, and swings can be left until you get a better sense of your baby's preferences. You're likely to want at least one of these items so you can free yourself to attend to

household chores, but remember that they're not baby-sitters; use them only under supervision and for no more than short periods at a time.

Safety standards don't exist for many equipment extras, so you'll need to be careful about the ones you get for your baby. Judge items for yourself; high prices and big-name endorsements don't necessarily guarantee quality or safety. Be sure that you always follow the safety instructions provided by the equipment manufacturer, especially any weight and size guidelines.

One piece of additional equipment you'll eventually need is a high chair. Whatever type and model you decide on should have a wide base so it can't be tipped over if it's accidentally bumped. If the high chair folds, make sure that its locking device is secure each time you set it up.

OUTFITTING THE NURSERY

• **Think safety over style.** Equipment standards alone don't guarantee safety; not all elements of design, structure, and use are covered. Be cautious when choosing equipment and careful in using and maintaining it. For example, cribs featuring high corner posts or headboards with decorative curves or openings should be avoided because of the risk that the baby's head could get caught.

• **Think function over form.** You don't have to possess every possible piece of equipment, nor is everything needed right away. For the first three months, the baby can sleep in a simple bassinet—even a lined laundry basket. Multipurpose equipment such as dressers with change table-tops that convert to shelf space and infant seats that double as swings can be space- and cost-efficient.

If your change table is the right height, you won't have to do a lot of bending while attending to your baby.

Your toddler may insist on getting into and out of a stroller by himself, so get one with wheels that lock.

Your infant's car seat must be installed facing the rear of the car.

CHILDPROOFING

There's some truth to the old saying that a toddler is an accident looking for a place to happen. But since your toddler can't be faulted for simply pursuing his natural urge to explore, you're the one who must take the responsibility for ensuring that he has a safe environment in which to satisfy his curiosity. In order to protect him from potential dangers, you'll need to keep thinking ahead to the next stage in the development of his skills and abilities.

Preventing Accidents

An accident can befall your baby faster than you think, so you need to be vigilant in your safety-mindedness. The best precaution of all is to keep a close watch on him at all times. You can't predict the first time that he'll roll over, so don't turn away from him for even a moment when he's on the change table. Take him with you—however inconvenient or short the time—rather than leave him at any height from which he might fall.

Once your baby can grab things, you need to be careful about what's within his reach. He'll put everything into his mouth, so be sure he doesn't have access to anything he could choke on. While you're handling him, don't eat, drink, or hold anything hazardous. Move his crib and playpen away from drapery and electrical cords that he might pull on or get entangled in. Remove pins and other sharp objects from his change table.

Before your baby starts crawling, survey every room in your home at his eye level and take action to eliminate potential dangers. Perform the same exercise outdoors, too. Both safety inspections should be conducted again before he begins walking and routinely as he grows. You'll be making a good start in childproofing his environment by using the many safety devices available to lock doors, cabinets, and drawers, eliminate falls, and prevent electrical shock.

Limits set by a safety gate provide her a secure environment where her curiosity doesn't have to be restricted.

Cabinet latches may deter him from getting into places that he shouldn't, but don't count on them for total prevention.

Unused electrical outlets invite him to stick things in unless you fit them with safety caps.

Eliminating Hazards

All your best childproofing efforts won't spare your toddler the occasional bump or bruise, but they can help to ensure that he doesn't suffer a serious accident:

• **Nursery:** Be sure that all furniture is sturdy; install protective guards on sharp edges. Use only short cords to attach things to his crib and remove items strung across it once he can stand. Store playthings on a shelf that he can reach without climbing; don't use a chest that isn't fitted with supports to hold the lid open. Restrict his access beyond play areas with safety gates.

• **Kitchen:** Don't allow him near the stove; use back burners whenever possible and turn pot handles toward the rear. Install a safety latch on the refrigerator. Unplug appliances when they're not in use and keep their cords out of his reach. Store household cleaners in a locked cabinet. Keep sharp utensils, plastic bags, and garbage out of his reach.

• **Bathroom:** Prevent him from venturing in alone by shutting the door and using a doorknob guard. Install a safety latch on the toilet. Line the bathtub with a slip-proof rubber mat. Store medicines in a locked cabinet. Keep razors, hair dryers, and cosmetics out of his reach. Set the water heater thermostat below 130°F.

• **Backyard:** Install locks on fence gates. Store all gardening tools and supplies in a locked shed. Get rid of plants and shrubs with poisonous leaves or berries. Set up his play equipment on grass or sand, not a hard surface. Cover his sandbox when he's not playing in it and empty the water out of his pool right after each use.

Place anything harmful that he might be tempted to touch safely out of reach.

Cushion his falls against sharp corners by installing protective edge guards on furniture such as tables.

	SAFE FROM FALLS
✓	Never leave your baby unattended anywhere but in his crib.
✓	Raise the sides of your baby's crib when he's in it. Lower the level of the mattress in your baby's crib as he grows.
✓	Always use the restraint strap on an infant seat, change table, high chair, and stroller.
✓	Limit clutter on floors.
✓	Anchor floor rugs with carpet backing or double-sided masking tape.
✓	Restrict the waxing of floors to prevent them from being slippery.
✓	Place a slip-proof rubber mat in the bathtub.
✓	Keep halls and stairways clear of obstructions.
✓	Install safety gates at the top and the bottom of staircases.
✓	Put away stools and other furniture that can be climbed to reach hazards.
✓	Move furniture away from windows.
✓	Open windows from the top instead of the bottom, if possible.
✓	Secure windows and screens with guards.

SUPPLEMENTARY CARE

Your devotion to your baby may be so strong that you wish to shower him with constant attention. But you'll find that you can't possibly accomplish everything you need or want to if he's always at your side. Sooner or later you'll have to give up some of the responsibility for his immediate care—even if it's just for a night out. Breaks in your parenting duties won't be as trying on your peace of mind if you find reliable, experienced baby-sitters.

First Sitter

Whatever the occasion, your first time away from your baby may be nerve-racking. You may be skeptical about letting anyone else look after him, but you shouldn't worry that he'll feel abandoned and unloved. Until he's six months old, he's unlikely to be troubled if someone else keeps him fed, dry, warm, and cuddled. Even once he's old enough to begin experiencing anxieties of his own, he's not likely to be upset by your absence for very long if he's comforted by a competent baby-sitter.

You'll cope better with uncertainties about being apart from your baby if you find the right person to mind him while you're gone. Other than checking qualifications and references, however, there's no best way of searching for a baby-sitter. If you have family living nearby, you may have easy access to someone familiar who's both loving and free; make sure, though, that you don't abuse the privilege. You may locate someone you can trust by asking for recommendations from parents in the neighborhood and at work. Local churches, schools, and professional child-care agencies are other possible sources; some communities have baby-sitting cooperatives.

When you're interviewing baby-sitter candidates, don't ignore your basic instincts. If you have reservations about someone's character or individual style, the person isn't the right baby-sitter for you. And if you're not comfortable with the person, odds are your baby won't be either; he'll have preferences, too, that you should respect. You'll never be able to relax and enjoy yourself away from him if you have doubts about the person you've left him with.

Afterthoughts...

"I felt like I'd lost my wife after our baby was born. She just couldn't bring herself to have someone else mind him for an hour or two so we could go out together. After weeks of coaxing, she finally agreed to getting a baby-sitter. She had such a good time that now she makes sure we get out alone at least once every two weeks."

"All my friends seemed trapped at home with their babies at first and I was determined that it wouldn't happen to me. From the time my daughter was born, I've had a sitter come in regularly so I could go off by myself. My daughter adores the sitter and I don't feel as pressured by motherhood because of the breaks I get."

The time that your baby spends without needing your full attention helps prepare him to be apart from you.

First Sitting

Once you're gone from the house, your baby-sitter takes over all responsibility for the care of your baby. So, you'll need to be very clear about your expectations and your baby's routines in order to eliminate as much uncertainty as possible—for all of you. You'll also want to treat a good baby-sitter well: Be back at the agreed time and be prepared to pay the agreed hourly rate on your return. Pay for time you cancel at the last minute if you'd like assurance that the baby-sitter will consider a request to come at a future date.

Ask a baby-sitter you're having for the first time to arrive a little early for a get-aquainted session. Conduct a tour of the house, pointing out safety and security features such as locks, utility shutoffs, and smoke detectors. Post a list of emergency telephone numbers with your address at the top for quick reference; leave a number where you or a trusted neighbor can be reached.

Inform your baby-sitter of your baby's preferences and show where essential supplies such as diapers and blankets are kept. Demonstrate and leave written instructions on how he should be fed, burped, and held, and what works best to calm and comfort him when he cries. Prepare bottles in advance and give details on bedtime routines. Don't forget to indicate his favorite playthings.

List the rules for your baby-sitter's use of the television and stereo, and eating of snacks. Don't suggest chores that might be done or presume the house will be any tidier than it is when you leave. State clearly that you expect the telephone to be kept free for your check-in calls and that there is to be no entertaining of visitors.

INTRODUCING A BABY-SITTER

3 As his initial wariness of the baby-sitter gives way to curiosity, he won't worry as much about your going away.

1 Get him ready to meet a baby-sitter with rehearsals of the fun he'll have while you're gone—and with you when you're back.

2 The more relaxed you are with the baby-sitter, the more comfortable he'll feel about interacting with both of you.

3 EARLY YEARS OF CHILDHOOD

FROM TWO TO SIX

Bouncing your delighted toddler on your knee one day, you'll suddenly notice how much heavier he seems and how big he's getting. No sooner are you into comfortable routines for feeding, dressing, and playing with him than he starts to take on responsibility for them himself. Through his preschool years, his physical growth will slow, but you'll marvel at the dramatic advances in his thinking and social abilities.

PHYSICAL GROWTH
- *Has attained more than half adult height.*
- *Last primary teeth appear; needs help with brushing.*
- *First visit to dentist; checkups with pediatrician now scheduled annually.*
- *Sensitive to tastes; may enjoy odd food combinations.*
- *Usually sleeps anywhere from 9 to 13 hours per day.*

2 YEARS TO 3 YEARS

THINKING AND UNDERSTANDING
• Aware of self as separate person; identifies self in photograph.
• Matches objects to pictures.
• Comprehends opposites such as up and down, large and small, and open and closed.
• Shows some awareness of difference between "mine" and "his" or "hers."

SKILLS AND ABILITIES
• Takes longer steps when walking and runs with greater confidence; can kick ball.
• Capable of standing on one foot for a few seconds.
• Speaks well enough to be understood by parents; has a word for almost all common objects.
• Begins toilet training.

PERSONALITY AND BEHAVIOR
• Broadening range of emotions; expresses affection openly.
• Easily upset by major changes in daily routines.
• Adventuresome and impulsive; needs to have clear limits set to prevent injury.
• Plays alongside playmates with little interacting.
• Imitates adults and playmates.
• Experiments with wide variety of roles in pretend play.

THINKING AND UNDERSTANDING

- *Beginning to grasp concept of time; talks about yesterday and tomorrow.*
- *Understands principles of same and different.*
- *Approaches problems from single point of view.*
- *May often experience difficulties in distinguishing between fantasy and reality.*
- *Lacks full comprehension of rule consequences.*
- *Developing imagination may lead to fears of monsters and the dark.*

PHYSICAL GROWTH

- *Appearance maturing; gains muscle and loses baby fat.*
- *Jaw begins widening in readiness for permanent teeth; starts having regular dental checkups.*
- *Stronger capacity for observation of details.*
- *Becomes more able participant at mealtimes.*
- *May enjoy baths, but hate having hair washed.*
- *Needs little help dressing.*
- *May not nap during day.*

PERSONALITY AND BEHAVIOR
- *Separates easily from parents.*
- *Emerging sense of empathy brings capacity for limited cooperative play.*
- *Vivid imagination leads to rich fantasy play.*
- *May display signs of hero worship toward older sibling or rivalry with younger sibling.*

SKILLS AND ABILITIES
- *Able to jump with both feet; may be capable of hopping on one foot.*
- *Catches ball with arms extended and throws without losing balance.*
- *Greater hand control; can cut with scissors.*
- *Pedals tricycle easily.*
- *Says most sounds correctly and can be understood by people outside immediate family.*
- *Masters toilet training; may occasionally have accidents and wet bed.*

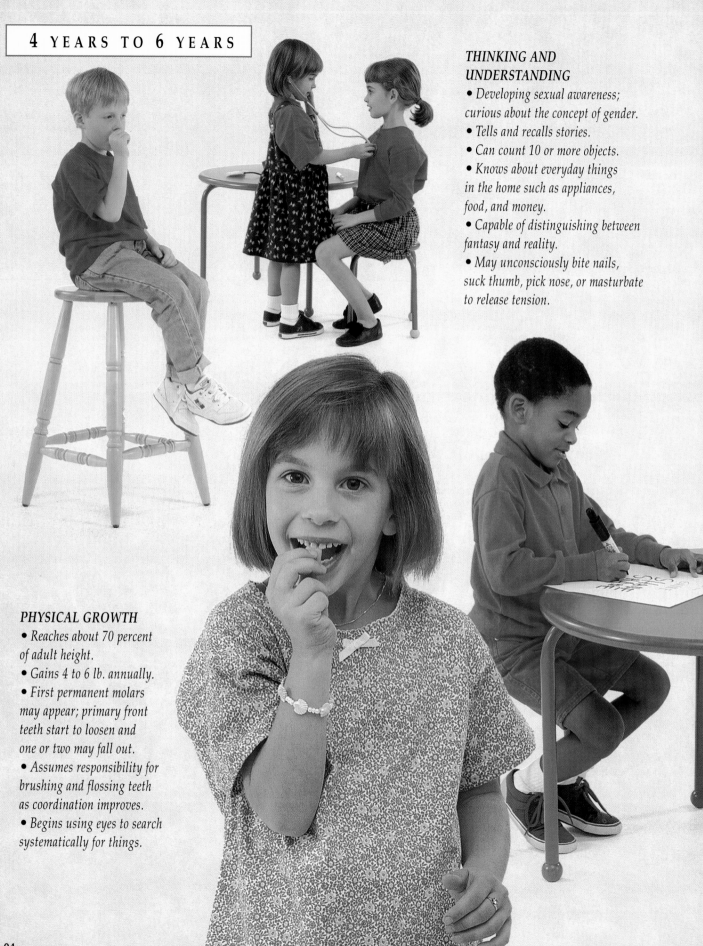

THINKING AND UNDERSTANDING

- *Developing sexual awareness; curious about the concept of gender.*
- *Tells and recalls stories.*
- *Can count 10 or more objects.*
- *Knows about everyday things in the home such as appliances, food, and money.*
- *Capable of distinguishing between fantasy and reality.*
- *May unconsciously bite nails, suck thumb, pick nose, or masturbate to release tension.*

PHYSICAL GROWTH

- *Reaches about 70 percent of adult height.*
- *Gains 4 to 6 lb. annually.*
- *First permanent molars may appear; primary front teeth start to loosen and one or two may fall out.*
- *Assumes responsibility for brushing and flossing teeth as coordination improves.*
- *Begins using eyes to search systematically for things.*

DEVELOPMENT WATCH

Milestones don't predict development; they're only a guide to general changes that you can expect. Alert your pediatrician to signs of delay such as:

- *frequent falling and problems with stairs; can't jump, hop, or ride tricycle*
- *doesn't speak in sentences of more than three words or understand simple two-part commands*
- *displays resistance to dressing, sleeping, or using the toilet*
- *shows no interest in fantasy play, other children, or interactive games*
- *doesn't separate easily from parents or respond to people outside family*
- *displays no emotional self-control; lashes out whenever frustrated or upset*

PERSONALITY AND BEHAVIOR
- *Often may swing between extreme emotional highs and lows; alternately demanding and eagerly cooperative.*
- *Shows particularly strong fondness for parent of opposite sex.*
- *Eager to please friends; wants to be like them.*
- *Enjoys singing, dancing, and acting.*
- *More inclined to be accepting of rules; enjoys games with rules and making rules for activities.*

SKILLS AND ABILITIES
- *Walks with swinging steps; more poised and in control of movements.*
- *Uses alternate feet to come down as well as go up stairs; somersaults, climbs, and may skip.*
- *Learns to tie own shoes.*
- *Copies shapes and prints some letters; draws people with bodies.*
- *Capable of increasingly complex construction projects.*
- *Communicates easily; uses detailed sentences of four or more words.*
- *May begin to independently express interest in learning how to read.*

TOILET TRAINING

Successful toilet training is principally a matter of timing. Once your child turns two, you'll probably have had enough of diapers. But be forewarned: If she isn't ready to be toilet-trained, pushing her to start early may just prolong the entire process. She must want to take this major step toward becoming more independent; she will eventually, so be patient.

With a relaxed, unpressured attitude to toilet training, the process is likely to go smoothly. Praise your child for her successes at self-control; don't even comment on her mistakes along the way. If she's scolded or made to feel bad about an accident, the added stress will only slow her progress. The best way to encourage her to be toilet-trained is simply to not overreact.

POTTY PROTOCOL

Most children who start toilet training at age two master the process by the time they're three years old. Your child may begin to be toilet-trained sooner, but you shouldn't expect her to learn more quickly; on the contrary, the process is likely to take several months longer. Don't worry if she isn't completely toilet-trained by age four or experiences occasional setbacks; they're normal and not a reason for concern about her development.

Giving Up Diapers
Your toddler is likely to show indirect signs of readiness for toilet training early into her third year. She'll become interested in the notion that certain things belong in certain places and seem keen on imitating and pleasing you. If she hasn't passed the early-toddlerhood stage of resistance and extreme negativism, you're better off to wait a while before starting to get her out of diapers.

You'll be doing your toddler and yourself a favor if you approach toilet training calmly and keep your emotions in check. Introduce

1 *Set up a potty chair in the bathroom and explain to her what it's for and when it's to be used.*

2 *If she's willing, let her try sitting on the potty chair; leave her diaper on if she wants.*

Afterthoughts...

"My son insisted from the beginning on standing up to urinate, but couldn't keep still and aim properly. He got a lot better once I started throwing a piece of toilet paper into the bowl first as a target for him to practice shooting at."

"We thought we were lucky when our first child started using the potty chair at two, but she had routine accidents until she was almost four. We never got her little sister to show any interest in the potty chair, but at three she was out of diapers and using the toilet."

3 *Don't force her to use the potty chair; she'll let you know when she's ready to try it.*

4 *Let her play without a diaper near the potty chair and remind her to use it when she needs to.*

her to a potty chair and let her know what it's for. Allow her to observe the use of the toilet by other family members, especially those of the same sex. Ask her every so often if she wants to try using the potty chair, but don't pressure her; if she doesn't seem interested, wait a while before bringing up the subject again.

Once your toddler is ready to begin using the potty chair, you may want to introduce routine sittings about 20 minutes after every meal, just before bed, and right after waking up in the mornings and from naps. Even if she doesn't go at first, she'll be developing the habit of using the potty chair. Also encourage her to come and let you know when she thinks she needs to go.

When your toddler uses the potty chair, don't force her to remain seated or sit for longer than she wants; if she hasn't gone within a few minutes, you shouldn't insist that she wait until she does. Once she's using the potty chair

regularly, gradually switch her from diapers to training pants during the day. Soon, she'll also be able to use the toilet—but for a while may need a trainer seat and help to get on it.

Keep in mind that your role in toilet training is to suggest, remind, encourage, and praise; pressure or frustration only makes the process more difficult. You'll naturally be interested in your toddler's progress, but try not to seem overly enthusiastic. If she senses that her actions control your feelings, she may feel anxious or insecure. Remember that toilet training is a learning process; avoid talking about her progress with others so she doesn't think you're judging her.

5 *When she starts asking regularly to use the potty chair, switch her from diapers to training pants during the day.*

ACCIDENTS AND BED-WETTING

Some children are completely toilet-trained within a few weeks, but don't be disappointed if your child isn't one of these exceptions and takes several months longer. Toilet training is a bewildering and complicated learning process, so be sensitive and try not to be taken aback by odd behavior or setbacks. Be understanding about her accidents and bed-wetting; they're likely to decrease in frequency after she's four and may stop before she's five.

Gaining Self-control

Your toddler may need a few months of getting accustomed to the potty chair before she uses it reliably. Give her all the time she needs to feel comfortable; she'll catch on to the routine soon enough if you stay relaxed. She'll probably learn to control her bowel movements before her urination and at first may have a little difficulty distinguishing between the two acts. Don't worry; as long as she views the process as natural and doesn't feel threatened, she won't be afraid to make the effort to figure it out herself.

When your toddler has an accident, you should treat it casually and clean it up without commenting negatively. Keep your feelings of frustration or disgust to yourself; she's likely to be far more upset by a mishap than she seems, so don't add to her sense of failure. She needs your support and comfort when she has an accident; don't think that by showing her your disapproval or making her feel ashamed you can prevent these incidents from happening.

If your toddler is like most, her nap and nighttime toilet training will take the most time to complete. Once she's routinely using the potty chair and developing daytime control, don't be discouraged if you need to persist a while longer before she's able to control herself during her sleep. Your best approach is to continue encouraging her to use the potty chair right before and after bed. Using training pants instead of relying on a diaper may help her to develop nap and nighttime control, so put a plastic mattress cover on her bed to minimize the cleanup of an accident. Restricting how much she drinks before going to sleep and waking her to use the potty chair aren't likely to stop her from wetting her bed; if she's agreeable, though, you may want to try these measures anyway.

Backsliding in your toddler's toilet training can result from any event that

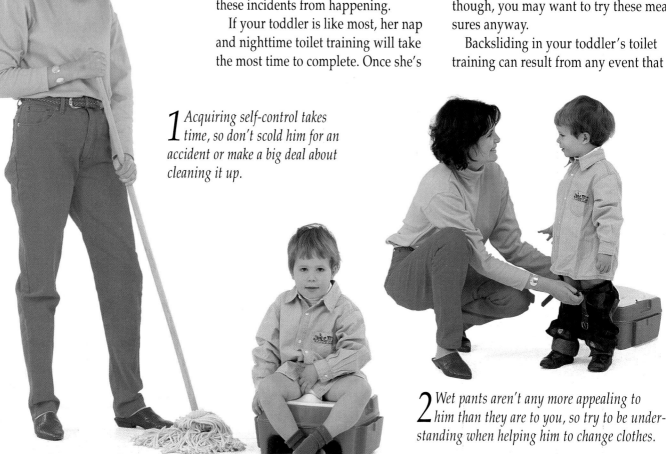

1 Acquiring self-control takes time, so don't scold him for an accident or make a big deal about cleaning it up.

2 Wet pants aren't any more appealing to him than they are to you, so try to be understanding when helping him to change clothes.

House Call

My five-year-old daughter still wets her bed at night. Is this a sign of some physical or emotional problem?

There isn't likely to be a physical or emotional cause for your child's bed-wetting unless she suddenly begins to do it after she's been completely toilet-trained for more than six months. If she's been persistently wetting her bed, she probably just needs more time to develop full bladder control. Reassure her that her nighttime mishaps are nothing to be ashamed of and let her know of any family history of bed-wetting. If she doesn't start soon to have more nighttime control, you may want to talk over your concerns with your pediatrician.

causes even temporary tension—for example, a family illness, a vacation, or a change of baby-sitter. Occasional setbacks are normal, so don't be too alarmed by them; overreacting or belittling her can bring about further stress and greater loss of control. But if you're patient and understanding, you can help her to overcome mishaps and quickly resume her progress. Take heart; the diaper era will soon be left behind for good and with its passing you'll both feel a lot more confident about facing other challenges.

5 Occasional bed-wetting is likely and won't be as problematic if you put a plastic mattress cover under her sheets.

4 If she wets the bed during the night, reassure her that you know she couldn't help it.

3 Encourage him to use his potty chair right before going to bed and as soon as he wakes up.

EATING HABITS

By encouraging your child to be aware of his appetite, to eat a balanced diet of wholesome foods, and to recognize when he's hungry and full, you're giving him a lifetime's training in good eating habits. And simply by practicing good eating habits yourself, you're providing him with the best possible example of healthy attitudes toward food—a lead he's sure to follow.

If you take a relaxed approach to eating, your child can develop his natural self-feeding rhythms. If you don't use food as a way to prove your authority, he won't use food as a way to assert his independence. Remember that there's a big difference between eating habits and table manners, but keep in mind that the right setting for fostering both is a pleasant mealtime.

BALANCE WITHOUT BATTLES

Between the ages of two and six your child requires three meals and two snacks every day. He needs to eat a balanced diet, but you may have to go to great lengths to keep food from becoming an emotional issue. What's most important is that he develop a healthy attitude toward eating.

You may find that your toddler is more cooperative at mealtimes if he's allowed to feed his favorite stuffed animal first.

Minimizing Food Fights
Your child's appetite and tastes may not stabilize before he's six years old. But you should try not to be alarmed by his erratic and unpredictable eating patterns. Swings from day to day both in how much and what he'll eat aren't things that you need to be overly concerned about; they're a natural result of normal changes in the pace of his development. Don't worry about fluctuations in his intake of food; he won't starve himself or eat so much that he bursts.

As long as the foods are healthy, let your child eat them in any combination that he wants.

Your youngster's eating patterns are unlikely to be a cause for medical concern, but they may pose challenges for you. He may eat everything you offer at breakfast, then want almost nothing for the rest of the day. After insisting for weeks on having the same kind of sandwich for lunch, he may suddenly refuse it and ask for something else. Relax; as long as what he eats is good for him, his health won't suffer.

Getting your child to eat a balanced diet doesn't require turning mealtimes into sparring matches. He needs to eat nutritious foods, but he doesn't need a lot of them; nor does he need to eat them all at one time. Be patient when he turns down food you've prepared; he's not rejecting you, so don't take it personally. And the harder you try to get him to eat, the less likely he'll be to do it. Spare yourself a lot of unhelpful hassles: Just offer him as wide a selection of healthy foods as you can and let him choose what he wants. If you stay calm, he'll soon learn that refusing food isn't the way to get your attention.

Maximizing Food Variety

Your child's food preferences are likely to become more pronounced and stronger as he gets older, so you should try to provide him with a balanced diet that contains as much variety as possible right from the start. Just don't expect him to eat everything that's offered or insist that he eat beans, tomatoes, or any other single food. You'll eventually find nutritional equivalents he likes, so don't worry.

As your youngster develops a taste for different foods, he'll be forming judgments using other senses, too. Tempt him with foods that are visually appealing—for example, cut into interesting shapes or arranged into a face on his plate. If he doesn't like the texture of baked potato, try mashed. Keep your efforts simple; he's not likely to be impressed with anything too fancy.

You might want to encourage variety in your child's diet by establishing some rules about having to taste foods. But while you may insist that he sample everything offered, never try to force him to finish anything he doesn't like. As long as he complies with your "minimal-amount" rule, permit him to have more of what he does want. You may withhold dessert until he samples a new vegetable, for example, but you shouldn't make dessert conditional on his eating absolutely everything on his plate. Your best response to confrontations over food is simply to withdraw, allowing him to discover that the natural consequence of not eating what's offered when it's offered is to feel hungry. Try to be patient; if he's otherwise healthy, he'll soon start developing more reasonable eating habits.

FUSSY EATERS

• If your toddler insists on eating the same things for dinner every night, serve him an additional food along with one he likes.

• When your child asks for something else no matter what you serve, respond calmly that you'll make what he's requested another time and he can have as much of what you've offered as he wants.

• If your child doesn't eat whenever you go out visiting, give him a little to eat before you go and encourage him to try one or two things when you're there.

• If your toddler refuses new foods, you'll be more likely to get him to at least try them if you involve him in helping to prepare them.

Your toddler may be more willing to drink her juice if she gets to pour it herself.

Instead of pressuring your child to try something new, provoke his curiosity by letting him observe you eating it.

As your child's food preferences and eating skills evolve, he's likely to become good company at mealtimes.

MEALTIME MANNERS

Mealtimes can be relaxed and pleasant if you simply take into account your child's self-feeding capabilities and allow him to express his own food preferences. He's old enough now to begin learning how to behave at the table. Just make sure that the limits you set are on conduct—not on what does or does not get eaten. And don't ever use food as a source of either punishment or reward.

Enlist your child's participation in mealtimes by letting her help to set the table.

ETIQUETTE

Do make mealtime an occasion for socializing. **Do** include your child at the table and give him opportunities to speak. **Do** be a model of good eating for your child. **Do** allow your child to eat at his own pace. **Do** correct your child's manners calmly and show examples of good habits matter-of-factly. **Do** praise your child's politeness. **Do** make the development of good eating habits your goal for your child.	**Don't** make mealtime a sideline to the television. **Don't** oblige your child to stay at the table once he's had enough to eat. **Don't** try to take control of your child's eating. **Don't** pressure your child to eat more quickly. **Don't** try to teach your child manners at one sitting or correct more than one habit at a time. **Don't** reward your child with food. **Don't** make issues out of what your child does and doesn't eat.

Tabletime Tact

Your child needs you to show him how to behave at mealtimes; but he can't learn all at once, so be patient. As long as you set a good example at the table, he'll soon conform to your standards. You may include a few lessons at each sitting, but try not to let them spoil the pleasure of eating together.

Mealtimes are most likely to be enjoyable if you're reasonable in your expectations. As your toddler develops his coordination, don't be critical of the mess he may make while practicing his eating skills. You may need to help him with using utensils as well as getting up and down at the table. And while he's mastering his eating skills, he isn't likely to be too keen on new foods, so don't introduce them too quickly.

By the age of three, your youngster is probably ready to learn some basic table manners. More adept with his eating skills, he's also likely to be interested in the rituals of mealtimes. If simple guidelines such as "chew with your mouth closed" are given pleasantly—not in a heavy-handed way—he may respond with enthusiasm. Be straightforward with your reminders, too, and don't be discouraged if he needs lots of them; learning social graces, like anything else, takes time.

Before your child turns four, he's likely to become a more able participant at mealtimes. He'll probably be capable of sitting at the table for 10 to 15 minutes at a time and want to engage in conversation. Learning not to interrupt, though, will be hard for him. Your best strategy is to bring him into your table talk and thank him when he manages to wait his turn to speak. Remember that his attention span is short; don't think he's just being rude if he talks before someone else has finished what they're saying.

Tabletime Tactics

Your child's eating habits are likely to become more flexible as he gets older, but you'll find that mealtimes are easiest to manage if you stick to a regular eating schedule. You should provide him with his three main meals at predictable intervals during the day— as many of them as possible with other members of the family. You may allow him

Adapt your toddler's place at the table to her abilities by using a booster seat, unbreakable dishes, and easy-to-grip utensils.

When serving your toddler, keep the portions small and let her know she can have more if she wants once she's finished.

Encourage your child to take control of how much he eats by letting him serve himself.

to have nutritious between-meal snacks, but don't let them take the place of his breakfast, lunch, or dinner. Be sure that you give him frequent praise for his efforts to behave well at mealtimes; keep in mind, too, that you're less assured of his best behavior if he's too hungry, too full, or too tired by the time he's at the table.

Between the ages of four and five, your child may become more difficult to handle at mealtimes. If he behaves unacceptably, you may need to take away his plate or send him from the table before he's finished eating. Stay calm and matter-of-fact, letting him know that he's responsible for the consequences of not follow-ing the rules. Try not to be too discouraged by setbacks; he'll soon outgrow the need to test the limits so relent-lessly if he doesn't get the attention he wants. Remember that this, too, is progress—he understands the rules well enough to deliberately challenge them.

Give your child permission to leave the table after a reasonable amount of time—even if he's barely touched the food on his plate.

BATHTIME AND DENTAL CARE

At the age of two, your child may begin to participate more in her own grooming and hygiene. She'll naturally want to feel comfortable and look good; compliment her on her appearance and she'll probably swell with delight. As she becomes more efficient at washing her face and hands, she's likely to seek even greater responsibility in caring for her body.

Keep in mind that your child's early routines are the basis for lifetime habits. Let her proceed at her own pace; she won't see grooming and hygiene as unpleasant chores forced on her if you don't push too hard or too soon. Show enthusiasm for her efforts at combing her hair and brushing her teeth, but be patient as she gains the coordination needed to do them properly.

TUB TRIALS

Suit your child's bath routine to her needs as well as your schedule. Active youngsters who play a lot outdoors might call for a bath every evening. But a nightly bath isn't always convenient or practical; and most youngsters would just as soon opt out on occasion in favor of a good washing up. Being a little flexible won't cause any harm; the only important thing is for your child to get into the habit of bathing regularly and thoroughly.

1 Run the bath for him and help him get undressed. Make sure the water isn't too hot or too deep.

2 Wearing swimming goggles may assure him that shampoo won't get in his eyes while his hair is washed.

Good Bathing Habits
Your toddler may get by with a bath two or three times a week. Until she's toilet-trained, you'll have to change her diaper frequently to keep her bottom clean. She'll also need your help to get into the habit of going to the sink to wash her hands before eating and after going to the bathroom—as well as to complete the routine properly.

As your youngster gets older, she's likely to become more active in her play. You'll probably be astounded by how dirty she can get in a day and want to increase the frequency of her baths. Summertime usually prompts a need for more baths, too, since grime-clogged pores in hot, sticky weather often result in skin irritations. But she'll also start taking more responsibility for washing herself and your job will be increasingly one of simply making sure she cleans adequately.

3 *Bubbles and hand-puppet washcloths help make baths fun for her and reduce the scrubbing that you need to do.*

4 *The bathtub is a natural learning environment and simple games help teach him the names of all his body parts.*

BATHTUB FUN

✓ Water experiments: Containers, funnels, and measuring spoons help her explore concepts such as full-empty and principles of volume. Things that float and things that sink invite her to learn about properties such as density.

✓ Word and number games: Describe things and ask her to guess what they are. Get her to count items in the bath, then ask how many there would be if you took away or added some.

✓ Conversation and songs: Talk over events of the day and encourage her to express her thoughts and feelings about them. Singing songs together helps exercise her memory—and may serve as a pleasant distraction from the business of having her hair washed.

5 *Wrap him in a warm towel and dry him. Let him study his reflection in a mirror to see how good he looks.*

Having a bath is likely to be fun for your youngster; she may enjoy being in the water so much that she doesn't want to get out of the bathtub. But if she isn't fond of baths, she may need a little coaxing to have one. Be patient; trying to force her to have a bath isn't the way to win her cooperation. Give her some advance notice of bathtime so she can start to make the transition from what she's doing; don't just march her off to the bath in the middle of her play. Enhance her fun in the bathtub by providing water toys and adding a little bubble bath—making sure it's a specially formulated type that won't irritate her skin.

Your toddler's early attempts to wash herself won't be very effective, but show her how and encourage her anyway; discouraging her efforts will only prolong her sense of dependence on you. A good start is simply to let her play with the soap and washcloth. As she gets a bit older, she'll be ready to learn how to lather herself with soap and rinse herself off. She'll gradually become more adept at washing herself and may not need your help at all by the time she's six. But no matter how quickly she develops the capacity to wash and entertain herself in the bathtub, your presence is necessary to ensure her safety.

Even if your toddler enjoys her bath, she may hate having her hair washed. Be patient; with a little ingenuity, you'll soon be able to alleviate her concerns about getting shampoo in her eyes or having water poured over her head. Don't be too worried if she develops a fear of the bathtub; if you're understanding, she's likely to soon outgrow it. If she accidentally slips or is scalded, for example, she may need some time before she can again feel safe in the bath. Or, until she understands size relationships, she may fear being sucked down the drain and panic if the plug is pulled before she gets out of the tub.

TEETH BRUSHING AND FLOSSING

Your child should be accustomed to a dental-care routine by the time she's two. Her baby teeth are important to her eating habits and speech, as well as to the formation and position of her permanent teeth. A child who has a baby tooth removed because of decay may suffer ongoing problems from having nearby teeth move into its space. Guard against such consequences for your child with preventive care—which includes proper diet, brushing, and flossing.

Good Dental Habits

Soon after your toddler turns two, she will be ready to start learning how to brush her own teeth. She may even become a little frustrated at having you always brush for her and insist on trying her own hand. For the first few times, lead her through the proper brushing procedure without using toothpaste on her toothbrush—which should be specifically designed for baby teeth, featuring soft, end-rounded or polished bristles. Then, put a small, pea-sized amount of fluoride toothpaste on her toothbrush and encourage her to repeat what you've shown her. If she just sucks or swallows the toothpaste, let her try brushing with only water.

You shouldn't expect your child to master full control of her toothbrush right away. Your goal should be simply to help her get into the habit of brushing her teeth and take on responsibility for her own dental care. Teach her to be consistent about brushing after eating, letting her do as much as she can on her own and then finishing up for her. Until she's at least six, she's not likely to have the capacity to brush properly all by herself.

Flossing is as important for your child as it is for you, but she may need you to do it all for her until after she turns six. You may find flossing her teeth awkward and time-consuming at first, but don't be overwhelmed; she'll take on the responsibility soon enough. Take heart; by flossing regularly for her now, she will quickly come to see it as routine and won't need constant reminding to do it once she's able to herself. As with all the lessons on dental care that you want her to learn, your best encouragement is to set a good example yourself. If you eat properly, brush and floss routinely, and see your dentist regularly, she'll get the message.

House Call

Despite religious brushing, my three-year-old has little white flecks on her teeth. What could be causing them?

A likely cause of your child's problem is too much fluoride. Although fluoride provides important protection against cavities, too much of it can result in a slight mottling of the teeth's enamel. Ask your pediatrician or dentist for advice: If your water supply is fluoridated, your child shouldn't take fluoride as a supplement, nor should she use too much fluoridated toothpaste when brushing.

Encourage your toddler's routine cooperation by making a game of brushing teeth.

BRUSHING YOUR YOUNGSTER'S TEETH

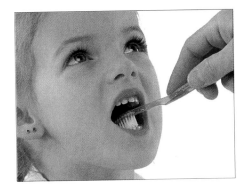

1 *To clean inside front surfaces, hold the toothbrush perpendicular to the gumline. Stroke up and down between the gumline and top of each tooth.*

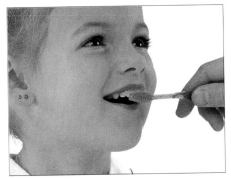

2 *Hold the toothbrush horizontally at an angle to the gumline to clean outside surfaces. Make short up and down strokes to get at plaque along the gumline.*

3 *Brush the tongue lightly from back to front a few times, being careful not to trigger reflexive gagging. Provide a glass of water for rinsing the mouth.*

TOOTH-CARE SCHEDULE

Age	Basic Requirements	Skills and Responsibilities
2 to 3 years	Brushing after meals Flossing before bedtime First dental checkup	Make dental care a habit. Encourage her to practice using a toothbrush so she gains coordination, but brush and floss for her. If she doesn't like the taste of toothpaste, just use water.
3 to 4 years	Brushing after meals Flossing at least once daily Dental checkups every 6 to 12 months	Make dental care routine. She'll be able to do some brushing herself, but will need help to finish the job properly. Floss for her before bed and encourage her to do it herself in the morning.
4 to 6 years	Brushing after meals and snacks Flossing at least once daily Dental checkups every 6 to 12 months	Promote dental care responsibility. As she gains coordination, encourage her to brush and floss on her own. Monitor her techniques and continue helping her to brush and floss before bedtime.

FLOSSING YOUR YOUNGSTER'S TEETH

1 *Pull off about a 12-in. length of dental floss and wrap the ends securely around the tops of your middle fingers.*

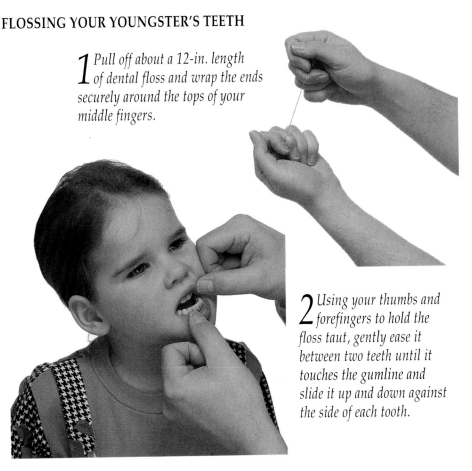

2 *Using your thumbs and forefingers to hold the floss taut, gently ease it between two teeth until it touches the gumline and slide it up and down against the side of each tooth.*

DAILY ROUTINES

You'll quickly discover the importance of routines to your preschooler. Routines, even for everyday tasks, provide him with stability and security: Because he knows what to expect, he can participate with greater confidence, and because of the added sense of control he gets, he's encouraged to take on more responsibility. Getting himself dressed, looking after his own things, and helping out with chores all give him a greater sense of independence and make him feel like a contributing member of the household. You don't have to worry too much about routines stifling spontaneity; they can't prevent the unexpected from happening, but they can bring you the liberty of taking the unpredictable in stride and enjoying it.

MORNINGS AND GETTING DRESSED

Morning routines can set the tone for the rest of the day—not only for your preschooler, but the entire family. With a little advanced planning, you can help to get things started off on the right note. Besides, you'll avoid a lot of last-minute scrambling to be ready on time.

Mastering morning mayhem requires a schedule with ample time for your preschooler to wake up, get dressed, and have breakfast. He'll be more agreeable if he feels a part of the routine, so give him some responsibilities. To be on the safe side, build in some extra time as a cushion.

2 *She may be more inclined to cooperate and eat a nutritious breakfast when the things she needs are left out within her reach.*

1 *Mornings are likely to get off to the smoothest start if she's encouraged to make decisions about what to wear the night before.*

Starting Off Well

The best morning routines both accommodate and take advantage of a child's developing self-help skills. You may face time constraints in the morning, but why not let your youngster's insistence on doing things himself work for you? If he doesn't feel a sense of control, his testiness is likely to cost you even more time anyway. And by allowing him to do as many things as he can by himself, you'll be encouraging his independence.

Most two-year-olds are capable of taking on some responsibility for dressing and feeding themselves in the morning. As your youngster's motor skills improve, gradually let him do as much as he can to get himself ready for the day. By helping him put his energy and enthusiasm to constructive use, you'll be doing yourself a favor. And if he knows that you're there to assist him when necessary, he's not likely to feel as frustrated by his limitations.

A preschooler is most inclined to do things for himself in the morning if he can get at what he needs. Keep items your youngster requires to dress and feed himself within his reach so he isn't automatically forced to ask you for help. Hang his clothes on pegs at his height in the closet. Put his favorite cereal on a low shelf in the pantry and leave a pitcher of milk where he can get it in the refrigerator.

Sanity Saver

Until your youngster can tell left from right and tie bows, he may have problems getting his shoes on and done up by himself. Instead of having to correct him when he puts his shoes on the wrong feet, mark the inside edges of the soles and show him that he can always put his shoes on the right feet by making sure the marks face each other. Although shoes with Velcro® straps are easiest for him to do up, shoes with laces don't have to mean endless hassles. He'll find the shoes a lot easier to slip on and off himself if you replace the laces with strong rubber bands; just cut the bands, thread them through the eyelets, and sew the ends together.

Preschoolers usually need prompting and reminders to get themselves ready. Keep your youngster's morning routines simple and leave time in your schedule to step in when he asks for help. If he's a dawdler, you may have to make a rule of being dressed before eating breakfast or make a game out of being ready before a timer goes off. And doing as much preparation as possible the night before—such as making lunches and putting out clothes—goes a long way in easing morning pressure.

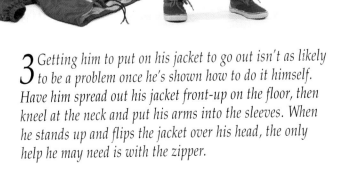

3 *Getting him to put on his jacket to go out isn't as likely to be a problem once he's shown how to do it himself. Have him spread out his jacket front-up on the floor, then kneel at the neck and put his arms into the sleeves. When he stands up and flips the jacket over his head, the only help he may need is with the zipper.*

HELPING OUT AND FIRST CHORES

Everyday routines provide invaluable opportunities for your preschooler to learn about things, practice using skills, and become a contributing member of the family. Being able to pitch in with household work makes him feel competent, helping to build his sense of pride and responsibility.

If your youngster knows there's a place for everything, he's more likely to help ensure that everything is put in its place.

Staying On Track

Spending quality time with a preschooler doesn't mean abandoning all other household duties. Doing too much for your youngster can impede his development, so you shouldn't think that you're depriving or harming him by having him help out around the house and giving him chores to do. On the contrary, when he can participate in meaningful ways with your adult tasks, he's likely to feel more grownup—at times even privileged.

Excluding your preschooler from household duties on the grounds of efficiency often turns out to be short-sighted. He may not have fully mastered many skills, but don't discount his capabilities; he's quite likely to surprise you in the number of ways he can and wants to help you. Doing laundry or making dinner may take you less time by yourself. But if he insists on having your attention, trying to keep him out of the way can be just as time-consuming as including him in the job. And if you wait for the time when he's not around, the job just might not get done at all.

Involving a preschooler in household duties contributes to his sense of belonging and helps strengthen his bond with the family. The earlier you start getting your youngster into the habit of helping out, the less resistant he's likely to be in taking responsibility for chores as he becomes older. Begin with small, occasional tasks that he can do to help out and build up to routine chores that he can take full responsibility for. At the age of two, for example, he might sometimes help to set the dinner table or put dirty clothes in the hamper. By the time he's six, for instance, he might

By sorting and matching socks while you fold laundry, your youngster gets to spend time with you and feel that she's making a contribution.

110

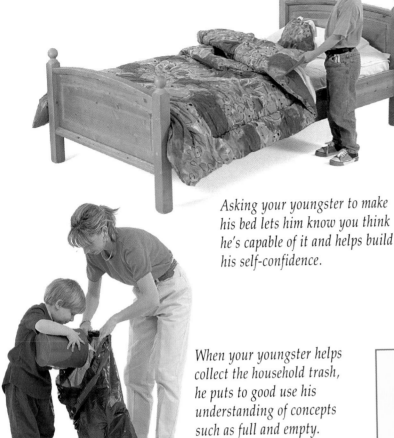

Asking your youngster to make his bed lets him know you think he's capable of it and helps build his self-confidence.

Involving your youngster in food preparation is a way of helping her to become responsible for what she eats.

When your youngster helps collect the household trash, he puts to good use his understanding of concepts such as full and empty.

make his own sandwich at lunch or take out the trash on collection days.

Household duties that your preschooler can do with confidence are vital to his sense of competency. Having him clean up his room may seem a good way for him to help out, but he's not likely to have the independence and self-discipline required for the job. He'll do better if you work alongside him at a more defined task such as picking up his toys. Encouraging him also means accepting the standards that he's capable of; try not to undermine his confidence by criticizing the way he does things or by redoing them.

Preschoolers often balk at household duties once the novelty wears off. Letting your youngster get away with not helping out may spare you some aggravation, but it isn't in his best interests. If your encouragement, gentle reminders, and praise aren't enough to keep him interested and motivated in his routines, try giving him more choice in the tasks he does or varying his schedule of tasks. Be patient; he needs your support to see tasks through to completion and feel good about himself.

Winning Ways

RESPONSIBILITY

• Assign chores to your child according to his abilities and what he thinks he can do. If he's given tasks that are too difficult, he'll feel frustrated. Tasks that he doesn't consider as meaningful help to the household can undercut his sense of self-worth.

• Make your child's chores duties that are required, not optional. Explain to him that his ongoing help is necessary to the household, that he has a say in how—but not whether—he'll routinely contribute.

• Reward your child for doing chores with words, not money. You may want to give him money for a special job such as raking up leaves in the yard, but his routine contribution to the household isn't something that he should be paid for.

• Don't punish your child if he doesn't do his chores. Since he's still developing an understanding of cause and effect, there's no benefit in having him face consequences. If he refuses to do a task right away, ask him when he thinks he can do it. To help him maintain interest in contributing to the household, you might consider a weekly rotation of his chores.

PAJAMAS AND BEDTIME

Nothing is more satisfying at the end of a busy day than tucking your sleepy preschooler into bed; sometimes, however, nothing may seem as difficult to accomplish. Problems in settling down and going off to sleep are likely to be temporary and tend to resolve themselves quickly, so be patient; they won't be overcome any sooner if you get exasperated. In most instances, a little encouragement to stick to his bedtime routine is all the reassurance he needs.

Ending Off Well

A child's bedtime can make or break a day. And whether a day has had more up or down moments, a pleasant bedtime helps your youngster and you feel positive about it—as well as welcoming of tomorrow. A familiar pattern at the close of a day is relaxing and comforting, so keep bedtime routines as simple and predictable as possible—for his sake and your own.

Not all preschoolers need the same amount of sleep at night; some can get by with only nine to 10 hours while others do best with as much as 12 to 13 hours. Set a bedtime hour for your youngster that makes sense for his age and needs. Give him enough time to get through his routines at a comfortable pace; don't wait for overt signs that he's sleepy and then expect him to hurry into bed.

2 With a little quiet time in her room, she can relax and unwind after a busy day.

1 Fresh out of the bath, she's squeaky clean and ready to get into her pajamas.

3 Choosing clothes for the next day helps her anticipate tomorrow's coming—and gives her one less decision to make in the morning.

Many preschoolers need a little notice to finish up what they're doing before beginning bedtime preparations. When your youngster's warning time elapses, get him started on his routines. To minimize distractions, have him proceed through his routines in the same order every night; he'll likely need a few reminders to stay on track, so be patient. End with a shared activity that he enjoys, such as reading a story. If he takes too long to get ready for bed, shorten the time for the shared activity; don't leave it out entirely, though, or the day may end with tears.

A preschooler may go to great lengths to prolong his bedtime. But as long as you're sure that your youngster's real needs have been met during his routines, you shouldn't find resisting his ploys too difficult. Be firm about his staying in bed and going off to sleep. If he gets up, lead him calmly back to bed without scolding him; the less attention he gets from diversions, the sooner he'll give them up. You may leave a light on if he's afraid and comfort him if he has a bad dream, but you should insist that he stay in his bed; you don't want to suggest to him that he has any reason to be fearful.

NIGHTMARES

Do reassure and cuddle your child when he awakens from a bad dream.
Do encourage your child to talk about a bad dream during the day.
Do help your child to imagine a good ending to a bad dream that he has repeatedly.
Do try to protect your child from violent and frightening movies.
Do advise your pediatrician if your child's bad dreams seem to be worsening or disrupt his daytime activities.

Don't awaken your child from a bad dream to comfort him.
Don't stop your child from returning to sleep during the night.
Don't expect your child to remember a bad dream or impose an interpretation on one that he does.
Don't limit your child's imagination by interfering in his fantasy play.
Don't be overly concerned about your child if he experiences occasional bad dreams.

4 *A comforting bedtime story gives her the kind of escape that's a helpful prelude to getting a good night's sleep.*

5 *Being apart from you during the night is easier for her if she has some of her favorite things in bed with her.*

6 *The reassuring ritual of being tucked in and given a goodnight kiss is your signal that she can safely drift off to sleep.*

PERCEPTIONS AND LEARNING

A child's powers of thought advance rapidly during the preschool years. By the time your child turns six, her perceptions are sharper, she has greater control of her memory and imagination, and her capacity for reasoning is growing. In everything she does—alone, with you, and increasingly with friends—she's developing a sense of the world and her place in it.

How your child views the world and what she thinks of herself aren't matters that you can or should try to dictate. But since she'll test a lot of her viewpoints with you first, your sensitivity to her character, interests, and comprehension can go a long way to assuring that she gets the positive correcting, modifying, and affirming of perspectives she needs.

CONCEPT OF SELF

A child's increasing awareness of herself as an individual begins her drive to define herself. As your preschooler gains powers of thought, she's free to explore the abstract domain of ideas—including notions of herself as well as the very concept of self. Since your interactions with her so greatly affect how she perceives herself, your day-to-day efforts to show her that she's valued go a long way in helping her form a positive self-image.

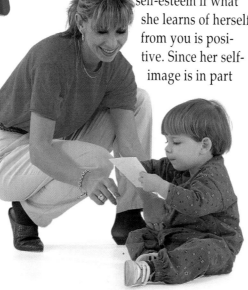

A youngster's early family portraits often feature exaggerated representations of himself.

When a child first begins to distinguish himself from others, he doesn't yet understand that others think and feel differently than he does.

Self-perception
Your child's notions of self and self-worth evolve from her sense of being different from others, but also in various ways similar to some of them. She'll always perceive herself in relation to others, and her early ideas of herself and her own value may change as she gets older. But since she forms her first impressions of herself mostly in relation to you, she'll get a lifetime's head start in building self-esteem if what she learns of herself from you is positive. Since her self-image is in part shaped by her own temperament, you can't expect to completely control how she perceives herself. But just by reflecting positively toward her, you can encourage her to think favorably of herself.

As early as two, your toddler is likely to show signs of her increasing self-awareness. She may point to herself in a photograph and refer to herself by name. Soon after, she'll probably begin to have some notion of body image—a sense of, for example, being tall or

Children's first friendships tend to be based more on shared activities than on similar outlooks.

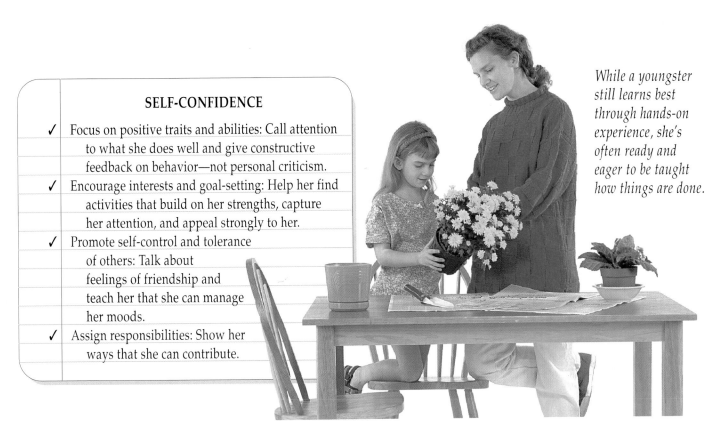

SELF-CONFIDENCE

✓ Focus on positive traits and abilities: Call attention to what she does well and give constructive feedback on behavior—not personal criticism.

✓ Encourage interests and goal-setting: Help her find activities that build on her strengths, capture her attention, and appeal strongly to her.

✓ Promote self-control and tolerance of others: Talk about feelings of friendship and teach her that she can manage her moods.

✓ Assign responsibilities: Show her ways that she can contribute.

While a youngster still learns best through hands-on experience, she's often ready and eager to be taught how things are done.

example, being tall or short, chubby or skinny. She may know her sex and age as well as routinely use the words "me," "I," and "mine." Her sense of herself isn't likely to be very secure and she won't be able to cope with rejection easily, so she'll need lots of reassurance from you. Help

build her self-esteem by recognizing and acknowledging her worth. Putting up her drawings on the kitchen bulletin board, for instance, is a simple way of showing her that her work is valued.

Until your child is six, she'll probably think of herself and others primarily in physical terms. Her descriptions of people, for example, are likely to be limited to features such as hair color, freckles, and being big or little, and to the things and activities that they do. She'll slowly begin to describe how she feels, but isn't likely to understand that others might feel differently. As her ability to reflect on herself improves, she may start to evaluate her skills and compare herself to others.

Since your child's self-judgments are so greatly influenced by her ability to interpret how you and others feel about her, encouraging her self-esteem can be a little tricky at times. If you're too protective, she may feel inadequate. If you leave her too much to herself, she may think that what she does is not very important. You may not strike the right balance every time, but keep trying; she needs a sense of self-worth strong enough to override occasional frustrations and setbacks.

LANGUAGE AND IMAGINATION

A child's powers of thought expand rapidly with advances in her language and imagination. As your preschooler gains experience of the world and becomes more sophisticated in her thinking, you'll find the content of what she says increasingly complex—taking in, for example, notions of past, future, and might-have-been. Her ability to think abstractly and form mental images unleashes her imagination, a safe and always available way to try out ideas.

Words and Communication

Within a year of turning two, your child is likely to have mastered most of the basics of language. She may command a spoken vocabulary of as many as 1,000 words and take great satisfaction in using the words she knows to make statements, ask questions, and issue demands. What she says is likely to be mostly factual in nature, her prime intent to simply express herself. She may talk as much or more than you,

A youngster's overreaction to something that breaks may be prompted by concern about his own intactness.

and even talk to herself when there's no one else around.

By the time your child reaches the age of six, she'll probably be using language to truly communicate. Her spoken vocabulary may have doubled or tripled and she'll likely be less self-centered in her outlook. More capable of talking about concepts such as yesterday and tomorrow, most and least, and here and there, she will also have developed a sense of empathy, learning to give and take in conversations that reflect more than just her own views. She may begin to adjust what she says and how she speaks according to the listener—for example, using simpler words with younger children and different tones of voice with her friends.

Your child's improving language skills are sure to result in a lot of questions for you. At first, she'll ask mostly "who," "what," and "where" questions that call for straightforward, factual responses. Her "why" and "how" questions, which start next, are likely to be much more challenging, since they often

will require complicated, interpretive answers. As she begins to grasp the concept of time and also asks "when" questions, you may be tiring of her inquisitiveness. But while she may seem to ask questions constantly until she's six, try not to feel too overwhelmed; as she makes friends and starts going to school, you won't be her only source of answers.

Fantasy and Fear

Your child's questions reflect not only her increasing command of language, but also the growing capacity of her imagination. Throughout her preschool years, her ability to imagine expands, deepens, and becomes richer. By the time she's six years old, you'll find that she's gained much more flexibility in her thinking and awareness of the world than you would've thought possible just a few years earlier.

Being able to imagine opens your child to an entire kingdom that exists only inside her mind. There, she contends daily with such imaginary complexities as monsters that chase her and friends who are visible just to her. At the same time, she struggles within her internal realm to figure out and control powerful impulses and feelings. Love, jealousy, and other emotions that she doesn't yet fully comprehend blur with fantasy to cause her anxiety and fear.

As a child gains a sense of self, she may show a strong, early interest in learning how to spell her name.

"Foots" is the kind of logical speaking error a child may make as she begins recognizing and trying to apply the rules of language.

House Call

My three-year-old sometimes has trouble getting her words out when she's excited. Should I be worried about her stuttering?

Many children experience occasional disfluency—unintended pauses or repeated sounds in their speech. Such disfluency is normal as a child gains language skills and attention shouldn't be drawn to it. But a child who develops a persistent pattern of repeating or prolonging sounds may have a stuttering problem. Talk to your pediatrician about your concerns; if there's a family history of stuttering, you may be referred to a speech specialist.

A flourishing imagination is essential to your child's well-being; don't think it's evidence of a problem. Freedom to imagine both helps her adjust to the world by sheltering her from it and gives her the courage to continue exploring and investigating. When she imagines herself as an evil witch or lost in the woods, for example, she has a safe way of applying her creative and problem-solving skills.

Fears arising from your child's imagination occur as she struggles to distinguish between what's real and what isn't. Lacking an understanding of certain things, she's apt to invent fantastic explanations and believe improbable stories. And while her world view is chiefly self-centered, she tends to perceive herself as the key player in all events and imagine how everything might affect her. Broader in her world outlook by the age of six, she will probably be better at separating reality from fantasy. But if she has difficulty overcoming imagined fears or if they interfere with her routines, you should talk to your pediatrician.

Your child's reactions to experiences can't always be anticipated. But you should try not to expose her to things that may incite imagined fears. For example, don't let her view realistic scenes of violence on television. And avoid making statements that are alarming when taken literally—such as "he'll kill me when he finds out." Respect her imagined fears without taking them so seriously that you reinforce them. She may need your help at times to overcome imagined fears, but don't underestimate her ability to work them out herself.

A youngster who is afraid of the dark may be reassured if she's given help in conducting a "monster check" and is allowed to sleep with a light on.

CURIOSITY AND REASONING

Information a child gathers by observing, experimenting, and seeking answers to questions helps expand her powers of thought. As your preschooler's memory grows, she can reason and form plans of action. Gaining the ability to think abstractly, she'll experiment increasingly with concepts. When she shares her perspectives on the "hows" and "whys" of things, you'll find that intuitive thinking is beginning to shape her understanding of the world.

Conceptual Awareness

Between the ages of two and six, your child will become steadily better at organizing and remembering information—skills that enable her to make increasingly finer distinctions and classifications. Language helps, too, so encourage her efforts to put her perceptions into words. Once she has a name for something, she can more easily classify and remember it; later, she can recall it using the word as a trigger.

Your child will develop a lot of understanding on her own; don't think that you have to teach her everything. Since she learns best by doing, she'll gain many lessons just through basic, hands-on experience. For example, by taking things in play and placing them together, separating them, arranging them in groups, and recombining them, she'll develop an effective understanding of mathematical concepts and begin learning the skills of adding, subtract-ing, multiplying, and dividing. And there's little she doesn't learn from: Through observation of happenings around her, she'll absorb and develop notions of people's roles and attitudes as well as ideas of right and wrong.

However, not all the information your preschooler will acquire will be self-taught or -learned. She'll probably spend many of her waking hours questioning you about everything that happens around her. She won't be capable

FACTS OF LIFE

• Address your child's questions matter-of-factly. Ask her what she thinks to get an idea of her real concerns. Don't jump to quick conclusions about her motives.
• Give your child appropriate answers. Straightforward, simple responses are best. Don't overload her with details; if she wants to know more, she'll ask.
• Respond honestly to your child's concerns. Be factual and use correct terms for body parts. Instead of making up stories, find answers with her.

Getting a correct total isn't easy for a child until she's able to keep track of what she has and hasn't already counted.

Although there's no difference in the number of candies she'll get, a youngster is likely to think that the most spread-out group is bigger.

Until a child understands that volume isn't affected by shape, she'll probably think a tall, narrow glass holds more than a short, wide one.

of grasping lengthy explanations, so keep your answers simple and to the point; you'll know that you're getting too detailed if she starts to stare off into space or turns her attention to something else. Faced with a learning challenge, she's likely to be one-sided in her reasoning; until she's older, she may have difficulty viewing issues from more than one perspective as well as solving problems that require considering more than one factor at a time.

Your preschooler may begin to explore many basic concepts that she'll be taught in greater detail later on at school. Before she goes to kindergarten, she's likely to know some days of the week and the differences between the seasons. She also may understand the essentials of counting, the alphabet, and some geometrical shapes. There are many ways that you can help her learn about concepts, but follow her lead and don't try to rush her education; if she feels pressured to perform, she's likely to resist learning. Your best approach is to offer her a wide range of learning opportunities that respect her special interests and natural talents.

Sexual Awareness

Growing awareness of the differences between males and females sets the stage for your preschooler's curiosity about the concept of gender. As she becomes toilet-trained, she's naturally more conscious of body parts once hidden by diapers; and combined with increasing opportunities for interaction with others, she naturally discovers that people are made in two distinctly different ways.

Your preschooler may begin to show an avid interest in basic sexuality, both her own and that of the opposite sex. She's likely to ask where babies come from and why girls' and boys' bodies are different. She may be curious about the organs involved in reproduction. Try not to be embarrassed or too serious when you respond to her questions; keep your answers simple, but use correct terms. She doesn't need to know the details of intercourse, but she should feel free to ask questions and know that you'll give her direct, accurate answers.

Awareness of sexual identity is important to your child's sense of self. And your influence on her sexual development and adjustment extends far beyond simple sex education. From the tone of your talks to the types of toys you buy, you're helping to shape her attitudes toward her sexuality in many, many subtle ways every day. You'll want her to understand that she belongs to one sex and appreciate the positive aspects of her gender. But you shouldn't make her feel that any special restrictions or expectations apply to her because of her gender.

Your child may experiment with—and sometimes even reverse—sexual roles, but you shouldn't overreact; it's a natural part of reaching a healthy norm. Stereotyping sex roles limits her and can damage her emotional development, so don't react negatively to her cross-gender play; she'll probably outgrow it soon anyway. Regardless of how she behaves, just make sure you communicate to her that she's valued for the individual she is—not because of her gender.

Children's developing self-awareness evolves into a curiosity about the body that's often reflected in their play.

BEHAVIOR AND DISCIPLINE

Effective discipline will guide your child toward good behavior. Discipline shouldn't be thought of as a lot of stern measures such as scolding and spanking; punishment is only a small part of it, a last resort that doesn't depend on severity or harshness to be successful. Discipline should bring out the best in a child, so think of it as a caring and creative process.

Effective discipline calls for unqualified love and reasonable limits; applying both, you'll be giving your child strong encouragement to behave well. There are many positive ways for you to influence behavior, so save punishment as an end-of-the-line fallback. And if punishment is needed, you'll find that a child can be taught a lesson without being humiliated.

RULES AND VALUES

Your preschooler's behavior can't be totally controlled, but with a little foresight a lot of problems can be avoided. What he requires most from you is a loving environment in which good behavior can flourish. You'll need to establish routines that help him stay on track, keep temptations that could get him into trouble out of his way, and provide clear, warm communication that lets him know where he stands and what's expected of him.

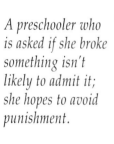

A preschooler who is asked if she broke something isn't likely to admit it; she hopes to avoid punishment.

Teaching Values

Good disciplining involves the imposing and enforcing of rules that help teach your preschooler how to control his own actions. Knowing what he can expect of you and of himself strengthens his sense of security, so you shouldn't think that rules are a burden to him or detrimental to his well-being.

If you set reasonable rules on behavior, apply them consistently, and spell out the consequences of not adhering to them, your preschooler will gain self-control and independence—as well as self-respect. As he internalizes the rules you teach him, he'll also be incorporating your values, enabling him to make increasingly effective decisions about his own behavior by himself.

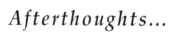

Afterthoughts...

"My daughter was impossibly bossy until she started playing with an older girl who lives down the street. Now that she has been on the receiving end of someone who will stand up to her, she's not as much of a sergeant-major around children her own age and younger."

"Refusing to change into his pajamas was my son's way of trying to get around his bedtime. Rather than battle with him, I let him go off to sleep at the usual time in his clothes. After a few nights, we worked out a compromise: If he's in pajamas a half hour before he has to go to sleep, he can have an extra five minutes of storytime."

Your preschooler needs time to assimilate rules and understand the potential consequences of his actions, so be patient. You'll be less inclined to overwhelm and confuse him if you keep in mind a few rule-making principles:

• Set behavior priorities. Make rules that are fair and attainable; don't give him too many at once or expect behavior that he isn't yet capable of. Your highest priorities initially should be issues of personal safety—such as not running into the street—and the prevention of harm to others. Rules for clumsiness or poor pronunciation, for example, simply aren't constructive.

• Focus on specific behavior. Make rules that are clear and concrete, giving him examples of what's desired—not just what's unacceptable. Vague characterizations such as "Don't be mean" or "Be polite" aren't helpful. What works best are instructions that offer a direct action for him to take, such as "Give your brother a car so he can play nicely with you" or "Look at a book while I'm talking on the telephone."

• Ignore irrelevant behavior. Avoid making rules that can become the basis for no-win power struggles. Trying to end his bed-wetting or thumb-sucking with rules, for instance, simply won't work. Keep in mind, too, that you're better off not making too much of an issue of behavior he's likely to outgrow on his own. For example, making rules to stop him from swinging his legs at the table or slurping when he drinks isn't likely to be worth the effort. The fewer rules he has to attend to, the more likely he'll try to abide by them. A lot of rules to follow can call for constant reminding and criticism, nagging that isn't effective.

Achieving just the right balance of rules that can be applied consistently may take time, so don't worry too much about setbacks or shortcomings; your skills will only improve with use. As long as you openly express your love for your preschooler and shape your expectations for his behavior out of respect for his unique needs, you won't go too far wrong.

A youngster who doesn't yet understand the limits of ownership often thinks he has a right to have whatever he wants.

While a preschooler may know he shouldn't take things without asking, he's still too young to fully appreciate the seriousness of the consequences.

Until a child grasps more than the rewards of winning, he may not be capable of abiding by all the rules of a game.

Sharing and Taking Turns

Good behavior depends on a sense of responsibility, which evolves as your preschooler recognizes that there's more to life than immediate gratification of his needs. Assuming responsibility for his own actions is a basic social requirement. He needs to understand that aggressive behavior such as hitting, kicking, and pushing aren't acceptable ways of dealing with frustration. To get along with others, he must cooperate by sharing and taking turns.

Learning Cooperation

Your unconditional love makes your preschooler feel special and worthy, which contributes to his self-esteem—a vital prerequisite for good behavior, as well as getting along with others. If he feels good about himself, he'll be motivated to behave well; without a positive self-image and reputation to live up to, he has little incentive.

Out of your loving bond with your preschooler, he gradually begins to recognize that you and others in his life have needs and feelings, too. Although he won't comprehend the full implications of his behavior on others for many years, you'll see signs that he's learning how he can make someone feel happy or sad through his actions. He's not likely to be capable of true empathy before the age of six. But the earlier he's taught and encouraged to interact respectfully with others, the sooner he'll develop the ability to identify personally with others' emotions.

Learning to behave responsibly starts at home. The compassion and courtesy that you show for others is behavior he's likely to copy, so be alert to the powerful influence of your own actions.

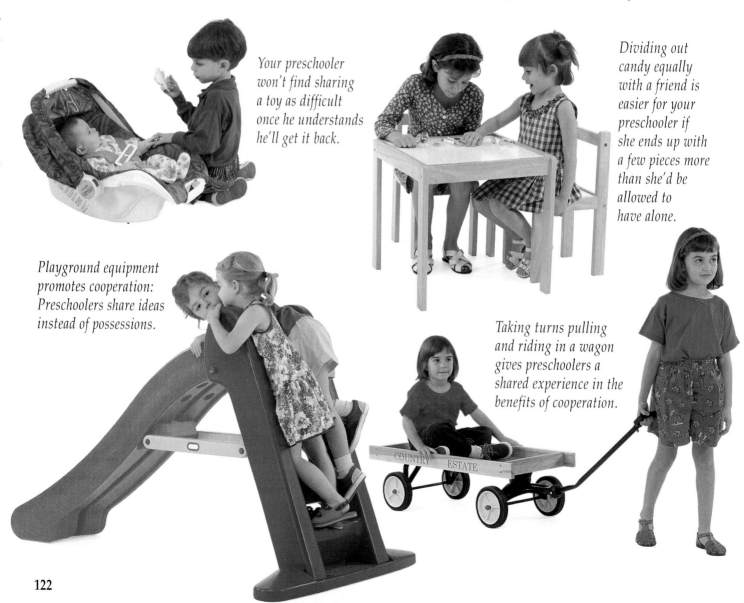

Your preschooler won't find sharing a toy as difficult once he understands he'll get it back.

Dividing out candy equally with a friend is easier for your preschooler if she ends up with a few pieces more than she'd be allowed to have alone.

Playground equipment promotes cooperation: Preschoolers share ideas instead of possessions.

Taking turns pulling and riding in a wagon gives preschoolers a shared experience in the benefits of cooperation.

Although he may have difficulties with some social niceties for years to come, you're setting a good example for him when you telephone to ask after a friend or allow someone to go ahead of you in the check-out line. By giving him simple duties such as putting away toys or bringing in the newspaper, you're showing him ways that he can help share the household work load—and feel like a proud, contributing member of the family.

Through play with other children, your preschooler gains experience in the benefits of sharing and taking turns—as well as the drawbacks of not cooperating. While standards of fairness, honesty, and trustworthiness are beyond his grasp now, he needs to start learning about them early if he's to grow up in harmony with others. He'll benefit most from rules that are simple and clear, with a generous allowance for the many missteps he's bound to

make. Don't expect a lot at first; he'll need time to develop the reasoning ability required to understand the basis of the rules. Eventually, though, he'll begin to incorporate moral principles and won't make as many errors on rules about things such as lying and cheating. If he's encouraged to show respect for property, for instance, he'll learn about ownership and will soon feel a sense of responsibility that will stop him from taking without asking.

TENSION OUTLETS

Some of your preschooler's most annoying behaviors may not be done deliberately. Bed-wetting, for example, isn't done intentionally. Likewise, thumb-sucking, nose-picking, and nail-biting are types of behaviors that may start as responses to stress and simply become habits. Patience is your best strategy; these behaviors are normal and usually outgrown. Your relaxed attitude will do more to help end the behaviors than nagging or punishment.

Discouraging Habits

Self-comforting behaviors that your preschooler developed during his infancy often evolve into unconscious habits. Thumb-sucking, nail-biting, and rocking back and forth to sleep are common examples. Keep such a habit in perspective; with or without your help, he'll probably stop it before he begins elementary school.

If your preschooler's habit is more pronounced at certain times of the day, you might consider changing his routines. Or, a chart that tracks his daily progress toward ending a habit, along with a system of rewards, may be just the boost in incentive that he needs. Usually, though, the best way to discourage a habit is simply not to draw added attention to it. If you're embarrassed in public by a habit such as masturbation, the best approach is to try diverting his attention to something else or encouraging him to go somewhere private.

An unhelpful power struggle may be avoided if a habit such as nose-picking is allowed in the bathroom.

Calling too much attention to nail-biting can add to the tension causing the habit and make it harder to stop.

House Call

"My five-year-old boy falls asleep at night sucking his thumb. Is he ruining the shape of his mouth?

Thumb-sucking isn't likely to cause a distortion of your child's mouth and he'll probably give up the habit all on his own before there's any need for you to worry about its effect on his permanent teeth. If you haven't already made a big deal of his thumb-sucking, he may accept your help in trying to stop. A simple solution such as wrapping adhesive tape around his thumb and leaving an extra tab to chew on may do the trick. Or, since he sucks his thumb to fall asleep, you might try modifying his bedtime routine.

ACTING UP

Teaching good behavior to your preschooler calls for you to keep his bad behavior in perspective. Not only should you accept that misbehavior is a normal part of his growing up, but you'll need to look for its reasons. His misbehavior isn't likely to be random; it will almost always serve some purpose for him. By figuring out his motives, you'll be better equipped to deal with his misbehavior—and help him find alternatives.

Encouraging Practices

Some of the most common reasons for your preschooler's misbehavior may not be obvious: a need for your attention, simple curiosity, mistaken ideas on how to win friends, sibling rivalry, family tension, a bad role model, and feelings of frustration. In analyzing the situations in which he misbehaves, be sure to assess your own feelings during them; often you'll find helpful clues to understanding what's going on between him and you.

If you take a thoughtful, methodical approach to your preschooler's misbehavior, you'll usually come up with something to do about it. Begin with a clear, precise definition of the problem behavior. Don't just label him as stubborn, for example; specify what he does that is stubborn. Does he dawdle over going to bed? Does he refuse to come when called? With the misbehavior defined, you can then assess what leads up to and follows after it. Is there a pattern? What part do you and others play? If you find that there are several problem behaviors linked together, pick one to deal with first; odds are that if you solve it, the others will disappear.

Once you've identified a problem behavior of your preschooler, studied its circumstances, and examined the responses of you and others to it, you're ready to try ways of bringing about the changes you want. Don't be surprised, though, if you discover that your behavior, as well as his, needs to be modified. For instance, you may find that you need to scold less, praise more, or set a better example.

There are several useful disciplining techniques that you can apply to your preschooler's misbehavior:
- Distraction: Side-step the problem behavior by directing his attention away from the cause. For example, bring along things for him to play with on outings so he's not tempted to go after things he shouldn't. Provide him with something to do when you know you're going to be busy with something in which he can't be included.
- Ignoring: As long as the problem behavior isn't hurtful or destructive,

She can't anticipate a lengthy telephone call any better than you, so try to be understanding when she interrupts.

She may need to learn that being rude and hurtful aren't acceptable ways of expressing herself, but she shouldn't be discouraged from communicating her feelings.

try to simply ignore it. If you don't respond to misbehavior such as whining, yelling, or rudeness, he'll eventually learn that it's not the way to get your attention. The problem behavior may intensify until he recognizes the need for an alternative, so be patient and don't give in. When he changes to an acceptable behavior, reinforce it by giving him praise and acknowledgment.

• Logical consequences: Letting him experience the natural, negative results of his own misbehavior can be extremely effective. Good examples include: Coming late to dinner means the food is cold; eating sand leads to an unpleasant taste; breaking a toy means it no longer works; and not wearing mittens leads to cold hands. Learning from mistakes, though, isn't appropriate if there are risks to his safety—such as playing with matches or running into the street.

• Time-out: Remove him from the circumstances of the problem behavior by having him sit in a chair or sending him to his room. Apply an isolation period of a minute per year of age to give him and you time to regain control. Used appropriately and consistently, this technique is especially effective for problem behavior that is harmful, aggressive, or otherwise impossible to ignore. When his time-out is over, treat him normally and don't bring up his misbehavior; if it recurs, though, repeat the time-out.

Spanking and other forms of physical punishment are never acceptable disciplining techniques; nor are they effective. If you think of spanking as a possible last resort that can force a change in him or break his will, you'll probably end up only being surprised by the strength of his determination. Physical punishment promotes aggressive misbehavior by teaching him to strike out when angry; and it does nothing constructive to encourage him to feel guilt or remorse. Spanking also carries the risk of unleashing unrelated, pent-up anger, setting off a rapidly escalating chain reaction that ends in abuse.

Winning Ways

SHORT-FUSE PRESCHOOLER

• Keep routines predictable. He won't get as frustrated if he knows what to expect and has time to make transitions between activities.

• Give limited choices. His frustration builds if he doesn't feel a sense of control, so let him select which sweater to wear or whether to have peas or carrots at dinner.

• Encourage problem-solving. Involve him in finding solutions to frustration. Ask him what he thinks would help to improve a situation in which he's having difficulty.

• Reduce self-help obstacles. Look for ways around things that thwart his independence. For example, give him a stool so he doesn't get frustrated trying to reach the sink.

If you simply ignore her when she bangs her cup on the table, she'll eventually learn that the strategy isn't an effective way of getting more juice.

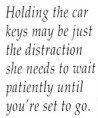

Holding the car keys may be just the distraction she needs to wait patiently until you're set to go.

PLAYTIME AND ACTIVITIES

Play is as vital to a child's development as nutritious food and proper sleep. Most of your preschooler's learning comes from play—it's a way for her to have fun and experience adventure, and to gain a sense of competency and control. Through play, she learns about the workings of objects and people, knowledge she can begin to apply within the world around her.

A child doesn't need to be told how to play. But while your preschooler is her own best teacher, there's a lot that you can do to promote her learning through play. The greatest contribution you can make is simply to be a resource; just by providing her a safe, stimulating environment in which to play, you're giving her all the instruction she requires to learn.

ARTS AND CRAFTS

Your preschooler possesses a natural ability to create. All she needs from you to unleash her creativity is a supportive environment. Almost any type of arts-and-crafts project is likely to appeal to her love of making things. And as she paints a picture, cuts and glues bits of paper, or rolls and shapes a ball of playdough, she's not just amusing herself but also developing her imagination, sharpening her perceptions, and improving her physical skills.

Child Artistry
The simple act of creating something tangible is a tremendous boost to your preschooler's self-esteem and offers a way for her to express her innermost self. With arts and crafts, she has results to show for her efforts at organizing a response to the world. Not only does she learn about the properties and qualities of materials she uses, but she gains insight into her own abilities to change and affect them. Simple choices along the way—such as what color to use— help build her sense of independence. "Look what I made!" is her proud statement of achievement that lets you know just how much the process itself helps her to define her identity.

The depth of self-expression in each stroke of a preschooler's paintbrush can be astonishing.

A preschooler's playdough sculptures can take you far into the world she inhabits.

HOMEMADE SUPPLIES

✓ Fingerpaints: Mix 1/2 cup cornstarch and 3 Tbsp. sugar, then add 2 cups water. Stir over low heat until blended. Divide into 4 or 5 portions and add to each a different food coloring and—for easy cleaning up—a pinch of detergent.

✓ Playdough: Mix 1 cup flour, 1/4 cup salt, and 2 Tbsp. cream of tartar. Combine and add 1 cup water, 1 Tbsp. vegetable oil, and food coloring. Stir over medium heat for 3 to 5 minutes until loose ball forms, then turn out and knead on lightly floured surface. Store airtight.

✓ Modeling clay: Mix 1 cup salt, 1/2 cup water, and 2 Tbsp. vegetable oil, then add 2 cups flour. After shaping, bake at 250°F for several hours. When cool, seal with shellac or clear nail polish and decorate using water colors or acrylics.

FANTASY PLAY

Rapid advances in your child's powers of thought influence her imaginative play, which takes on an especially important role during her preschool years. Whether in the form of pretend play, humor, or an imaginary friend, fantasy is a way for her to experiment and gain understanding of the world. Remember that she doesn't perceive things the way you do; she's still learning to distinguish between what is real and what she has imagined.

Child Imaginings

A strong focus of your preschooler's pretend play will be her developing awareness of her place in the world. She may alternate between male and female roles, for example, in exploring her sexual identity. As her world expands, she's likely to assume the parts of a doctor, shopkeeper, firefighter, and other characters. Some of her pretending may involve positions of power, symbolic of her desire for control. Her fantasy play allows her to work out things on her own; it's important to her sense of independence and self-confidence, so don't interfere.

Pretend play is a way for your preschooler to release tension and claim a sense of personal power—even master an unpleasant memory or fear. You may not always see the humor in her acting silly or her ridiculing imitations, but be patient; the exercises are a way for her to relieve anxiety and feel more in control. Try to be sympathetic if, for instance, she scolds, spanks, or throws a doll to release feelings of jealousy and hostility toward a new sibling; she needs your support to understand and accept things that can't be changed.

In make-believe games such as playing "house," children get the opportunity to role-play and experiment with their identities.

As children develop interest in people outside the home, their role-playing becomes more realistic and complex, with a number of characters taking part in the same story.

By acting the part of an all-powerful superhero, a child fulfills her longing for control.

STORYTIME AND TELEVISION

Your interest in your preschooler's learning will naturally include important decisions about books and television. Habits that she develops now may last her lifetime, so you'll want to assure her a strong start. Until she can read, television may seem to have advantages, but don't be fooled; books are far more beneficial. She'll be best served by your diligent efforts to build her familiarity with books and limit her exposure to television.

Book Freedom

Books aren't the source of all your preschooler's learning, but there's no substitute for the stimulative interaction they can promote. When you read aloud to her, your voice engages her in thinking about words and how ideas can be expressed in ways other than speech; along with looking at the pictures, she's encouraged to apply her powers of imagination. How you hold a book, turn pages, and proceed left-to-right, top-to-bottom, a page at a time introduces her to the mechanics of reading.

Books also provide your preschooler a measure of control over her own learning. Respect her sense of ownership of books that she feels belong to her. Make a variety of books always available to her so she feels empowered by having choices. Be tolerant of her requests to have entire books or certain passages read again and again, as well as her interruptions with questions. Take advantage of the opportunities for interaction that books provide; what other medium affords her such learning freedom?

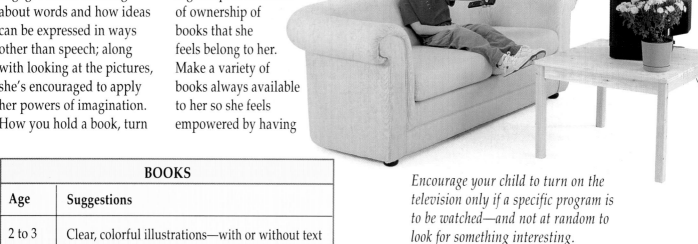

BOOKS	
Age	**Suggestions**
2 to 3 years	Clear, colorful illustrations—with or without text Rhymes and poems; text with repetitive phrases Sensory appeal; stories with sounds to imitate, textures to feel, or scents to smell A-B-C labeling books
3 to 4 years	Stories told in short, simple sentences; text that matches illustrations Fairy tales and humor; ridiculous characters and bizarre situations Friendly animals—real or imaginary Sorting and classifying books
4 to 6 years	Stories about everyday experiences; illustrations that give clues to unfamiliar words in text Simple action and adventure plots Personality appeal; characters of the same age that can be identified with Fears and feelings books

Encourage your child to turn on the television only if a specific program is to be watched—and not at random to look for something interesting.

The warmth and affection that comes from reading aloud to your child promotes her affinity for books.

Television Limits

Limiting your preschooler's watching of television is justifiable on the basis of TV's sheer passivity. Set a good example yourself and encourage her to develop critical viewing habits. Restrict her television to no more than an hour or so per day and preselect appropriate programs. Promote shared, participative viewing and avoid letting your preschooler watch alone; sit with her whenever possible and encourage discussion about the program. Keep the television in a common room where its use can be monitored and don't leave it on unless it's being watched.

GAMES WITH RULES

Rule-based games and play are likely to become increasingly popular with your child during her preschool years. Through such activities she cannot only improve her skills, but experience the excitement of competition, the challenge of devising strategy, and the virtue of cooperation in shared ventures.

Children are quick to exercise their basic social skills and rule-making abilities when they want to play together with a ball.

Even though children might not know how to play by all the rules, they often enjoy board games that require them to think before they act.

Fun Rules

Your preschooler's interest in rule-based activities evolves naturally out of her developing memory and capacity for understanding instructions. Playing games gives her a chance to exercise physical and cognitive skills, as well as learn about sharing, taking turns, and sportsmanship. A game's healthy sense of competitiveness encourages her to build self-discipline and can be balanced by the need for a cooperative social spirit to keep the game running.

Game playing is a safe context for your preschooler to practice making judgments and adhering to principles—and can be revealing of her inner self. Arguments about rules, for example, help her to negotiate differences and make compromises. If she disrupts a game with a display of temper, she may feel frustrated and need more time to handle losing; until she can be more philosophical, she's better off playing simpler games that involve more chance and less strategy.

A game of hide-and-seek helps improve children's running and coordination, and tests their abilities to be observant and find good hiding places.

OUTDOOR FUN

Your preschooler will thrive on outdoor play, so don't feel obliged to keep her indoors simply because the weather isn't perfect. She'll benefit enormously from some fresh air and the freedom to run, jump, skip, hop, climb, ride, and be a little wild every day. Just be sure that she's dressed properly and has a secure setting in which to play. Even so, she'll require your constant supervision to ensure that her outdoor fun doesn't entail safety risks.

Playground Safety

Your preschooler's safety outdoors depends on your caring supervision. But while you must always keep her in sight, you shouldn't be overprotective. She needs to be allowed to attempt things on her own; some risk-taking is necessary to her development. For example, she may turn too sharply and fall off her tricycle a number of times before she masters it, but she'll never learn how to ride it at all if you don't let go and allow her to try by herself. Don't be overly cautious or prevent her from taking normal risks; you may undermine her sense of self-confidence.

However, your preschooler doesn't perceive risks the way you do and may not always see the possible consequences of her actions. Just because she can repeat your instruction not to throw rocks, for instance, doesn't mean that a few moments later she won't try. Until she is capable of thinking logically and making the connections between actions and results, she needs you there to make judgments for her. You needn't spend a lot of time explaining to her why something is dangerous; she'll probably end up more confused than enlightened. But while you don't have to justify safety rules, you do have to be available to ensure they're followed.

To a youngster with colored chalk, any patio, sidewalk, or driveway is a canvas awaiting his artistry.

Training wheels help boost a child's riding confidence during the transition from tricycle to bicycle.

STREETPROOFING

Your preschooler isn't streetproof instinctively or quickly; she needs a lot of training in how to be traffic-wise and people-cautious before she's capable of looking after herself. Start early to work with her on establishing personal safety guidelines; you won't be able to supervise her activities forever.

A tricycle provides a youngster with the riding stability that's needed to practice pedaling and steering.

Water-filled balloons in the warm sunshine can engage preschoolers in mischievous learning about concepts such as volume and density.

Street Safety

Everyday outings are your opportunities to build your preschooler's safety consciousness. She isn't able to apply safety principles herself, but if you set a good example and constantly repeat the rules, she'll eventually develop the awareness required to protect herself.

Always cross streets properly and explain the procedures to your preschooler: Stand well back from the curb, look both ways and listen for traffic, and cross only when the street is clear. Show her the safest places to cross and teach her not to run out between parked cars.

There are some risks your preschooler must be warned against. Rules about strangers, for example, are best given simply and clearly to avoid making her overanxious. Tell her she must:
• never accept anything offered by a stranger;
• always keep a distance from a stranger—at least an arm's length;
• never, ever go anywhere with anyone unless she first asks you or the person you've left her in the care of.

STREET-SMART RULES

✓ Always go out with a grown-up. Supervise your preschooler's outdoor play. Teach her never to go off on her own, even if it's only to a neighbor's house or the corner.

✓ Never play near the road. Make sure your preschooler plays in a safe, enclosed area with gates that shut securely. Explain to her the importance of not stepping out into the street or chasing after a ball or other plaything that goes astray.

✓ Stay close on walks. Have your preschooler walk on the inside, farthest from the street. Get her to hold your hand so there's no chance of her becoming separated from you.

If guidelines to activities aren't established, a preschooler may not recognize the risks of going off to the store without permission.

DAYCARE AND PRESCHOOL

Entrusting your preschooler to the care of someone else is always a big decision. Whether you're leaving him half or full days for part or all of the work week, you'll want the care he gets to be the best. To get on with your work and other responsibilities, you'll need to be sure that he's safe and comfortable in pleasant surroundings, busy with his own learning and play.

Finding just the right setting for your preschooler may take some searching around, so give yourself plenty of time to explore all available options. Whatever place you eventually select, you'll need to help him adjust and settle in. No arrangement is ideal at all times; but if you stay informed and attentive, you'll be assured that he gets the care he needs.

SCHOOLING HOMEWORK

You'll have to weigh for yourself the many pros and cons of child care outside the home; no one else can decide what's best for your preschooler and you. His personality and needs may be your highest priorities, but you'll also have to consider practicalities such as cost and location in making your choice of the best setting. Self-doubts and second thoughts are normal, so try not to feel anxious; getting used to any decision can take some time.

Initial Inquiries
Develop your own list of care options and don't settle for the first place you come across. No matter how highly a setting is recommended by others, what works for their children may not be what's best for your preschooler and you. By comparing care options for yourself, you'll feel more confident about your choice—and have some possible alternatives to pursue should the need ever arise.

Write up a list of practical questions, including concerns such as licensing, flexibility of hours, and costs, then use the telephone to make a decision on places worth investigating in person. The answers you get to your questions

2 Touring prospective places with your preschooler gives you both the opportunity to form insightful, firsthand impressions.

1 Narrow down your list of options by getting answers to all your practical questions on the telephone.

will help you weed out options that clearly aren't suitable for your preschooler, but a phone call can't give you more than a vague sense of a setting, so don't be too quick to make judgments. Only by a personal visit and interview can you find out what you need to know about a place.

Give yourself ample time for tours. Spend at least a half hour interviewing the director and teacher of the class your preschooler would enter, and a minimum of an hour observing the children in their program. If you're discouraged from making a long visit or showing up unannounced to observe, eliminate the place from consideration.

Specific questions that you should ask and have answered to your satisfaction include:
• What is the philosophy on child care and discipline?
• Is there a formal educational program? If so, what are its components?
• How many part- and full-time children are there? What is the teacher-to-child ratio?
• What training and education is required of the staff and how long have they been employed?
• What are the policies on sickness, lunches, and changes of clothing?
• Is there an active parent board involved in operating the program?

3 Your preschooler won't feel as anxious about the transition to a new setting if you ease her entry into activities.

4 Once your preschooler feels secure, she'll feel much more comfortable about participating in things by herself.

133

EARLY SCHOOLING DAYS

The best child care outside the home will enable your preschooler to enjoy himself while he develops his abilities and learns to get along with others. Make sure that whatever program he's in provides plenty of opportunity for social interaction. The setting in which you leave him should be safe, clean, and relatively tidy, but remember that fancy toys and equipment are neither a guarantee nor requisite of a quality program.

First Feelings

Your perceptions on the general environment of a place are important, so take a good look at the space, materials, and activities. Is there adequate room and time for routines? The outside play area should be fenced, its equipment sturdy and safe. Are materials plentiful and age appropriate? Activities should be varied, with a balance between structured time and free play. Is a child given the freedom to pursue something on his own if he finds a group activity too demanding? Above all, you'll want to watch the children: Do they work and play together happily?

Observe the staff at the place closely, too—especially the teacher with whom your preschooler would have the most contact. Is the teacher enthusiastic, energetic, and positive? How much effort does the teacher make to include as many children as possible? Does the teacher look at the children while speaking and kneel down or sit to talk to them at their level? Does the teacher intervene appropriately to stop a child from hurting himself or someone else?

Take as much time as you need to feel confident about your judgment of a place. Trust your instincts and feelings about whether your later questions, ideas, and suggestions would be welcomed. Ask yourself how suitable the environment would be for you if you were a child again. Watch your preschooler's reactions and ask for his opinions; even if all his comments can't be taken too literally, you should still be respectful of his views.

Indelible Impressions

Whatever place you choose for your preschooler, preparing him in advance is your best assurance that his experience will be positive and get off to a good start. Talk about the activities he'll do and the friends he'll make to encourage his sense of optimism and excitement. Take him for visits a week or so before he's scheduled to begin going to help him get acclimatized; stay just long enough for him to be eager to return.

When the big day arrives for your preschooler to start, make sure that your schedule is carefully arranged so there's no last-minute scrambling to get out the door. Allow enough time for you both to dress, eat a relaxed breakfast, and share a few quiet moments before heading out. Stay calm and don't

1 Special items he needs for school can give him a sense of self-importance that translates into a positive attitude toward going.

try to rush him; hurrying may upset him and make him feel anxious.

Despite all your preparations, both your preschooler and you may find the initial separation difficult. Arriving a little early may be helpful; he's likely to feel less overwhelmed if he doesn't have to enter a hubub of activity. Plan to spend an hour or so with him. Be relaxed and cheerful, greeting and introducing him to his teacher and the other children. Don't try to pressure him into playing with anyone. You may help him find some suitable playthings, but minimize your participation; don't start him on a project that requires your ongoing assistance. If he's playing independently or with another child before you leave, your departure won't be too difficult for him to take.

Your preschooler may not give you a happy welcome on your return; instead, he may cry or ignore you. Stay calm at his displays of resentment toward you for leaving him. Give him a warm greeting and a hug. Ask him about his day and listen closely to what he has to say. Avoid rushing him home; he needs as much time to adjust to being together again as he did to the separation.

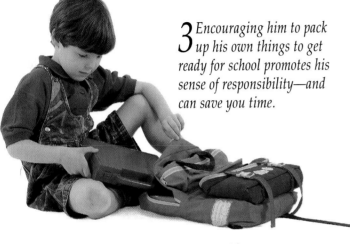

3 *Encouraging him to pack up his own things to get ready for school promotes his sense of responsibility—and can save you time.*

2 *Calm morning routines that allow for time together at breakfast can help you both feel good about his going off to school.*

ADJUSTING	
Do let him know when you're about to leave. **Do** keep good-byes brief and go even if he's upset. **Do** allow him to take along something comforting from home. **Do** be understanding if he responds poorly on reunion at the day's end. **Do** expect him to need at least a few days to fully adjust to the routine.	**Don't** slip away without saying good-bye to him. **Don't** prolong good-byes or return to comfort him. **Don't** call to talk to him if your faraway voice may upset him. **Don't** be alarmed if he exhibits behavior that is immature or regressive. **Don't** worry if he's still adjusting to the routine after a couple of weeks.

4 *Taking along a favorite plaything may help him to overcome feelings of anxiousness about going to school— even if he never unpacks it.*

FRIENDSHIPS AND FAMILY

During a child's preschool years, her attention turns increasingly to the world outside home. Secure in the bond of her family and familiar with the way they do things, she's ready for new challenges and broader experiences. The forming of friendships becomes possible as she gains awareness of herself as an individual and an understanding that others are different.

Siblings, too, play an important role in the development of a child's social skills during her preschool years. Competition for attention may lead siblings into power struggles that get out of hand if they're not handled sensitively. But siblings aren't just rivals; they also interact positively. With your love and guidance, your children can build and enjoy a special relationship.

PLAYMATES

Playmates are important to your preschooler's development. With friends she has an opportunity to learn in ways she never can with adults and a standard against which she can measure her performance. Her interactions with friends won't always go smoothly. But as she and her playmates mature, antisocial incidents will become fewer and less physical; just remember that awareness of others' feelings comes long before the ability to handle them well.

Peer Dynamics
Your preschooler's developing social abilities prompt a natural interest in spending time with others her own age. Although you'll need to supervise her play to make sure she's safe, you're likely to find that she becomes much more capable of interacting with playmates on her own. Conflicts gradually happen less often and will tend to be waged primarily with words.

When a conflict erupts between your preschooler and a playmate, you should resist the impulse to step in and settle it; save your intervention for situations that are getting out of hand. By giving her the chance to work out her own problems, she'll learn about the challenges of getting along with playmates. As well, she'll get good practice in thinking and fending for herself. Remember, too, that the best way to discourage an antisocial act is to offer a praiseworthy alternative.

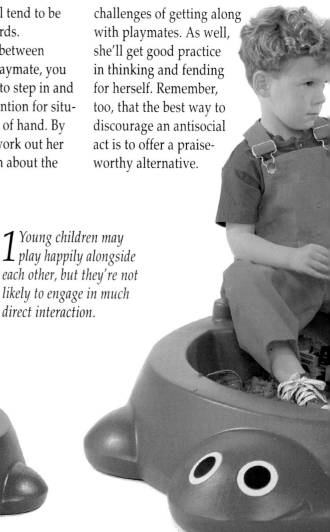

1 Young children may play happily alongside each other, but they're not likely to engage in much direct interaction.

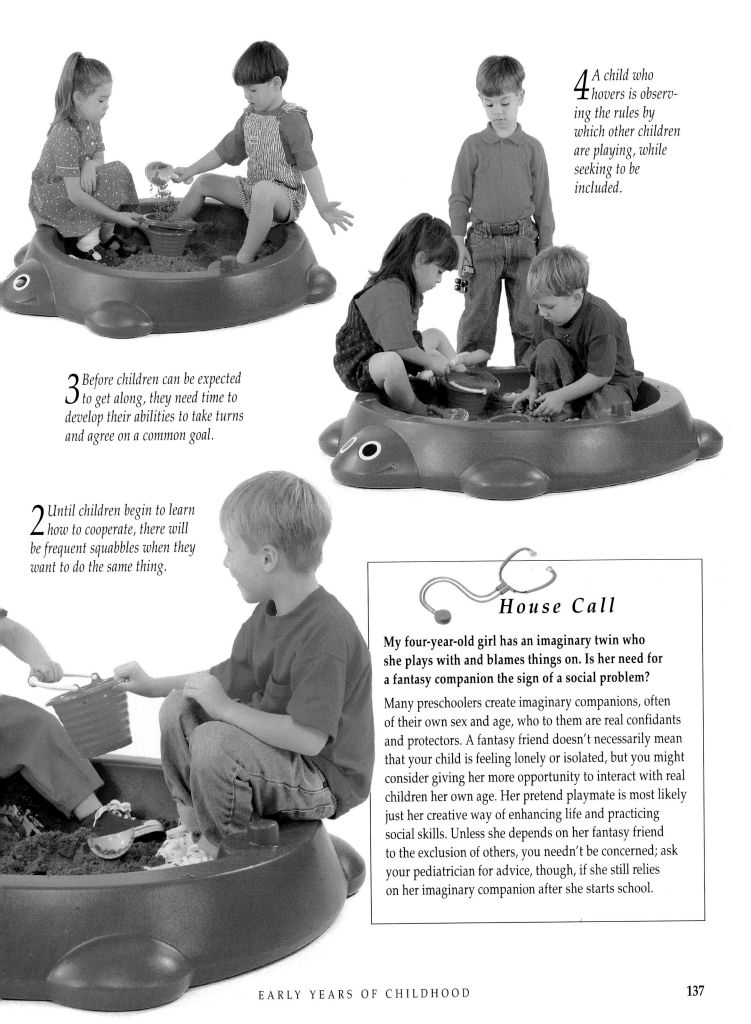

4 *A child who hovers is observing the rules by which other children are playing, while seeking to be included.*

3 *Before children can be expected to get along, they need time to develop their abilities to take turns and agree on a common goal.*

2 *Until children begin to learn how to cooperate, there will be frequent squabbles when they want to do the same thing.*

House Call

My four-year-old girl has an imaginary twin who she plays with and blames things on. Is her need for a fantasy companion the sign of a social problem?

Many preschoolers create imaginary companions, often of their own sex and age, who to them are real confidants and protectors. A fantasy friend doesn't necessarily mean that your child is feeling lonely or isolated, but you might consider giving her more opportunity to interact with real children her own age. Her pretend playmate is most likely just her creative way of enhancing life and practicing social skills. Unless she depends on her fantasy friend to the exclusion of others, you needn't be concerned; ask your pediatrician for advice, though, if she still relies on her imaginary companion after she starts school.

Parents and Siblings

Birth order, age gap, and gender are important factors in sibling relationships; of even greater influence, though, is the temperament of the individuals and the quality of each child-parent relationship. Two children who live under the same roof don't automatically like each other, so you shouldn't expect them to always get along. Nor should you worry about trying to treat your children exactly the same way; fairness, not equality, is what they need.

Home Dynamics

A preschooler's growing independence usually brings an easing of resistance to her parents' wishes. Often, she develops an intense fondness for both her father and mother. As she gains self-confidence and an understanding of what's expected of her, she's not as troubled by separating from her parents; at home, she even may spend less time with them than with her siblings.

The relationship of most siblings ranges between extremes; they fight one minute, play happily together the next, then erupt in argument a short while later. Don't take the volatility of your children's interactions as a sign of your failure; to expect them to live together in perfect harmony isn't realistic. Their personalities can be as different as unrelated children; just because they're related doesn't make them any more likely to be compatible. You can't change who they are or force them to get along, so keep things in perspective. Sibling rivalry is natural and can be healthy; and don't overlook or underestimate the strength of the love and loyalty that's also a part of their bond.

Accepting the inevitability of sibling rivalry, though, doesn't mean there's nothing for you to do about it. Your children need you to ensure that their

NEW BABY	
Do make sure that you're the one to inform your child of the pregnancy. **Do** encourage your child's curiosity and interest in the pregnancy. **Do** give your child praise for mature behaviors such as feeding, washing, and dressing herself. **Do** involve your child in getting the house ready for the baby. **Do** answer your child's questions matter-of-factly and honestly. **Do** point out to your child the special privileges and advantages of being the older sibling. **Do** let your child know that having mixed feelings about a baby is normal.	**Don't** risk having your child hear about the pregnancy from someone else. **Don't** worry your child by trying to hide or downplay the pregnancy. **Don't** start making any demands on your child to learn new skills such as toilet training. **Don't** shelter your child from household changes needed for a new baby. **Don't** hide the truth from your child or make unrealistic promises. **Don't** hurry your child to grow up by overstating the responsibilities of having a younger sibling. **Don't** expect your child to have only positive feelings about the new baby.

Open, mutual displays of warmth, love, and affection make for a strong relationship between you and your child.

Helping out a younger sibling can boost a child's self-confidence, but she shouldn't be pushed into taking too much responsibility.

rivalry is kept within strict bounds and doesn't get out of hand; left unchecked, it can result in damage to them and the entire family. Encouraging your children to find positive ways of getting the attention they need is the basis for some of the most practical steps that you can take to limit their rivalry:

• Create opportunities for cooperative interaction. Suggest games and activities that they can do together—for example, where one benefits by learning from the other, who gains a sense of responsibility that comes from being the teacher. Praise them when they're getting along to reinforce cooperation as a way to get positive attention.

• Set clear, firm limits on behavior that's unacceptable. To be effective, their rules about no hitting, screaming, and throwing things must be frequently repeated, consistently enforced, and also apply to you.

• Encourage cooperative resolution of conflicts. Don't engage in or allow yourself to be drawn into every little disagreement. If they can't settle a difference, separate them or remove the item of contention until they can work out a fair compromise. By discouraging tattling and not trying to get to the bottom of disputes, you'll avoid charges of favoritism.

• Promote same-age friendships. When they're fighting too much and won't leave each other alone, invite a friend over for each of them. They're likely to be better company for each other if they can sometimes play apart.

A younger sibling's pestering and taking of things aren't as likely to be problems if a child has a place to retreat and safeguard prized possessions.

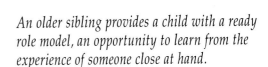

An older sibling provides a child with a ready role model, an opportunity to learn from the experience of someone close at hand.

Even when siblings aren't pleasant with one another, they should be given a chance to work out their differences on their own.

4 FROM CHILD TO ADOLESCENT

SIX TO PRETEEN

The door flings open, the books drop to the floor, and a voice yells "Hi, I'm home!" Before you can ask about your child's day, the door bangs shut and she's gone again. She's making dramatic intellectual and social advances; her world is broadening beyond immediate family. But as school and friends become priorities, she still needs a secure base at home and you hold a vitally central place in her life.

SKILLS AND ABILITIES

- *Has good sense of balance and control of movements; learns to ride bicycle without training wheels, and may enjoy hopscotch and skipping games.*
- *Starts assuming responsibility for bathing and dressing.*
- *Capable of taking on routine household responsibilities—such as feeding a family pet, taking out the garbage, or setting the table.*
- *Learns fundamentals of reading, writing, and arithmetic.*

THINKING AND UNDERSTANDING

- *Conscious of own gender; asks factual questions about sex and reproduction.*
- *Begins to grasp concept of money; may start getting a regular allowance.*
- *Sorting and classifying becomes more refined.*
- *Comprehends basic mathematical principles; shifts from concrete to abstract applications.*

PERSONALITY AND BEHAVIOR

- *Thrives on physical activity; enjoys rough-and-tumble play.*
- *Relationships at school take on increasing importance.*
- *Gradually becomes less egocentric; slowly develops capacity to interpret feelings outside own immediate experience.*
- *Shows increasing self-control and displays growing sense of personal responsibility.*
- *Friendships tend to be based on mutual benefit; "best friends" may change often.*

PHYSICAL GROWTH

- *Grows 2 or 3 in. taller on average each year.*
- *Gains about 5 lb. annually.*
- *Begins period of hormone adjustment that precedes onset of puberty.*
- *Permanent front teeth start to appear; acquires three or four permanent teeth a year.*
- *Facial bones begin developing and noticeably altering in shape.*
- *Amount of fatty tissue beneath the skin starts to increase.*

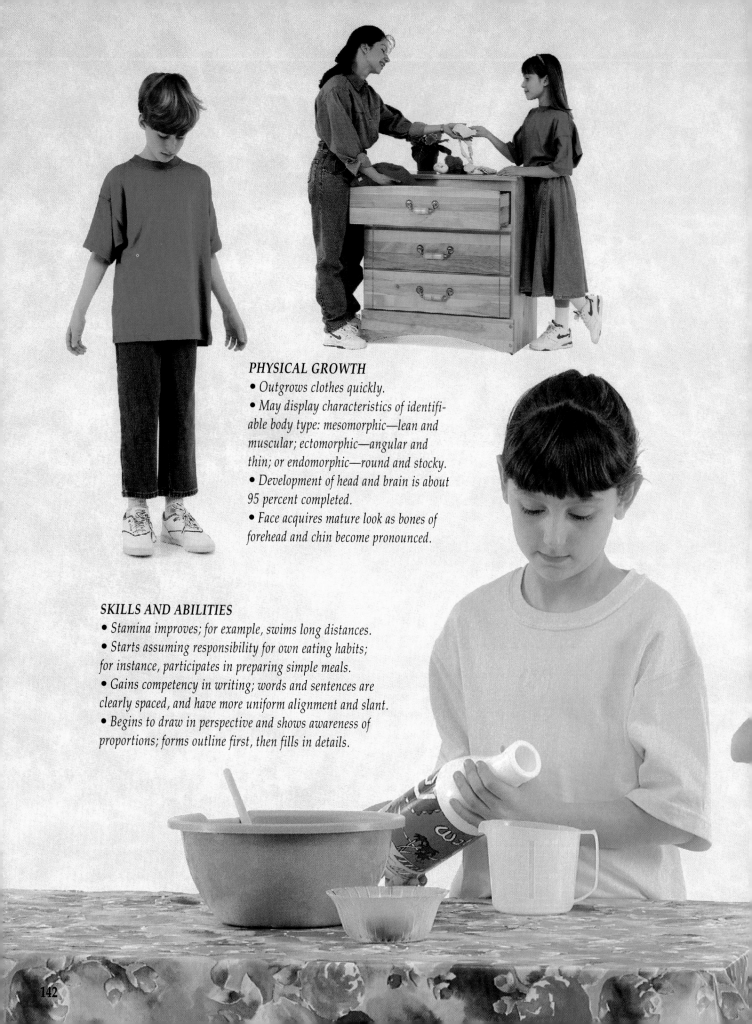

PHYSICAL GROWTH

- *Outgrows clothes quickly.*
- *May display characteristics of identifiable body type: mesomorphic—lean and muscular; ectomorphic—angular and thin; or endomorphic—round and stocky.*
- *Development of head and brain is about 95 percent completed.*
- *Face acquires mature look as bones of forehead and chin become pronounced.*

SKILLS AND ABILITIES

- *Stamina improves; for example, swims long distances.*
- *Starts assuming responsibility for own eating habits; for instance, participates in preparing simple meals.*
- *Gains competency in writing; words and sentences are clearly spaced, and have more uniform alignment and slant.*
- *Begins to draw in perspective and shows awareness of proportions; forms outline first, then fills in details.*

PERSONALITY AND BEHAVIOR

- *Ability to follow rules often leads to interest in games of strategy.*
- *Applies increasingly less rigid notions of reciprocity and fairness to relationships.*
- *Seeks inclusion in groups of same-sex peers and may belong to tight-knit clubs and gangs.*
- *"Best friends" stabilize; more intensely distressed by problems with close friends.*

THINKING AND UNDERSTANDING

- *Becomes sexually self-conscious; insists on privacy and may be curious or anxious about the onset of puberty.*
- *Begins to distinguish between "private" and "public" self; more accepting of personal responsibility for self-care routines.*
- *Searches less randomly and more systematically for details.*
- *Increasingly capable of logical thought; deliberates on experiences, draws conclusions, and applies learning to new situations.*

8 YEARS TO 10 YEARS

PERSONALITY AND BEHAVIOR

- *Becomes image conscious and often may be preoccupied with appearance.*
- *Gains increasing emotional self-control; less inclined to throw tantrums as conflict resolution skills improve.*
- *May take health or safety risks to win peer acceptance.*
- *Friendships grow, becoming longer lasting and deeper.*
- *Develops interest in opposite sex; may start attending mixed-gender parties.*
- *Often less demonstrative in showing affection toward parents and more openly critical of them.*

PHYSICAL GROWTH

- *May enter growth spurt and jump as much as 4 in. in height in one year; onset earlier for girls than for boys.*
- *May have full set of permanent teeth— except wisdom teeth.*
- *Face changes in overall shape, altering in length more than in width; more dramatic in boys than in girls, especially as lower jaw becomes bigger.*
- *Amount of fat beneath the skin begins to diminish in boys; continues to increase in girls as their bodies fill out.*
- *A girl may begin to menstruate.*

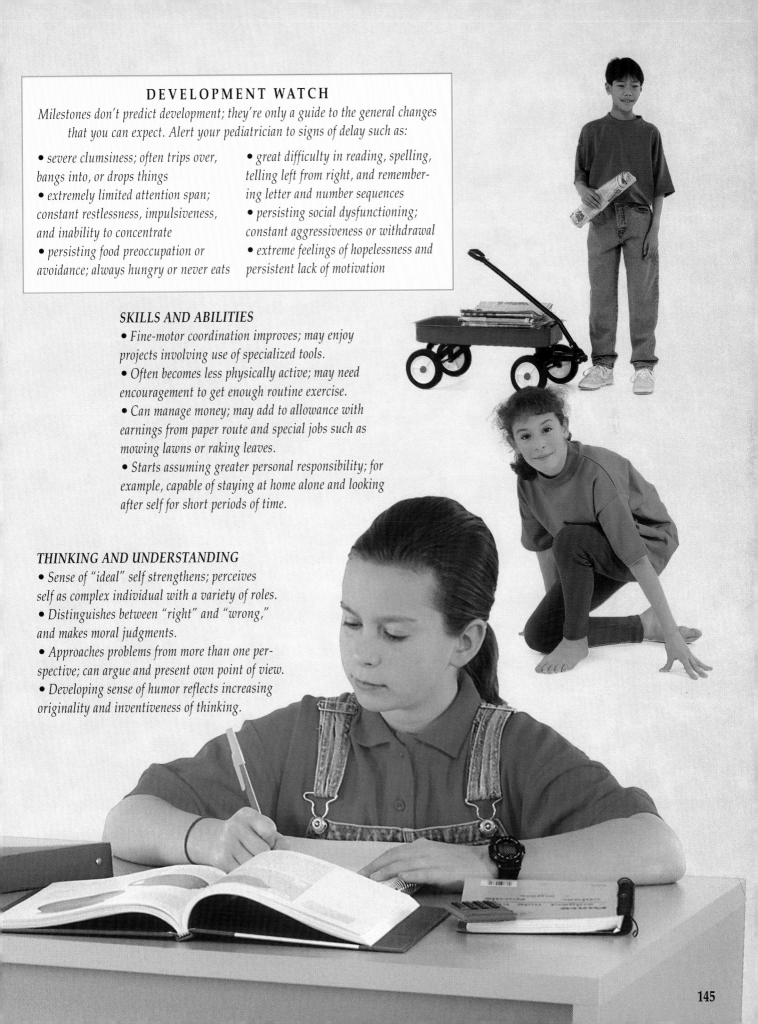

DEVELOPMENT WATCH

Milestones don't predict development; they're only a guide to the general changes that you can expect. Alert your pediatrician to signs of delay such as:

- *severe clumsiness; often trips over, bangs into, or drops things*
- *extremely limited attention span; constant restlessness, impulsiveness, and inability to concentrate*
- *persisting food preoccupation or avoidance; always hungry or never eats*

- *great difficulty in reading, spelling, telling left from right, and remembering letter and number sequences*
- *persisting social dysfunctioning; constant aggressiveness or withdrawal*
- *extreme feelings of hopelessness and persistent lack of motivation*

SKILLS AND ABILITIES

- *Fine-motor coordination improves; may enjoy projects involving use of specialized tools.*
- *Often becomes less physically active; may need encouragement to get enough routine exercise.*
- *Can manage money; may add to allowance with earnings from paper route and special jobs such as mowing lawns or raking leaves.*
- *Starts assuming greater personal responsibility; for example, capable of staying at home alone and looking after self for short periods of time.*

THINKING AND UNDERSTANDING

- *Sense of "ideal" self strengthens; perceives self as complex individual with a variety of roles.*
- *Distinguishes between "right" and "wrong," and makes moral judgments.*
- *Approaches problems from more than one perspective; can argue and present own point of view.*
- *Developing sense of humor reflects increasing originality and inventiveness of thinking.*

PREPARING FOR PUBERTY

Your child begins adjusting to the onset of puberty years before he experiences the physical growth spurt and other bodily changes that signal its arrival. Early into his preadolescence, you may start to sense a certain remoteness developing in him. More reserved about sharing his every thought and feeling with you, he may at times even spurn your kisses and hugs.

Don't be alarmed by your child's seeming withdrawal from you; it's not a sign of rejection. In coming to terms with his gender, he just needs a little distance from you to build a healthy sexual identity. Respect his desire for privacy, but keep yourself open to communication. Be sensitive to his feelings of confusion and be as direct as you can when giving him information about sex.

EMERGING SEXUALITY

By the time your child turns six, he understands that his gender is permanent and begins to develop a sense of himself based on his sex. You'll want him to grow up with positive feelings about his sexual identity, without having gender-based expectations of himself or others. Encourage him to respect both sexes and not to typecast; using labels such as "sissy" and "bruiser," for example, isn't acceptable because it implies gender-based behavior rules.

Gender doesn't determine a child's interests or talents, so don't qualify your encouragement of his knitting and her carpentry.

Sexual Consciousness
How your child perceives himself in terms of his gender will influence his views on such things as his abilities, strengths and weaknesses, and popularity. At six years of age, he'll probably prefer to play with others of the same sex; the reasons aren't easy to define, though, and there are many exceptions to the norm. Try not to worry about him becoming sexist; his choice of friends during preadolescence is based primarily on shared interest in activities and his seeming exclusion of girls probably isn't a deliberate decision. Encourage him to have individual friendships with girls, but allow his selection of group activities to evolve on its own.

However, your child probably will have begun to develop stereotyped views on what is acceptable behavior for boys and girls by the time he reaches school age. Television, teachers, peers, and the dynamics of your own family all play a part in shaping his consciousness and undoubtedly will influence his perceptions of gender. What he's exposed to during the course of a single day at school or at play with friends will become increasingly impossible for you to control; but while the negative influences on his views of the sexes can be subtle, so, too, are the ways that you can exert a positive influence. If both parents simply take an active role in raising him, for example, he'll grow up with a healthy notion of sex roles and behavior. And by hav-

146

ing him sometimes take out the garbage and sometimes help with dinner, he won't be inclined to view any household responsibility as associated with a particular gender.

Sexual Self-consciousness

Your child's increasing sexual consciousness may be expressed by a sudden insistence on privacy. For instance, he'll start closing the door when using the toilet or undressing. While once he wanted you always with him, now you may seem unwelcomed. A "Keep Out" sign may appear on his bedroom door, he may start a diary, and his conversations with friends may stop abruptly when you enter the room. His secrets, a sign of his growing awareness that his life is his own, also reflect his recognition that you don't know everything.

Respect your child's need for privacy; it's a healthy sign of his maturing sense of self, so don't feel threatened or rejected. He isn't shutting you out of his life, just developing

a stronger inner world that will help him broaden his capacity for intimacy. If he feels that you're respectful of his privacy, he probably will be more eager to share his thoughts, ideas, and opinions with you on his own volition.

Just as your child needs a safe place in which to play and exercise his body, he now also requires a secure environment in which to think and exercise his mind. Establish some household privacy rules that you both agree to observe. For example, knock before entering a bedroom, even when the

door is half open. Always obtain permission before borrowing belongings and make it a policy to not read each other's mail or personal papers.

Be available to your child without intruding on his privacy. For instance, wait for him to come to you with a problem rather than insist he tell you what's on his mind. Take care of your household bills alongside him at the kitchen table while he does his homework. By respecting his privacy, you're showing trust and confidence in him, as well as promoting his independence.

Respect your child's telephone privacy and don't eavesdrop on his conversations with his friends.

Having a personal diary allows your child to record the important events of her life as well as express her private hopes and dreams.

House Call

Every so often, my seven-year-old son complains of an aching in his shins. What's causing his discomfort?

Your son probably has so-called "growing pains;" their cause isn't known, but they're not serious. The cramp-like pains are deep in the muscle and usually occur in the shins, but also may affect the calves and the front of the thighs. The pains typically come during the night and last for only a few minutes; on occasion, they may persist for an hour or so. He may suffer periodic bouts for several years, but will outgrow them eventually. Try easing his discomfort with a heating pad or gentle massage.

SEX EDUCATION

Your child probably won't be very interested in sexual relationships before he's a teenager, but don't think he isn't curious about sex just because he doesn't ask you questions. In deciding how best to handle the subject of sex with him, be forewarned that discussions will only get more awkward for both of you as he grows older. But if you're sensitive to his need for information, you'll be able to judge when and how much he should know.

Sexual Understanding

As your child approaches puberty, he may become interested in the changes that will occur in his body. But even before then, he probably will display a growing curiosity about sex that's based largely on his recognition of taboos. For example, he'll understand that he isn't supposed to walk around with nothing on and shouldn't say "bad words." And he might wonder, for instance, why talking about some things is "not nice," or even seem to think there might be reasons for him not to be too friendly with children of the opposite sex.

Although you aren't your child's only source of information about sex, you are in the best position to provide him with it. You're a far better authority than his friends and can give him information that's a lot more accurate than they do. His teachers at school are a reliable source, but they may be limited by an official policy on what information can be taught and how; and the rigidity of a classroom schedule tends to impose unnatural restrictions on discussion.

By providing your child with information about sex at home, he is much more likely to adopt the attitudes and mores you believe are best; remember that the education he receives from you includes powerful implicit lessons on your morals and values. At home, you have the freedom to pursue the subject with him in the way you wish, using whatever books and resource materials you find helpful. And the continuity of your day-to-day relationship means that you can provide him with information in manageable doses, when and as he needs it; the subject can be dropped and easily picked up again at an appropriate moment.

A children's book about sex is a helpful way of introducing him to the reproductive process and preparing him for the arrival of a baby.

During your child's preadolescent years, he probably will be interested primarily in the "facts" of sex—the basics of reproduction, such as how babies are made. Most of his questions will be fairly straight-forward and he isn't likely to be very self-conscious, so respond-ing to him and correcting his misperceptions shouldn't be too difficult or awkward for you. Later on, though, he may need encouragement to talk about his feelings and the emotions involved in the sexual experience. As he gets older and more interested in sexual relationships, such discus-sion probably won't be very easy or comfortable for either of you.

No two children are alike, however, so you shouldn't think that there is any one "right" way to handle the subject of sex. If you simply trust your sense of your child, you'll figure out what he needs to know and how best he should be informed. You may want to be entirely open with him and not have a problem talking to him about sex in

Your casual attitude toward feminine pads and tampons will help dispel any anxiety she may feel about the onset of her menstruation.

If children understand basic hygiene principles, they won't be afraid to share a drink because of misconcep-tions about sexually trans-mitted diseases.

simple terms—such as "you grew in mommy's tummy." But don't be sur-prised if you find participating in dis-cussions about how he got there and came out a little more challenging. Both of you may become much more reticent about discussing sex as he gets older; and you also will find that there are fewer opportunities for the subject to come up casually.

Your child needs to know that his interest in sex is healthy and normal. He must be warned about the risks involved in sexual experience, but don't put so much emphasis on the hazards that he worries about his sexu-ality. If he is taught to simply guard against disease, pregnancy, and getting a "reputation" by avoiding sex, he may view his natural desires as harmful.

Long before a child's first romantic interest, she may become an avid reader of love and heartache stories.

Your child's curiosity about the physical changes ahead for him may prompt a fascination in your shaving habits.

FOOD AND FITNESS

Encouraging your child to develop self-motivated healthy attitudes toward food and fitness should be one of your most important objectives during the years leading up to adolescence. Whatever eating and exercise habits she learns now will probably last her lifetime; by starting to accept responsibility for them, she takes a big, positive step toward independence.

The benefits of physical activity to your child aren't restricted to just the health of her body. Exercise is as vital as food to her physical growth and also contributes to her psychological development. Enjoyable participation in physical activity during her formative preadolescent years will have a positive influence on her self-image, confidence, and general well-being.

NUTRITIOUS EATING

Your child's appetite and food preferences probably will stabilize during her early school-age years. She may acquire a taste for a food she never liked before and pass up a long-standing favorite, but her habits aren't likely to be as erratic and unpredictable as they were when she was younger. More consistent in her appetite and maturing in her behavior, she probably will eat the same foods you do at most meals and enjoy socializing at the table.

Healthy Responsibility
Your child's appetite probably will increase slightly as she grows, but you're likely to find that the biggest influence on the amounts of food she eats is her level of physical activity. She still requires three meals a day and may ask for as many snacks—possibly more, especially if she's had a lot of outdoor exercise. Although you may begin to provide her with bigger portions at mealtimes, don't oblige her to eat more than she wants. She needs to start taking responsibility for her own nutrition—and she can't if you make all the decisions about food for her.

As your child starts spending more and more time away from home, monitoring what and how much she eats will become increasingly difficult for you. Try not to worry; if she has devel-

Encourage your child to contribute to the grocery list so she feels a sense of responsibility for the food she eats.

When your child helps with the food shopping, teach her to read package labels and select brand items for their nutritional value.

oped good eating habits at home, she'll continue to make healthy food choices when she's not around you. And if she feels that you trust her to be nutrition wise, she won't disappoint you.

The more you encourage your child to participate in food decisions at home the more likely she is to eat responsibly. Food shopping and cooking with her are two excellent ways for you to teach her about nutrition and the origins of the foods she eats. She may enjoy the fun of planting seeds and harvesting her own vegetables. And she doesn't have to be a master chef to assist in the preparation of meals; just imagine her sense of accomplishment when the dish that she helped make is set on the table. Learning about nutrition also will make her more inclined to taste and accept new foods—as well as more appreciative of food.

Healthy attitudes toward food develop naturally in your child if she participates in the preparation of nutritious meals at home.

Children aren't inclined to overeat if they learn that snacks are to satisfy hunger—and not a sideline to watching television.

Unhealthy Preoccupation
Your child's weight gains should approximate those of her peers and her percentile in the weight-to-height ratio shouldn't vary much from year to year. She probably will gain about five pounds a year until puberty, when the rate will accelerate. But keep in mind she's also getting taller: She may seem chubby just before a growth spurt and skinny just after one.

Just as food shouldn't be an emotional issue for your child, neither should her weight. The most important thing is to accept her at the weight she is. She may be naturally a little under- or overweight no matter how much her diet is adjusted. In the long run, she must learn to live with and like herself; she will if she's shown how. Let her know that she's special just the way she is.

DIETS AND DISORDERS

As long as your child's eating habits are healthy, there's little reason for you to be concerned about her weight. A wide range of weights are acceptable for school-age children, so don't worry if she seems to be a little on the skinny or chubby side. Obesity that persists beyond the preschool years, however, can be a problem. But before you consider putting her on any type of diet, you should always consult your pediatrician.

DISORDER WARNINGS
✓ Extreme preoccupation with weight, shape of the body, and calorie intake.
✓ Unusual eating habits—for example, frequent skipping of meals or repeated cycles of dieting and binging.
✓ Strict avoidance of certain foods—especially those considered to be fattening.
✓ Feelings of guilt or shame about eating.
✓ Fear of gaining weight or being fat; feelings of being fat when not overweight.
✓ Persisting irritability or depression; feelings of ineffectiveness or low self-esteem.
✓ Irregular menstruation or loss of periods.
✓ Noticeable and continuing loss of weight or frequent fluctuations in weight.

Physical Activity

Your preadolescent child probably won't need much encouragement to be active. She'll get enough exercise from jumping, climbing, running, and riding her bike with her friends. She may even place great importance on athletics and take pride in her prowess at turning somersaults or cartwheels. And she needs as much positive experience as possible in being active now if she is to develop and sustain an interest in fitness right through adolescence.

Exercise and Fun

Soon after your child turns six, she probably will have a good sense of balance and control of her movements. She might like gymnastics and develop a passion for activities that require precise motions—such as skipping and hopscotch. Her swimming strokes may start to improve; and as her stamina increases, she'll be able to swim longer distances. Whatever physical activity she does and whatever her performance level, the most important thing is that she have fun. If she enjoys a physical activity for its own sake, she'll gain a sense of well-being from doing it—and be far more likely to develop a positive attitude in general toward fitness.

Encourage your child to participate in as many different physical activities as possible. Your example is important, so be a good role model; if you're not inclined to stay fit yourself, you won't be in a position to help motivate her to remain active as she approaches adolescence. She won't always find satisfaction in simply running around in the playground with her friends, so start now to help her build an interest in physical activities that she can still enjoy as she gets older. Just make sure you encourage her to participate in physical activities that bring her pleasure and personal satisfaction; if too much weight is placed on competition, she'll feel pressured to perform and end up turning off to them.

If you focus on health and fitness—rather than organized games and sports—the range of physical activities possible for your child is tremendous. For example, dance, martial arts, skiing, skating, and swimming all involve self-discipline as well as the acquisition of complex skills and movement patterns.

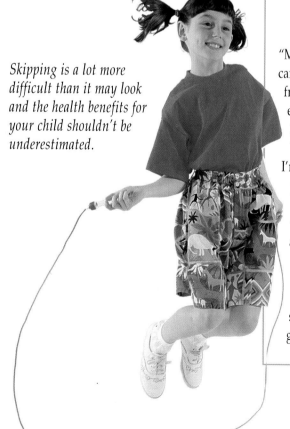

Skipping is a lot more difficult than it may look and the health benefits for your child shouldn't be underestimated.

Afterthoughts...

"My son used to spend most of the weekend watching cartoons on television. I felt he wasn't getting enough fresh air and exercise, so I got myself a bicycle and started asking him to come cycling with me in the mornings. Every Saturday and Sunday, we're now out and have been riding for miles by the time we used to wake up! I'm surprised at how much closer I feel to him—and pleased by how much better shape I'm in."

"I never even learned how to skate, so I was quite taken aback when my daughter began expressing an interest in playing hockey. I signed her up on a local team and couldn't believe how much of a natural at the game she is. She's turned me into an avid hockey fan. We follow the major league standings in the newspaper and look for televised games of our favorite teams to watch on weekends."

Your child may be drawn to an activity such as diving, where performance is strictly individual-based.

Just be sure that she's encouraged to set her own goals and enjoy improving her own performance. She may prefer to pursue a physical activity such as hiking or yoga that provides exercise benefits without being too strenuous or pressuring. And there are all sorts of outdoor and adventure-type expeditions that the whole family can participate in. Keep in mind, too, that during her preteen years almost any physical activity will be more attractive to her if you're also prepared to be involved.

Just by helping to lace up your child's skates, you show support for his participation in physical activity.

SPORTS AND GAMES

Your school-age child may want to play an organized team sport such as softball or soccer. Make sure that her approach to the game is relaxed and she doesn't feel pressured to perform. The rules and equipment must be suited to her age and ability, and her coach should be understanding of emotional and physical needs.

Competition and Sportsmanship

From the time your child first begins to play organized team sports, you need to be alert to the type of competitive pressure that can turn her off physical activity altogether. Your attitudes will affect her approach to the game, so be a role model of good sportsmanship:

• Make sure she knows that your love and acceptance aren't dependent on her performance or the outcome of a game.

• Attend her games and be a good spectator. Don't jeer the opposing team or the officials.

• Show interest in the game, not just who wins. After a game, talk about the quality of playing and caliber of both teams' efforts; ask her if she had fun and what she has learned from the experience.

• Comment favorably on her good plays and don't criticize her mistakes. Encourage her to focus on how much her skills are improving and not dwell on the disappointment of a loss.

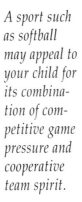

A sport such as softball may appeal to your child for its combination of competitive game pressure and cooperative team spirit.

Your child may spend hours and hours of his free time shooting baskets, all the while improving his coordination, balance, and aim.

PERSONAL HYGIENE

The habits of personal care and cleanliness that you have established for your child should become his responsibilities by the time he reaches adolescence. Let him take charge of as much of his own grooming and hygiene as he can—and remember that encouragement and cajoling work better than criticism and nagging in helping him develop the right attitude.

You will need to be especially tactful as he begins to develop an interest in his appearance. In making sure that he looks after himself properly, you'll have to be careful not to undercut his sense of autonomy. Be sensitive to his style and fashion statements; they're his way of experimenting with his identity, and your intervention isn't likely to be welcomed or helpful.

BATHING AND GROOMING

Having baths alone and starting to take showers are symbolic rites of passage that mark the increasing maturity of your child. He's learning that responsibility must be handled responsibly: Not only is he capable of looking after his own body, but he understands that attending to his needs requires being health and safety conscious. Don't try to hurry him through the process too quickly; he'll tell you when he feels ready for the next step.

New Needs

Early into your child's adolescence, he probably will want to start having baths by himself; he may also begin to express an interest in taking showers.

But while you'll want to assure him of his privacy and your confidence in his ability to wash himself, you'll also need to be assured of his safety. Make sure that your bathtub and shower stall are equipped with a slip-proof rubber mat. Teach him to double-check that he's got everything he needs before he gets into the bath or shower so he doesn't have to get back out. Show him how to run

As your preadolescent takes on more responsibility for his own hygiene, he won't need as many reminders to wash his hands before eating and after using the toilet.

A long, leisurely bubble bath may be just what your preteen needs on occasion to relax and calmly reflect on the events of her day.

the water and test its temperature before he gets into the bath or shower, and supervise his turning on and off of the faucets until you're certain that he can control them on his own.

Your preadolescent probably won't require a bath or shower every day; two or three times a week may suffice. Encourage him to take responsibility for how often he washes and help him to set a bathing schedule that makes sense for his age and level of activity. As he gets older, his recreational activity won't be as physically demanding so he isn't likely to become as obviously dirty. But as he gets older, he also will begin to perspire and have unpleasant body odors; he may need to concentrate more on keeping his skin and hair clean to discourage pimples, acne, and dandruff. He'll be better prepared for these eventualities of puberty if he is discouraged early on from considering a bath or shower as required only when he can "see" he needs one. Don't be too rigid, though, in insisting that he stick to a bathing schedule; as long as he washes regularly and well, a little flexibility in his routine won't hurt him.

Getting your child to assume full responsibility for his own bathing and grooming takes time, so be patient. The more you help him to feel in charge of his own cleanliness, the sooner his routines will become second nature to him. Promote his sense of self-control by giving him his own toiletry supplies, such as soap, shampoo, face cloths and towels. Minimize his need for your assistance by designating a place for him to store and keep track of his toiletry supplies. Encourage him to show consideration for others by teaching him to rinse out the tub and put away what he has used after he has bathed.

Praise your child to reinforce his efforts at keeping himself clean and tidying up after himself. Don't expect too much from him too soon; he's not capable of taking total responsibility for his own bathing and grooming overnight. Try not to feel exasperated by his seeming forgetfulness. He won't always remember to wash his hands before dinner, clean behind his ears while in the tub, place the cap back on the shampoo, and leave his towel in the laundry hamper. But you'll soon see signs of progress if you stay calm and acknowledge the efforts he makes in response to your reminders.

Your adolescent may balk at taking a few seconds to wash thoroughly behind his ears, yet eagerly spend a whole half hour drying his hair.

Giving your preteen her own manicure kit is a helpful way of encouraging her to take proper care of her own nails.

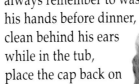

Sanity Saver

With a little commonsense planning and organization, you can help prevent your adolescent's preoccupation with his own grooming from turning the bathroom into a family battlefield. Avoid conflicts by scheduling baths and showers for family members at different times—such as on alternate days, or in the morning or evening. Minimize unnecessary demands for bathroom time by encouraging family members to dress and groom themselves in their bedrooms; for example, hang full-length mirrors on closet doors and provide a nearby place for keeping combs, brushes, hair dryers, and other toiletry items that can be used without the need for a sink. ★

DENTAL CARE

Every time your preadolescent flashes his gap-toothed smile, you may be reminded of how much he has grown. As he loses his baby teeth and his permanent teeth start appearing, routine dental care is especially important—and should become largely his responsibility. You'll probably still need to schedule his visits to the dentist for him, but brushing and flossing are procedures that he is now capable of doing all on his own.

Routinely monitor how your child brushes his teeth to be sure he is reaching the gumline and not applying too much pressure.

House Call

My son's first two permanent front teeth aren't coming in straight. Will he need braces?

Worrying about your child's need for orthodonture is probably premature. The problem may correct itself if there is space for the teeth and they're positioned where the natural, outward pressure of the tongue may help to align them. But if there is a family history of problems with crooked teeth, early treatment may prevent the need for more complicated measures later. Ask your dentist to recommend at least two orthodontists; you'll benefit from as much time as possible to consider all available options.

Weekly use of special plaque-disclosing tablets allows your child to self-test his improving teeth-cleaning capabilities.

New Responsibilities

Once your child turns six, he probably will have the dexterity required to brush and floss properly by himself. Encourage him to take over the routine care of his teeth and check periodically to confirm that he's doing a good job. As his six-year molars come in behind his baby teeth, monitor his cleaning techniques closely to be sure that he does these first permanent teeth especially well; he may miss spots on the far surfaces against his cheeks and along his tongue. Also ask your dentist about treating the molars with a sealant—a plastic coating that smooths bumpy surfaces and helps prevent cavities from forming in hard-to-reach crevices.

As your child's permanent teeth begin appearing, regular dental check-ups will alert you to early signs of a problem. Just from the position and fit of the six-year molars, for example, your dentist may warn you of an eventual overbite, underbite, or crossbite. Your observations, too, are helpful in the early detection of a problem, so be sure to point out any of the following:

• Excessive thumb-sucking: If he hasn't yet broken his thumb-sucking habit, the pressure of his thumb may push the front teeth forward.

• Grinding of the teeth: Persistent pressure can cause his teeth to move out of alignment in his mouth.

• Difficulty chewing: If chewing is painful or the teeth don't apply enough force to chew properly, the problem may be a misalignment of the jaws.

• Breathing through the mouth: If his tonsils and adenoids aren't enlarged, the problem may be that he's unable to close his mouth or lips due to improper growth of the teeth or jaws.

IMAGE CONSCIOUSNESS

Your child may become preoccupied with his appearance early into his adolescence. Until he reaches his teens and begins dressing to satisfy himself, he probably will dress to impress his peers—and no longer simply to please you.

Experimenting with new "looks" is your child's way of trying on different identities, so try to be understanding. Be sure you let him know that you love and appreciate him no matter what he wears or does with his hair.

New Issues

Clothing, hairstyle, and other grooming habits may be touchy subjects as your child starts to relate his appearance with his identity. Almost overnight, his carefree attitude toward his appearance may vanish; instead, he'll insist on wearing only a certain pair of jeans and preen for hours in front of a mirror. He'll experiment with his appearance as a way of expressing who he is, so be sensitive to his self-consciousness; a simple, offhand comment about his hair or clothes may be misinterpreted as a personal criticism.

Peer groups set the standards of style and fashion, and your child may feel strong pressure to conform. As long as

there's no risk to his health and safety, give him as much latitude as you're comfortable with; a trendy haircut or ponytail, for example, won't hurt him and shouldn't be embarrassing to you. Just as he needs the freedom to experiment with other aspects of his identity, he needs some room to try out different "looks." Avoid taking exception to his "statements;" by being tolerant and allowing him to take charge of his appearance, you're contributing to his sense of self-control and independence.

Your child's experimentation with his appearance won't last forever, so try to enjoy it; his tastes will change and eventually may even approximate your own. If you feel that you must set some limits, allow for compromise. For example, if you want him to dress in a certain way on occasions when he is with you, let him wear what he wants when he plays with his friends. Agree to have an older sibling or store clerk mediate clothing disputes; odds are both of you will win—and lose—half the time.

When your adolescent begins to experiment with cosmetics, try to be sensitive to her need to project a certain image instead of worrying about how it might be misinterpreted.

Your preteen may not be ready to start the day until he gets his hair arranged in just the right way.

As your adolescent becomes more self-conscious about her appearance, she may spend hours at the mirror trying to achieve the look she wants.

LEARNING AND COMPETENCY

Your school-age child's comprehension improves in subtlety, complexity, and flexibility. As she learns to think beyond immediate experience, she'll become capable of taking an overview of a situation. When watching a basketball game, for example, she'll not only notice a shot that has just been missed, but also consider all of the possible consequences for the entire game.

As your child matures, she'll be less easily distracted. She'll realize that success comes more easily when she does things in an orderly way, and she'll take a more systematic approach in general to problem-solving. At the same time, she'll acquire the capacity to consider and weigh options, skills that help her to become more flexible and creative in her thinking.

CONCENTRATION AND MEMORY

Throughout your child's school-age years, she refines her abilities to select, classify, absorb, and recall information. By applying her powers of concentration, she can begin to fully exploit the benefits of her memory.

A child's improving concentration helps him to find the not-so-obvious differences in details between illustrations in a puzzle book.

Knowledge
Your child's capacity to handle information improves naturally as she gets older—both because of her greater maturity and because of the practice she has had. As she learns to concentrate, her thinking will become progressively less haphazard and more systematic.
At six years,

for example, she may search two pictures randomly to find the differences between them; at 10 years, though, she'll scan more thoughtfully and pause to focus on details.

Your child's memory is an important learning tool—and to remember well, she must concentrate. Whenever she is learning new information, she will benefit from your encouragement to select details and focus on them. You can also help her to build on knowledge she already has by prompting her to make links between her past memories and what she now needs to learn. You don't have to make a lot of special effort; your day-to-day interactions and continuing interest in her thoughts provide natural opportunities for you to help her improve her concentration and memory without even trying.

A simple card game requires a child to pay close attention to cards that are turned over and remember their location.

For a child learning to play a musical instrument, rehearsal is a basic memory strategy that he must apply.

LOGIC AND CREATIVITY

Your school-age child's ability to come to logical conclusions will improve dramatically as she deliberates on her experiences and applies them to other situations. Her remarkable ability to combine ideas in different ways reflects growth in her creative thinking that is born of flexibility, spontaneity, curiosity, and persistence. Although always fascinating, her developing logic and creativity may alternately amuse and exasperate you.

Sense and Nonsense

Your child may seem impulsive at times. But even if she doesn't always think things through, you can still help her to learn from her experiences. Just by asking her thought-provoking questions and encouraging her to try out her own solutions to problems, she will get practice at analyzing and interpreting situations. By tactfully pointing out that she rarely seems to get what she wants by whining or being bossy, for instance, you can prompt her to think about alternative strategies that might better her chances of success. Be patient; she may need lots of gentle reminders to stop and think about the possible consequences of an action before she can plan effectively. She needs to be supported in her own thinking, too, so be careful not to assume responsibility for solving all of her problems for her.

Not all of your child's creative thinking may seem obvious or even appropriate. Don't overlook or discount, for example, the thought that she puts in to planning her weekend. And when she goes off on a tangent that she finds funny, for instance, try not to dismiss her divergent thinking as silly. You may tell her that jokes about bodily functions aren't acceptable at dinner, but don't make rules about what or how she should think.

Sophisticated classifying and sorting abilities are shown by a child as his knowledge and thinking develop.

CREATIVITY

Do encourage your child's sense of self-discovery by letting her find things out for herself.

Do show interest in the process of your child's thinking and activities.

Do follow your child's lead in activities and let her set the pace.

Do offer your child helpful ideas or suggestions if she asks for them.

Do engage your child in brainstorming about real problems and encourage discussions about hypothetical situations.

Don't discourage your child's experimenting by giving away the results of things she's about to do.

Don't express support for only your child's answers and results.

Don't direct your child's activities or pressure her to achieve.

Don't give your child so many instructions that you spoil her fun.

Don't dampen your child's developing sense of humor by making disparaging remarks about her clowning around or her jokes.

The artwork of a child more subtly reflects her emotions once she attempts to reproduce the detailed realism of what she sees.

INTELLIGENCE

Intelligence isn't a single capability, nor is it a predictor of success at school or in friendships. What will be of most practical value to your child is to consider intelligence as a collection of abilities—such as to recognize relationships among things, discriminate, think about abstract ideas, and act purposefully. If you simply take into account the strengths and weaknesses of her personal learning style, you'll be doing your best to help her fulfill her potential.

Strong spatial and pattern-recognition abilities may make the solving of complicated puzzles fairly easy for your child.

Your child's exacting financial records reflect great strides in her conceptual thinking and mathematical abilities.

Thinking Styles

As a parent, you undoubtedly know a great deal about your child's learning style—perhaps more than you realize. After all, you've been one of her first teachers. From your everyday interactions with her, you've observed a lot about how she learns. You know, for instance, if she is a good listener and enjoys routine. You also have a sense of how long she can sit still and pay attention, how specific to make her instructions, and what encouragement she needs. You know, too, if she does well in group situations, how much choice to give her, and whether she tends to think logically or imaginatively.

Your child's use of her senses can also bring you important insights into her learning style—information that you'll find especially helpful during her early years at school:

• Visual: Does she rely on her eyes to learn? If she remembers what she sees, likes pictures, charts, and maps, and prefers to write things down, she probably has a strong visual sense.
• Auditory: Does she learn using her ears and voice? If she has a keen auditory sense, she'll remember what she hears, follow oral instructions, and like talking through problems.
• Kinesthetic: Does she use her body to learn? If she likes to touch and manipulate materials, experiment, and act things out, she'll need lots of freedom to apply her sharp kinesthetic sense. Her learning style isn't completely defined by her use of senses, though, and will become a lot more complex as

she gets older. But just being aware of her basic strengths and weaknesses will help you stay in tune to how she learns best—and avoid the trap of trying to teach her in ways that you learn best.

Being sensitive to your child's learning style can benefit her enormously. If she is encouraged to learn in ways that respect her strengths, she'll develop a more positive attitude toward learning. She'll enjoy greater success at learning, which will strengthen her sense of competency and promote her self-esteem. And if learning isn't frustrating for her, she'll be motivated to try her best.

There are endless ways to apply your child's learning style. To help improve her verbal skills, for example, you can draw on one of her strengths. If she is musical, you can make songs out of spelling words. If she favors her sense of touch, let her spell out words by using her finger to trace letters cut out of felt or sandpaper. If she tends to be deeply self-aware, get her to see how many words she can spell using the letters of her name. Likewise, you can appeal to her strong suits to encourage her number skills. If she has strong visual and spatial senses, get her to measure and compare items such as her toys or the family's shoes. Or, appeal to her auditory and verbal skills by letting her read a recipe and measure the ingredients for you. If she is highly kinesthetic, match numbers to body movements as she adds or subtracts— three steps forward and two steps back could equal one, for instance.

THE THREE RS

Reading, writing, and arithmetic—the so-called "three Rs"—are fundamental learning abilities that your child will need to develop during her school-age years. Competency in these basic skills is vital to her academic achievement, but she won't master them any better if she is pressured. Respect her learning style and let her progress at her own pace. By encouraging her sense of self-control, you'll help her to build self-confidence.

Thinking Skills

Your child may learn to read easily—even seem to teach herself. But you shouldn't be concerned if she finds the process difficult; she may go slowly through the first stages and catch up quickly later on. However, if she turns seven and hasn't started to read after a year or so of teaching, you should alert your pediatrician. Don't be put off by arguments that she will outgrow the difficulty; a simple auditory test, for instance, might reveal a small hearing loss. There's no harm in investigating the reasons for a difficulty and if a problem can be diagnosed, the sooner she is helped the better.

Writing, too, is a complex phenomenon and she'll need time to become familiar with the way to form letters, and the structure of words and sentences—as well as figure out how to comfortably grip a pencil and which hand she prefers to use. By seven, she should be able to write smaller letters and numbers—about 1/4 inch in size—and align them horizontally. She probably will have learned to write her last name as well as her first, and may be starting to write very simple stories.

Basic arithmetic will be difficult for your child until she understands and can apply its special language and symbols. Don't worry if she counts on her fingers; they're a useful transition between concrete and abstract numbers. To fully grasp numerical principles, she'll need lots of practice.

Your child may capitalize on her visual learning strengths to pursue her talents as a photographer.

Your child's interest in books may be sparked once he is encouraged to see himself as his own publisher.

Letting your child measure recipe ingredients is good practice for her developing mathematical skills.

Winning Ways

COMMUNICATION SKILLS

• Encourage talking. Discuss events and feelings. Be a good audience to her stories, staged plays, and jokes. Talk to her about yourself.

• Encourage reading. Make weekly trips to the library and let her choose her own books. Ask her about the characters and plot of stories she reads. Don't stop reading to her, even when she can read by herself.

• Encourage writing. Let her help with lists and invitations. As she gets older, she can send letters to friends and keep a diary. Ask her to read stories that she writes out loud to you.

PERSONAL IDENTITY

As your child's world expands to include a broader mix of people and range of experiences, his concept of self will become increasingly sophisticated and complex. Not only will he gain a sharper sense of who he is, but he also will begin to see himself as a member of a social community. As he matures in his world awareness, he'll grow out of his insular self-centeredness.

Your child's developing understanding of himself and the world will bring inevitable changes to your parenting. Instead of being an almost exclusive influence in his life, you'll find yourself becoming more of a guide to him. But you will still play a vital role in his self- and world discovery, so don't discount the importance of your presence and continued support.

SEARCH FOR SELF

By the age of six, your child will start to become much more involved with the people around him and his self-perceptions will be based increasingly on comparisons of himself to others. Some of his comparisons will boost his sense of self-confidence; others, though, may feed feelings of inadequacy. Encourage him to make reasonable comparisons; if you help him to set realistic expectations, he'll develop a balanced, positive sense of himself.

Actual Self

As your child approaches adolescence, he'll tend to describe himself as much by inner feelings as by outward appearance. Growing in self-awareness through greater social experience, he'll begin to see himself as a complex entity playing a variety of roles—such as son, friend, pupil, and brother. As different people respond to him in different ways, he himself will behave in different ways in different situations. For example, you may notice that he shows a lot more bravado with his friends when he thinks you're not around. Or, his teacher, who has never seen how messy he keeps his bedroom, may make a comment to you on how neat and well organized he is at school.

Your child also will be constructing a system of beliefs. His beliefs about the world are an important basis for assessing situations. The beliefs he develops about himself help him to gain and

Your child's sense of identity evolves gradually out of her self-perceptions in a wide variety of roles—such as big sister, daughter, and best friend.

maintain a sense of identity as well as purpose. These beliefs are formed gradually, becoming more elaborate as he gets older. A mere suggestion that one of his central beliefs isn't true can bring a serious threat to his sense of well-being. For instance, he may seem to overreact to certain insults, yet take others in stride. If he has been brought up to believe that he is deeply honest, a charge of cheating may be very hurtful to him. Being accused of lying, though, might not upset him too much if his belief in his truthfulness is peripheral.

Ideal Self

Early into your child's preadolescence, he'll begin to become conscious of the distinction between "public" and "private" self. He'll recognize and appreciate that what a person says and feels can be quite different. For example, he'll see through the false protests of a friend who says he doesn't care about not being on the soccer team. He also will learn that he can keep his own thoughts private—and that you don't always automatically know what he's thinking. He may at times cover up his true feelings by putting on a brave front or crying so-called "crocodile" tears; when he doesn't tell the truth, he will expect you to believe him.

Awareness of a public and private self leads your child to also recognize and appreciate that he can understand his own feelings better than those of other people. This stimulates his thinking about not only who he is, but also who he would like to be. Through his comparisons of his actual self and his ideal self, he can assess how well he is measuring up to standards—thereby establishing a sense of self-esteem. A crucial factor in this ongoing process is the degree to which he feels that he or other people control his actions. You have an important role in providing a sense of balance: He needs to feel enough control that he is encouraged to assume responsibility for himself, but not so much that he develops unrealistic personal expectations.

Posters of your child's heroes show he is gaining an idea of who he wants to be. By comparing himself to others, he'll develop an increasingly stronger sense of who he is.

	DEPRESSION WARNINGS
✓	Feelings of inadequacy and worthlessness: If a child is to think well of himself, he must feel that he is loved, valued, and approved of by the people who matter to him.
✓	Lethargy and lack of motivation: A child needs to feel a sense of competency—that he can do some things well; he also must know that the people he cares about respect and appreciate what he does well.
✓	Social isolation and poor school performance: For a child to feel that he can be a positive influence on his and other people's lives, he requires a belief in his own self-virtue—that he is good—as well as a sense of personal power—that he can do good deeds.

FAIRNESS AND MORALITY

Guiding your egocentric child into the world outside your home is a big challenge. Complicating the task is his realization that the world isn't perfect—and that even you sometimes make mistakes. But if you provide him with a strong model of positive social behavior, you needn't be too concerned. Although you aren't his sole influence, he still identifies with you; the attitudes and values that he learns from you are ones he'll eventually adopt.

Right and Wrong

Your six-year-old child's rigid, narrow sense of right and wrong evolves from the set of rules for behavior that he has learned principally from you. Rules and authority are things he accepts absolutely; the notion of unfair rules or unjust application of authority isn't something he yet comprehends. For the most part, he does what is right to win approval and avoid punishment. And until he develops the ability to understand another person's point of view, he judges actions strictly by their effects. If his younger sister breaks his model airplane, for instance, his response isn't likely to be tempered by the circumstances that prompted her to touch it.

As your child starts school and spends more time with his peers, he won't be as egocentric. Learning how to cooperate in group activities and

Once your child can distinguish between intent and outcome, he may show compassion toward a sibling who breaks one of his playthings.

games, he'll begin to form relationships based on empathy and reciprocity. He'll begin to show more consideration for the feelings of others and realize that if he treats someone well, the person probably will act likewise toward him. As a result, a more sophisticated sense of fairness and mutual satisfaction will motivate him to try to do what is right.

Empathy and Justice

As your child learns to think in terms of fair exchanges and give-and-take, doing what is right won't be as much of an automatic response to authority. He'll increasingly find himself in situations where he must decide what is right and wrong on his own. And with

enough experience, he'll begin to realize that life isn't always fair or just. He'll see situations where wrongdoings go unnoticed and unpunished. As he gains awareness about such complexities of justice, he also will develop a growing capacity to appreciate another person's circumstances. He can sympathize with someone who is crying, for instance, and may try to offer comfort.

Approaching adolescence, your child's motivation to do what is right probably will include a desire to be perceived as a good person. Intentions will matter to him, sometimes much more than actual results. Caught having done something wrong, he may say "I didn't mean to"—a protest he thinks is

ETHICS	
Age	**Characteristic Stage**
6 to 8 years	Learning to distinguish between right and wrong; motivated to act in ways that might bring direct reward and avoid immediate punishment.
8 to 10 years	Beginning to internalize rules about right and wrong; motivated to act in ways that win approval of both parents and friends as well as conform to accepted conventions of peer group.
10 to 12 years	Learning to contextualize applications of rules about right and wrong; motivated to act in ways that are in accord with personal beliefs and also respectful of broader social values.

Your child's early sense of fairness probably will be a rigid notion of equality—for example, that everyone gets exactly the same amount of juice.

Sanity Saver

Family discussion is one of the best forums for learning morality—as well as a great way to enliven mealtimes and ease the boredom of long trips. By posing real-life and hypothetical dilemmas to your child, you can help to broaden his world outlook and strengthen his moral development. You'll gain your best insights into his emerging code of ethics if you try to avoid questions that presuppose obvious "right" and "wrong" answers. For example, ask him "Would you stop to help a friend look for something he lost on the way to school if the delay would make you late and get you a detention?" Have him give reasons for the course of action he would take.

enough to excuse the act. Eventually, though, he also will gain the ability to think in terms of the larger common good. At times, he'll do what he considers as right out of a sense of personal duty and social responsibility. Learning to weigh both intentions and actual results, he won't consider an act that causes someone harm to be justifiable simply because it wasn't meant.

Learning about the gray areas of right and wrong isn't easy for your child. In beginning to exercise his own judgments, he is bound to make some mistakes. He'll need time, for example, to resolve the confusion that arises when a friend's values don't match those he has grown up with. Be patient and don't underestimate the effectiveness of your good example. The day-to-

day concern you express for him, other family members, and people outside the family are powerful lessons. He also will benefit if you show him that you consider moral judgments important and are prepared to discuss them. Just by talking with him about your own right-and-wrong dilemmas, you can help him to learn a lot about moral responsibility and decision-making.

Your child's developing social awareness may prompt a sense of spirituality that she expresses through religious practices.

Putting kitchen scraps into the composter can help your child build a sense of environmental responsibility.

RESPONSIBILITY AND DISCIPLINE

The progress your child makes toward responsible behavior won't always keep up with her ability to reason. Self-disciplined behavior takes more than high-level cognitive skills and a capacity for sophisticated moral conclusions; it also requires a lot of practice. Be sensitive to the challenges she faces in trying to apply self-control within the accelerating pace of her life.

A number of factors will influence your child's behavior during her school-age years—including the example of her role models, consistent and reasonable guidance by you and her teachers, and her newly acquired ability to understand another's point of view. You can't always be at her side when she makes decisions, so reinforce her efforts to take responsibility for herself.

LIMITS AND SELF-CONTROL

In order for your child to behave responsibly, she must learn to control and discipline herself. As she matures in her thinking, she'll become better able to curb her impulses, defer gratification, and maintain a fairly consistent notion of right and wrong. But achieving this level of self-control isn't automatic or easy; even if she is exceptionally well behaved, she needs your encouragement and praise to learn how to make good decisions for herself.

Decision Testing
As your child starts showing greater self-control, your disciplining remains a vital part of her behavioral development. Ideally, your disciplining efforts will help her to learn how to make responsible decisions for herself. Since you can't forever impose your external authority over her, she'll need your support to build her own internal authority—her own conscience.

How well your child is able to exercise her own judgments and decide for herself between appropriate and inappropriate actions will depend on your approach to discipline. She will benefit most if your parenting is neither too controlling nor too permissive. The best way for her to learn how to think responsibly about her actions is to provide her with firm behavior guidelines along with the reasons for them.

Discipline should be applied in ways that help your child think for herself and achieve self-control—instead of being a simple asserting of your authority. For example, being told not to play ball too near the house because she might break a window encourages her to think about the consequences of an activity and to see

Your child builds a sense of responsibility for himself when he is encouraged to routinely make his bed and tidy his room.

By helping with household tasks such as putting out the garbage, your child develops a sense of family responsibility.

herself as having a role to play in deciding on a suitable course of action. When you explain your reasons, she benefits from hearing about your values and will try to apply them herself. So, if she asks you why she can't do something, don't feel threatened; it's a positive sign that she's becoming more responsible.

Being responsible includes helping out at home, and your involvement in your child's chores should diminish. By giving her more control over her tasks, you'll reinforce her developing sense of responsibility. Learning to plan and follow through on commitments are as important as doing the chores themselves. So, rather than tell her to stop her game and take out the garbage, give her a list of tasks to do by the end of the day or before the weekend.

If your child neglects her household responsibilities, discuss the problem calmly and try to work out a mutually agreeable solution. For instance, she may need to set aside designated times for chores or be reminded on the day a task is to be done. Be firm and consistent in disciplining her for failing to meet her responsibilities. Avoid punishing her by giving her extra chores, though; she may simply come to see her responsibilities as drudgery. Instead, withdraw a privilege such as watching television until her chores are done. As she accepts greater reponsibilities, include her in family decisions on such things as how to spend a holiday or what should be a savings priority. Listen to her ideas and if you must reject them, give her the reasons why. Participating in grown-up decisions promotes her sense of responsibility for them—and means that she'll be more likely to cooperate in helping to carry them out.

Giving your child a modest weekly allowance helps him to learn about financial responsibility.

Watering plants and doing other special jobs are good ways for your child to earn a little extra pocket money.

Encourage your child to make her own financial trade-offs by allowing her to pay the extra cost of the more expensive item she prefers.

ALLOWANCES

Do give your child an allowance to teach her about managing money.	**Don't** give your child an allowance as a reward or behavior incentive.
Do encourage your child to earn extra money by doing special jobs such as washing windows or raking leaves.	**Don't** make your child's allowance conditional on her doing routine household chores such as tidying her room.
Do specify how much of your child's allowance is for discretionary spending and help her to set savings objectives.	**Don't** impose restrictions on your child's discretionary spending allowance or insist on too-far distant savings goals.
Do let your child live with mistakes so she learns to spend wisely.	**Don't** be insensitive to your child's out-of-the-ordinary spending needs.

SAFETY AND RISK-TAKING

As your child approaches adolescence, she'll face extreme decision-making challenges. Temptations to engage in reckless physical stunts or experiment with alcohol and drugs, for example, can be deadly if she hasn't learned to assess risks or places too much importance on impressing her peers. But if she's armed with a strong sense of personal responsibility and good decision-making skills, she'll be well equipped to make the right choices.

Self Testing

During your child's school-age years, her behavior and attitudes will be shaped increasingly by her peers—and your direct influence will diminish. But the more you help her to internalize rules and develop self-control, the better able she'll be to make her own independent judgments. Just by taking the time to explain to her why you believe certain types of behavior are good or bad, you help to instill your values in her. Adopting and applying your values for herself, she'll develop a capacity to weigh the pros and cons of situations where she faces pressure from her peers to behave in ways that are contrary to what she has been taught.

For your child to develop the independent coping skills she requires, good, open, and honest communication is essential. Your discussions with her should be conducted in a way that promotes mutual respect and allows for any subject to be raised. Talk to her about high-risk behaviors, using close-to-home, real-life examples that she can relate to—for instance, the neighbor's boy who was caught shoplifting or the teenage cousin who became pregnant. Encourage her to feel comfortable bringing up problems she faces—such as teasing at school or pressure from her peers to do something dangerous. Listen attentively to show that you take her concerns seriously and are willing to be supportive. Keep your focus on the outcomes of actions rather than lecture her about right and wrong; if you're overbearing and preachy, she'll simply shy away from conversation and stop approaching you.

As your child gets older, your capacity to listen will at times matter as much as your experience and wisdom. Neither should you trivialize her concerns nor should you attempt to solve all her problems for her. A little humor, however, often eases the way into an awkward conversation and laughing together can strengthen your feelings of closeness. You may help her to come up with possible options, but try to leave her in control of choosing an appropriate course of action. By showing her that you respect her ability to make decisions for herself, you'll make a tremendous contribution to her sense of responsibility and independence.

Maintaining real communication can be difficult as your child goes through her school-age years. As she starts spending more time apart from you, there will be fewer occasions for conversation. You'll have to not only listen attentively when she has something to say, but also pay attention to the unspoken signals she gives of having something on her mind—her behavior, attitudes, and body language. You'll have to persist at times when lines of communication seem closed. But if you lay the right groundwork, you can be assured that communication will go on—and never will it matter more than when she reaches her teen years.

Your child needs you to teach him that being responsible means never taking physical risks without proper protective gear.

Independence Testing

There's no bigger test of your child's sense of responsibility than when she begins to be left under her own supervision at home. Your decision on whether she can be entrusted with her own care should be based primarily on her maturity and common sense, along with other factors such as the overall safety of your neighborhood. At 10 years of age, she may be capable of handling some of the responsibility of caring for herself; remember, though, that maturity and common sense develop at widely varying rates.

Entrusting your child with her own care can boost her sense of independence and self-esteem—if she is ready to handle it. But while the decision isn't one to take lightly, you'll know when the time is right if you apply your own common sense and heed your instincts. Observe the following guidelines and start with short trial periods, increasing the time she spends alone as she proves herself able to handle the responsibility:

• Go over emergency procedures—and review them periodically. Rehearse what she should do in an emergency. Leave a number where you or a designated adult can be reached, and specify times for check-in calls.

• Work out a schedule of things to do and spell out off-limit activities. Routines will help her to pass the time and stay out of trouble. Give the reasons for your rules so she understands how you think and can manage the unexpected the way you would want.

• Revise your rules as she gets older and shows more responsibility. Once she has handled being alone for an hour or two on many occasions, she might be allowed to have a friend over—provided the friend is someone you know and will respect your rules.

Encourage your child's safety awareness by having him map out the best route to and from school.

Your child is ready to take on more responsibility for herself once she learns to check in with you at designated times.

Unless your child is shown responsible ways to satisfy his curiosity about potential hazards, his inquisitiveness may lead to risky experiments.

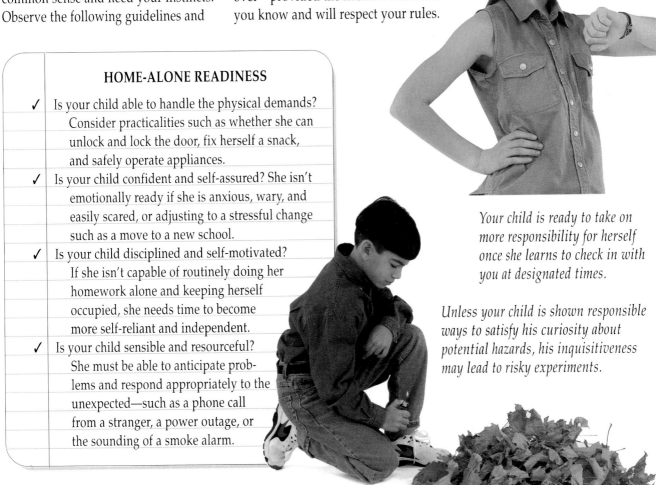

HOME-ALONE READINESS

✓ Is your child able to handle the physical demands? Consider practicalities such as whether she can unlock and lock the door, fix herself a snack, and safely operate appliances.

✓ Is your child confident and self-assured? She isn't emotionally ready if she is anxious, wary, and easily scared, or adjusting to a stressful change such as a move to a new school.

✓ Is your child disciplined and self-motivated? If she isn't capable of routinely doing her homework alone and keeping herself occupied, she needs time to become more self-reliant and independent.

✓ Is your child sensible and resourceful? She must be able to anticipate problems and respond appropriately to the unexpected—such as a phone call from a stranger, a power outage, or the sounding of a smoke alarm.

CONFLICT RESOLUTION

At one time or another during your child's school-age years, she will test the limits you've set on permissible behavior. Common misbehaviors as she nears adolescence include lying, cheating, and stealing. And she may defy your authority by simply refusing to follow instructions. Your conflicts may be upsetting, but they're a normal part of growing up; take comfort in knowing that as they're resolved, you're forming a more mature relationship.

Authority Testing

As your child's peers assume a greater importance in her life, the values of her close friends inevitably will compete with the ones she has been taught at home. And as she starts developing her own sense of internal authority, she'll inevitably test your limits and make decisions counter to your judgments. Try not to take her arguing, back talk, and defiance too personally; she is just trying to assert her independence.

In encouraging your child to take responsibility for herself, your goal should be to help her find acceptable ways of demonstrating independence. She still needs to know what behavior is expected of her and what is forbidden. You'll have to stand your ground, and not become overly rigid or give up. Your discipline will be most effective if you spell out the reasons for both rules

and consequences; you also will need to monitor and respond to her behavior consistently. Keep in mind, too, that even as she pleads or argues with you, she may at times actually want you to set a firm limit on what she is allowed or forbidden to do.

Discipline is easier as your child's ability to reason improves. By appealing to her cooperative spirit and modeling good behavior yourself, you can help to minimize conflict. For instance, as she develops a mature understanding of reciprocity and fair exchange, you might suggest that she invite over a friend whose house she has been to a couple of times. Keep in mind, though, her growing capacity to observe even subtle discrepancies in

your standards. For example, you can't raise your voice at someone and then tell her not to yell at people.

If your child breaks a rule, you should try to remain calm. Overreacting and becoming angry or using harsh punishment in response to even a serious offence such as stealing doesn't teach her how to obey rules. If you're too severe, her resentment of you will overshadow her thinking about what she did wrong. You may insist on her

Until your child learns how to resolve differences, he may express his frustration with you by packing his favorite things and threatening to run away from home.

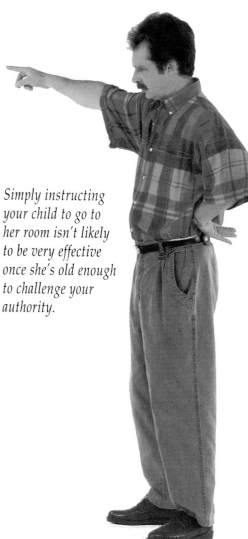

Simply instructing your child to go to her room isn't likely to be very effective once she's old enough to challenge your authority.

doing restitution for her wrongdoing, but make sure that you treat the misbehavior as an error that she can correct. If you force her to think of herself as a liar, for instance, you'll free her to continue behaving as if she's inherently bad. Talk to her about things she could have done so she can exercise better self-control next time.

Even when you intend to apply gentle reasoning, you may sometimes lose your temper with your child. You're not expected to be a saint, so be as forgiving of yourself as you would be of her. If you feel yourself losing control, tell her that you're very angry and insist on a cooling-off period. Remember that physical punishment won't correct her misbehavior; it will simply make her try to be much more careful about not getting caught again.

An angry confrontation with your child can be turned into an opportunity to model self-discipline by thinking things through and talk calmly with her afterward. When punishment is necessary, make sure it's appropriate to the misbehavior. For example, if she spends an evening at a friend's house without

telling you the parents were out, she might not be allowed to visit friends for a week. If she feels that she is ready for more unsupervised responsibility, you might later work out a compromise. By encouraging her to negotiate freedoms, you involve her in cooperative limit-setting; the resulting rules are ones

Trades of sports cards and other exchanges with friends are helpful ways for your child to improve his negotiation skills.

she'll most likely follow. She won't always see things the way you do, so disagreements will arise that you'll need to talk about and deal with over time. Show respect for her views—even when you disagree and must insist she abide by your limits—and be prepared to modify your rules as she matures.

Even if your child's conflict isn't with you, he'll appreciate your positive reassurance and efforts to help the day end in a spirit of reconciliation.

Winning Ways

RULE MAKING

• Set house rules and be consistent. Your child will respond best if she knows what's expected and if the rules—not you—are the authority. A house rule about cooperating to clean up after meals, for instance, will be more effective and provoke less argument than simply insisting that she clear her plate from the table "because I said so."

• Show respect for your child and allow her to air her views. If she participates in the making and modifying of rules, she'll be more inclined to abide by them. And if she knows she can express her perspectives openly without criticism, she won't feel as compelled to rebel.

• Teach your child to negotiate and put a penalty on her arguing. Be flexible and don't be afraid to bend if she comes up with conditions that make what she wants more acceptable. For instance, you might say no to having a friend over, but yield if she assures you that she'll tidy up afterward. But if she simply gives you back talk, you might tell her that she risks being refused the same request at a later date.

EDUCATION AND SCHOOLING

So much of your child's time is spent either at school or attending to school-related tasks that school will inevitably influence his sense of achievement, his self-esteem, and his values. As a caring parent, you can be of great benefit to him if you simply involve yourself in his education and respect his unique learning style. If he is motivated to learn, he'll be successful at school.

Especially during your child's early years at school, he'll thrive if he is allowed to develop at his own pace. There are many positive ways that you can strengthen and enrich his learning, but don't overload him. His chances of scholastic advancement aren't improved if he feels pressured and overwhelmed. Your goal should be to help him find self-fulfillment in doing his best.

SCHOOL READINESS

Learning doesn't happen only at school, but there are big differences between the ways of learning inside and outside the classroom. At school, your child is required to learn concepts apart from concrete references—all through structured information exchanges dominated by a teacher. His capacity for classroom learning, therefore, depends a lot on his abilities to listen and follow specific verbal instructions on how to carry out tasks.

One measure of a child's physical readiness for school is whether she can tie her own shoes.

Intelligence will be a factor in your child's performance at school; but of greater significance will be his interest in learning. What will most influence his success is the attitude he brings to the classroom—specifically, his inner drive to achieve. Even if he is one of the brightest in his class, he won't shine if he isn't motivated; if he is motivated, though, he may do a lot better than others in his class with equivalent brainpower.

The motivation to learn originates in the environment in which your child grows up. The values you pass along to him have a big impact on his attitudes, so instilling a positive inner drive in him is in many ways simply a part of good parenting. The more you encourage him to do well and offer him praise for his achievements, the better he'll perform scholastically. He'll set high standards for himself and be willing to work hard to achieve them. Along the way, he'll discover the self-satisfaction that comes from doing the best he can.

Self-reliance and confidence add to your child's motivation. If he feels in control of his own destiny, he'll apply himself to his schooling. Show him you place a high value on his education, and remember that praise for effort and accomplishment is far more effective than criticism for apparent failings.

The emotional demands of school are best handled by a child who can separate easily from his parents.

Personal Motivation

Your child's success at school depends on many things. For example, he needs to be in good general health and must be able to see and hear adequately. Sitting in one place for long periods of the day isn't easy, so social skills are also important. He should be able to separate easily from you, get dressed alone, control his bladder and bowels, play well with other children, and enjoy participating in games and activities. Language ability, too, is essential.

SCHOOL DYNAMICS

School provides much more than book learning; just as important is its enrichment of your child as a social being. Through his developing relationships with peers, he benefits from the chance to feel that he both is unique and has things in common with other children. Simply because of the variety of experiences he gets, school can be a tremendous boost to his self-esteem.

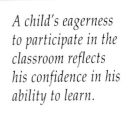

A child's eagerness to participate in the classroom reflects his confidence in his ability to learn.

Social Motivation

Your child's teachers and peers exert an enormous influence on his schooling. And the dynamics of the classroom consist of many variables—for example, the teacher's style and learning expectations, as well as the number, mix, and intellectual capacity of the students. A well-run classroom has a sense of order and purpose, charged with the excited energy of eager and respectful students.

Teaching methods and approaches will matter less to your child than the abilities and dedication of his specific teacher. Simply put, the best teacher for him is one who generates an atmosphere in which learning is

A child's grasp of classwork concepts may come quickly if she applies strategies such as counting with her fingers.

possible. You can be fairly sure that his teacher is effective if most class time is spent on studies, transitions between subjects are smooth and swift, and excessive disruptions aren't tolerated.

An element of your child's schooling to monitor closely is competition in the classroom. As he goes through school, he'll become increasingly aware of how his performance measures up to that of his classmates; as well, their opinions may shape his self-evaluations.

Some competition will benefit him; and if you help him to keep his successes and failures in perspective, his confidence won't suffer.

How well a child gets along with her classmates is a big factor in her adjustment to school.

	A GOOD TEACHER
✓	Treats every child as unique and encourages progress at each individual's own pace.
✓	Encourages children to evaluate their own work and involves them in group activities.
✓	Sets clear limits on children's behavior in a positive manner.
✓	Integrates regular curriculum with special projects, outings, and events that reflect and stimulate children's interests.
✓	Promotes classroom discussion and challenges children's responses in ways that help to foster their thinking.
✓	Acknowledges and respects children's social traditions and backgrounds; employs multicultural and non-sexist materials.
✓	Considers parents as partners; invites and welcomes their involvement.

AFTER SCHOOL AND HOMEWORK

Your child's education isn't best left to school experts. Nor does the ringing of the afternoon school bell signal an end to his day's learning. On the contrary, your active role in his learning is important and his everyday experiences outside school can greatly enhance his in-class performance. One of the biggest educational contributions you can make is simply to help ensure that his after-school hours include a balance of both structured and free time.

After School and Independence

Your child needs your help to get the most out of his after-school hours. But just how he should spend his time involves considerations that you'll have to weigh for yourself; no one else knows what's best for him and you. In addition to his personality and interests, practical concerns such as whether you can be at home for him after school will have to be a part of your decision.

Once your child is accustomed to full days at school, he may be ready to spend some of his after-school hours in a structured activity—such as music, karate, or swimming lessons. Too much organized routine isn't helpful, though, so don't overload him; he also needs unstructured time to simply unwind, amuse himself, and pursue interests on his own. Just by striking a balance between stimulation and relaxation in his after-school hours, you can both contribute to his learning and encourage his sense of independence.

Whether you're primarily seeking after-school enrichment or care for your child, he'll benefit from opportunities that provide the following:
• Security: He needs to be in an environment where he is both physically

Before a child is given unsupervised after-school responsibility, he needs to show he is capable of keeping track of things such as house keys.

To complete major assignments on time, a child must learn to organize, plan, and schedule her schoolwork.

For a child who arrives home from school to an empty house, a check-in telephone call is a reassuring ritual.

STUDY HABITS

Do provide your child with a comfortable place where he can routinely do his homework.

Do make sure your child's workspace is ample and well lit.

Do encourage your child to set aside regular times for doing homework.

Do show an interest in your child's homework and support his efforts to get it done on his own.

Do leave your child in control of his homework.

Don't inconvenience your child by obliging him to move from place to place when doing homework.

Don't clutter your child's workspace with a lot of tempting distractions.

Don't force your child to do more homework than his teacher gives him.

Don't get overly involved in your child's homework or undercut his initiative by doing it for him.

Don't be your child's homework policeman.

safe and emotionally protected from teasing and harassment.

• Physical activity: After sitting all day at school, he needs to be able to move and exercise his body.

• Competency and achievement: Experiences of doing something well will promote his sense of confidence and self-esteem.

• Social interaction: Positive friendships are important to his development and well-being.

• Creative expression: He'll benefit from activities that let him convey his individuality—not just art, but gymnastics, theater, cooking, and other forms of self-expression.

How your child feels about the way he spends his after-school hours is important, too, so take his views into account. Try to abide by his preferences; they're healthy signs of his growing sense of identity and independence. Rather than push him into an activity, let him choose an interest to pursue. The more he gets to participate in the decision-making, the more likely he'll be to go along with after-school plans.

Homework and Responsibility

To help your child learn how to get along with schoolwork on his own, you'll need to encourage him to take responsibility for his own homework. Homework should be an extension and consolidation of what he's learned at school, so he shouldn't require a lot of direct assistance or input from you. As his thinking advances and he becomes better able to reason in the abstract, he'll be capable of working through his own ideas. You may query or reinforce his understanding of a concept or principle from time to time with an appropriate explanation, but you shouldn't have to be constantly telling him what to do or giving him all the answers.

Your principal role in your child's homework should be to help him learn to study. There's no benefit to him if you become immersed in helping him do his day-to-day assignments; but he'll gain a lot if your support is targeted at helping him to improve his skills at organizing his workload and using his time productively. Simply establishing a proper

place and time to study is the best long-term contribution to his homework that you can make. Just remember that the most effective homework guidelines will be ones that he has a say in and agrees to; if nagging, badgering, or pressure from you is required to enforce them, they won't lead to lasting improvements in his study skills.

Homework routines and policies should evolve out of respect for your child's own best way of working. For instance, be sensitive to the time of day he finds most productive and the amount of time in which he can usefully concentrate. If he is wound up and restless in the afternoons, don't insist that he complete his homework before dinner. Forbid him to do homework sprawled in front of the television, but permit him to take a break to watch his favorite program. If he is easily distracted, discourage him from cluttering his work area, but don't object to him playing background music if it seems to help him to concentrate.

Your child is encouraged to take her schoolwork seriously if she has an adequate workspace.

Helping your child with her schoolwork means leading her to the answers—not simply giving them away.

175

TROUBLE AT SCHOOL

At school, your child should feel safe to express himself and able to experiment with his identity. He should have the opportunity to learn his strengths and weaknesses, and to find something at which he can excel. Your involvement can ensure the ideal is realized. Knowing when to step in and when to show restraint is intuitive; but you won't go wrong if you simply pay attention to whether or not he is flourishing and fulfilling his potential.

Aptitude and Attitude

There may be some rough times during your child's early school years. Even with a strong beginning, his outlook at some point may be shaken by personal frustrations, peer competition, or teacher evaluations. Keep track of changes in his attitudes; whether he approaches school positively or negatively has a big impact on his learning and performance. And since trouble at school can erode his sense of confidence, his self-esteem may suffer.

Your compassion and tact will go a long way toward helping your child overcome a problem at school. If he is having trouble making the transition between home and school, he may benefit from simply having you spend some extra time with him in the evenings. Listen sympathetically to his complaints about school; your sensitivity and reassurance may be all he needs to work things out on his own. Trouble at school that lasts more than a few weeks, however, should be discussed with his teacher. Often, the remedy is simple—for example, the clarifying of a rule or the reassigning of his seat.

Because grades are symbolic and not concrete, they're not likely to be a factor in your child's motivation at school. Sometimes, though, he may benefit from your help in modifying how he interprets his role in school achievement. Simply encouraging him to try harder next time—without berating his performance—may make a difference. In some instances, he may need your help to improve his study skills and to be reminded that difficulties can't always be immediately resolved. Be gentle in urging greater effort; he may be trying much harder than you realize. Take your cues from him and don't overpower him with your views; his incentive to do his best will come if he feels that his efforts are recognized.

Writing notes in your child's homework book is a helpful way for you to inform her teacher of specific problems.

House Call

My seven-year-old son starts every weekday morning by saying he is too sick to go to school. What should I do?

You need to look closely at what's going on in your child's life. Listen carefully to what he says is happening to try to pinpoint the problem. Take his complaints about school seriously, but tell him he can't stay home without a good reason. Explain to him that a problem at school can only be solved at school and do your best to enlist the support of his teacher. If the problem persists or what's bothering him isn't directly linked to school, you should seek help from a psychologist.

A child who tends to dawdle over her schoolwork may enjoy the challenge of simple self-conducted time tests.

LEARNING DISABILITIES

A poor report card is an obvious sign of learning difficulty; it isn't, though, the only indication. A child suffering from a disorder that interferes with his capacity to process, understand, or use certain types of information may manage to get by at school for quite some time before his disability is detected. Be alert to your child; keeping a close watch on how he does at school is your best assurance that he gets any special help he might require.

Aptitude and Ability

A child's learning problem is most likely to show up at a time of transition—such as his entrance into first grade or relocation to a new school. Often, a learning difficulty is reflected in his behavior. Resistance to going to school, irritability after school, and school disinterest or apathy are all signals of a possible problem in the development of a child's skills.

Because a learning disability has so little to do with intelligence, a child's weakness in basic reading or math skills may not surface until he advances into a higher grade and the work begins getting harder. Sometimes the symptoms of a disability are mistaken as simply signs of immaturity. But a child's ongoing reluctance to practice writing and arithmetic, difficulty in sitting still and listening to a story being read aloud, or problem with remembering and describing his school day shouldn't be too quickly dismissed as inconsequential.

A child's learning problem may be due to poor vision or hearing, so he should be taken for a complete physical examination. A suspected learning difficulty also should be discussed with his teacher; disability testing and evaluation usually are best arranged through the school. Once the nature of a child's problem is made clear, the school is a useful resource in deciding on a course of action. He may be provided with remedial instruction at no extra cost or be placed in a special class. If in-school assistance isn't available or suitable, the school can recommend the type of tutoring that will most benefit him.

The best tutor for a child with a learning difficulty usually is someone other than either of his parents. Few parents possess the information and skills required to tutor effectively, and most don't have the perspective that's needed to judge how well or poorly their child's work gets done. Attitude and expectations are other important factors: A child's parents are seldom capable of the patience that's demanded to provide him with the consistently supportive and encouraging tutoring he needs; their frustration or criticism will too easily erode his confidence and self-esteem. Parents shouldn't consider themselves as powerless, though; on the contrary, the special help that their child receives depends on their alertness and intelligent decision-making.

A child who has difficulty keeping focused on schoolwork will benefit from a minimum of distractions.

By recording and playing back story ideas, a child may become better able to organize her thoughts on paper.

Background music may help a child to concentrate, so let her have the radio on if it doesn't keep her from her schoolwork.

RECREATION AND PASTIMES

For your school-age child, play is still an important way of developing physical, language, and social skills. Play also brings emotional benefits in helping her to find self-satisfying pursuits and cope with personal challenges or difficulties. As she becomes more competent and mature, she'll be capable of sustaining interests and better able to keep herself occupied.

Play must bring pleasure to your child; if she feels coerced into an activity or pressured to perform, she won't get anything positive out of it. You may want to encourage some interests and discourage others, but try to respect her sense of control and independence. If she's not active enough, for example, don't insist that she take aerobics; let her choose a sport to play.

COLLECTIONS AND HOBBIES

Preadolescence is an age of collections and hobbies. Your child's collections may begin by her just keeping whatever comes to hand; gradually, though, she'll become more discriminating and organized. Hobbies will be of interest to her as she reaches higher levels of competency and seeks to use real tools for projects. Be supportive of the collections and hobbies that preoccupy her; they're her way of bringing order to the world and feeling in control.

Things of Fancy

During your child's school-age years, she may start to become a devoted collector. She already may have shown an interest in accumulating certain types of objects, and come home regularly with her pockets full of rocks, bottle caps, or other treasures. But while she'd never agree to throwing out the things she gathered, their purpose for her was fairly simplistic: She just liked having lots of similar-looking things around, and enjoyed the activity of arranging and rearranging them.

Sometime after the age of six, however, your child will bring a new perspective to collecting as she gains the ability to develop enduring interests. Once she has the capacity to sort and categorize, collections take on new meaning and can become the basis for improving a variety of skills—such as counting, analyzing, and serializing. She also is encouraged to apply her investigative and research skills to finding out about the things she collects—such as where they come from and how they're formed or made.

Pursuits of Passion

Like collections, toys take on new meaning in your child's school-age years and hobbies she pursues can become lifelong passions—even lead to a particular career or field of study. As she gets older, satisfying her interest in activities such as model-building, photography, or carpentry will depend on her having the right supplies and using the proper equip-

With collectibles such as sports cards that can be traded, a child can exercise his negotiation skills.

A child's collection of pressed wildflowers blends an interest in nature with her own artistry.

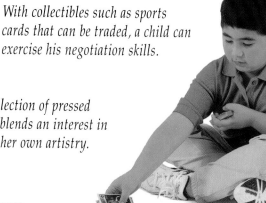

ment. Give her the freedom to pursue hobbies; being encouraged in self-directed interests helps her to focus time and energy on activities in which she finds something of worthwhile value.

Your child will need instruction on the safe use of tools required for her hobbies. She also will benefit from being shown correct techniques and encouraged to choose undertakings suit-ed to her mastery of skills. Until you both are sure she knows what she's doing, you'll need to keep a close watch on her progress. Try to guide her without inter-fering; if she needs you to do everything for her, she's picked a project that's too challenging. Don't under-mine her sense of competen-cy, though, by insisting she attempt something too easy or by criticizing her results.

BOARD AND COMPUTER GAMES

Games that involve second-guessing an opponent may become of interest to your child as she learns to think about what others are thinking. She may be a formidable strategist; don't be sur prised if she beats you at a game soon after you teach it to her.

Shows of Strategy

As your child's thinking matures, games requiring strategic skills will appeal more to her than games relying strictly on the chance throw of dice or spin of a wheel. Games of strategy are good tests of what she has learned about life; as such, they also reveal a lot about her values.

Playing games of strategy with your child allows you to observe her intel-lectual strengths and the values she practices. And if you detect short-comings in her abilities or values, such controlled activities are helpful ways of teach-ing her better strategies and desirable behavior.

Word games such as Scrabble help children to build vocabulary and improve their language skills.

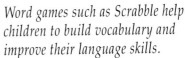

Chess and similar types of games become of interest to children as they learn to think strategically.

A good computer game challenges a child's logic, reasoning, and timing—as well as perseverance.

STRUCTURED ACTIVITIES

Sports, music lessons, and other structured activities can offer your child tremendous enrichment. The simple discipline of routine, regular practice carries over easily into other aspects of her life. Just be sure that you appreciate the value of exploration at this age, and keep your expectations geared to her interests and abilities.

Something in Particular

Structured activities provide your child with the opportunity to broaden the scope of her learning as well as achieve group status. In a team sport such as soccer, for instance, she has the chance to strengthen her physical and perceptual skills, improve her ability to play by rules, and develop a sense of good sportsmanship. Such experience helps her to learn that victory is achieved as much by cooperation with teammates as by competition with rivals.

Even if your child's artistic aspirations aren't exceptional, she might enjoy taking classes in drawing, painting, or modeling with clay. If she works intensely in one specific material, she'll have the opportunity for the in-depth exploration that best helps nurture creative impulses. Just by providing her with the chance to develop her own way of organizing information and elaborating on themes, her artistic endeavors can foster other forms of creativity in other areas of her life.

However, structured activities won't provide your child with effective learning experiences if she isn't genuinely interested or takes too many.

Just because an activity appeals to you doesn't mean that she'll enjoy it, so encourage her to make her own decisions. Don't fall into the "more-is-better" trap; overloading her with activities won't make her well-rounded.

Your child's structured activities also must be suited to the level of her skills so she can be successful; too big a challenge to her capabilities will undermine her sense of competency. In making assessments of activities, keep in mind as well factors such as time commitment, competitive elements, and characteristics of participating adults. An activity's learning potential won't be realized if results matter more than effort or the desire to win supersedes the developing and refining of skills.

A child perfecting complicated dance moves soon learns to appreciate the value of self-control, practice, and determination.

In an organized sport such as the martial arts, a child benefits a great deal from the emphasis that is placed on skills and discipline rather than on competition.

HANGING OUT

Hanging out will become important to your child during her school-age years. She benefits from unstructured time alone and with friends, so don't jump to conclusions about how she could be more productive. If she feels trusted to stay out of trouble, she'll be more likely to appreciate and respect your concerns for her safety.

Nothing in Particular

Hanging out is a welcome break in your child's structured routines and is more constructive than you may think; if her schoolwork doesn't suffer and she maintains other interests, no harm is likely to come from it. When she hangs out with friends, they'll mostly talk—about teachers, schools, pop stars, music, and other topics of currency. By helping her to develop a better understanding of who she is and how she relates to her peers, such conversation makes a big contribution to her thinking about her place in the world.

Being part of a group provides your child with a sense of security and belonging. This is an important step for her in becoming an individual—separate and distinct from her parents, but related to others and the world. The feeling of security and belonging that she gains by hanging out helps her to develop the confidence she needs to interact with others—both inside and outside her group—and to pursue her own personal goals.

Your biggest concern about hanging out should be your child's safety. Preparing her to socialize safely requires your continuing efforts to help her develop self-respect and respect for others. If she's encouraged to establish long-term goals, she'll try to avoid doing anything that might jeopardize them. Safe places to hang out are necessary, too. Encourage her to invite her friends home and when she goes out, insist on being kept informed about who she's with, where she is, and when she'll be back. If she understands that you're not trying to control her every move, she'll be sensitive to your safety concerns.

As children's understanding of language improves, they often find great amusement in absurd riddles and jokes that play on multiple meanings of words.

Children's cooperative spirit flourishes in activities such as cat's cradle where there are no winners or losers, goals, or end points.

Books and Magazines

The more your child reads, the better she'll read and the more pleasure she'll get out of reading. Unfortunately, though, the reverse is just as true: If she doesn't enjoy reading, she'll read very little and her reading skills won't improve. With a little tact and patience, you can help her to build and maintain an enthusiasm for reading. Just keep your focus on developing her interest in reading and don't be critical of her choices of reading materials.

Building a personal library can bring a satisfying sense of accomplishment to a proud reader.

Reading and Competency

Your child will enjoy reading if she finds something positive in it for her—a thrill, an idea, or a good laugh. Knowing her reasons for not liking or wanting to read can help you to encourage the self-motivation she needs to find how much pleasure reading can bring. If she thinks reading isn't fun, she may be under too much pressure to read for performance. Reading won't seem like a chore to her if she is allowed to be more relaxed about it. If she finds reading too hard, reading aloud to her can help prevent her discouragement about poor reading skills from dampening her interest in reading. If she complains that reading is boring, she probably needs a greater variety of reading than what's assigned at school—reading more related to her interests. If she feels that she is too busy to read, she may require help in arranging her schedule so she can include time for reading.

Nagging your child won't work, so don't turn reading into a campaign; she'll only resent your lectures. Under pressure, she may read only to please you rather than for herself—or simply refuse to read at all. Just helping her to enjoy reading is a worthwhile goal in itself, so encourage her to separate reading for pleasure and school performance. Don't criticize her choices; reading almost anything is better than reading nothing at all. If you offer praise for her reading efforts and don't try to bribe her, eventually she'll experience reading as its own reward. Make a wide variety of reading materials available to her. Leave books, magazines, and catalogs in conspicuous places around your home and take her to the library regularly. Use her hobbies and interests as starting points in scouting for things she might like to read. Don't expect dramatic changes in her reading habits; help her to set realistic goals and find satisfaction in her progress.

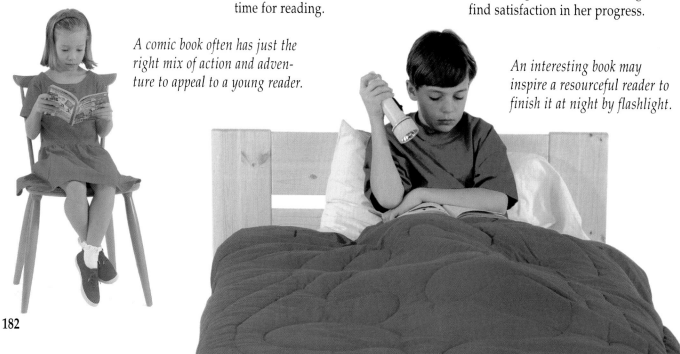

A comic book often has just the right mix of action and adventure to appeal to a young reader.

An interesting book may inspire a resourceful reader to finish it at night by flashlight.

TELEVISION, VIDEOS, AND POPULAR MUSIC

The media's influence on your child won't be problematic if you simply set reasonable limits on her viewing and listening habits. Strict bans and censorship aren't practical, and will become increasingly difficult to enforce as she gets older. But if you monitor what she is exposed to and encourage her to develop a critical response to the media, she'll learn to discriminate between the positive and negative effects for herself.

Television isn't of overwhelming appeal to a child whose parent is willing to play cards or other games with her.

Media and Influence

Television, videos, and popular music provide your child with a big window on the world; with your guidance, the influence on her can be positive. Show your interest in what she watches and listens to; your views and discussions with her about the content encourage her to think critically. If she learns to respond critically to what she sees and hears, she'll be better able to extract the elements of value—and less likely to simply absorb without thought whatever is presented.

Limits on television, videos, and popular music have merit not just because of what your child might be exposed to, but also because of activities she may be kept from pursuing. Encourage her to use what she watches and listens to as a link to other interests—rather than as a distraction from them. Television, for instance, can be used to complement and enhance her interest in reading by having her review weekly listings to find programs that build on subjects she's studying at school. Or, make her television interests the focus of a routine visit to the library and look for books that feature similar characters or adventure-type plots. Watch a news program together regularly and have her select a city or country that's mentioned, then find its location on a map and look up interesting facts about it in an encyclopedia or almanac.

HOME LIBRARY

• Set aside a special place for your child's books. Her own bookcase, shelf, or basket for books of particular interest contributes extra meaning and value to what she reads.

• Let your child choose books to read and add to her collection. Book-buying outings to yard sales or secondhand bookstores can be fun, inexpensive routines.

• Give your child books and magazine subscriptions as gifts. Also encourage her to give books as gifts to members of the family and her friends.

• Borrow books from your child to read. Your interest in her books shows respect for her reading. Likewise, she'll better appreciate books that you offer as of possible interest to her.

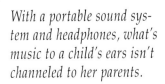

With a portable sound system and headphones, what's music to a child's ears isn't channeled to her parents.

FRIENDS AND RELATIONSHIPS

Your child's friendships and his relationship with you will change dramatically during preadolescence. Friendships won't be simply temporary partnerships based on shared activities; instead, they'll be deeply emotional, lasting experiences—some may be lifelong. What he learns about himself and the world by interacting with peers will be vital to his self-esteem.

As your child becomes more involved with his peers, the amount of time he spends with you will decrease; so, too, will his need for you to entertain and supervise him. Instead, you'll find yourself giving him much more periodic advice and guidance. But while he needs to be given room to assert his independence, he still benefits from your unconditional love and support.

GROUPS AND OUTCASTS

Being included in a peer group satisfies your child's growing desire for social acceptance and need for greater freedom from your control. As he compares himself and his abilities with those of his friends, he'll gain a clearer sense of himself as well as learn to deal with the ups and downs of inclusion and rejection.

Mutuality and Belonging

During your child's school-age years, making friends will become a major focus of his attention. Although the relationships sometimes may be short-lived, they play a vital role in his social development. Through friendships, he'll gain the necessary interpersonal skills to give and receive confidences, avoid or resolve conflicts amicably, and rely on and trust others.

Your child's ability to become part of a group is just as important to his well-being as building and maintaining one-on-one friendships. Feeling a sense of belonging with his peers gives him confidence and self-esteem, and contributes greatly to his enjoyment of school and his motivation to do well. But if he is shunned or excluded by his peers and feels lonely, there's a great risk of him losing interest and failing in school, or having other adjustment problems as he gets older.

Forming a special club allows children to feel superior—even though they're usually more critical of each other than of outsiders.

Children often strengthen their feelings of friendship by exchanging secrets, gossip, and confidences.

If making friends doesn't come naturally to your child, offer him advice on how to approach peers and start relationships. For instance, you might ask him what games his classmates like to play and probe to see if he understands the rules. His acceptance may involve a skill such as throwing or kicking a ball that you can practice with him. Show him ways to initiate conversations and not be coercive or argumentative. Stress the value of listening, taking turns, sharing, and compromise in being able to make friends and be part of a group.

Children who are close friends frequently lend each other their favorite music tapes, clothing, and other personal possessions.

A special handshake is one of the ways that children often signal their acceptance and approval of each other.

TROUBLE WITH FRIENDS

Good friendships will help your child to flourish. But rejection, too, is inevitable and happens to everyone at some time. You can't protect him from the lows in his relationships with peers, but you can help him to see beyond momentary rejection and prevent his self-esteem from suffering.

Discord and Rejection

Allowing your child to choose his own friends is an essential contribution to his sense of independence. But you should get to know his friends so that you can develop a sense of the pressures he faces and support him at times when he has a problem. He will need your help to understand that rejection is a part of growing up—and may find comfort in hearing about your own childhood experiences.

Not all of your child's friends will be to your liking; but unless a relationship is destructive or dangerous, try not to interfere. Don't judge his friends only by your standards; if they aren't suitable, he'll find out soon enough on his own. Challenging his choices of friends may simply cause him to defend them and continue the relationships longer than he otherwise might.

Friendship sometimes brings frustration, and a child needs sympathy and reassurance when he feels left out or rejected.

THE SHY CHILD	
Do assure your child of your unconditional love and support. **Do** encourage your child's efforts to rise to challenging occasions. **Do** prepare your child for new experiences by talking about them and listening to his concerns. **Do** encourage your child to develop one-on-one relationships and invite friends home.	**Don't** allow your child to feel that he somehow disappoints you. **Don't** overprotect your child or try to shelter him from difficult situations. **Don't** force your child into new situations and abandon him to either "sink or swim." **Don't** push your child to make friends by signing him up for team sports or other group activities.

BULLIES AND VICTIMS

A bully thinks that force works; sooner or later, your child may have a run-in with one. A bully usually requires the help of a psychologist to find acceptable outlets for his feelings. The victim needs help to understand that being singled out isn't his fault—that the problem is with the bully and not himself.

Harassment and Vulnerability

If your child is the victim of a bully, he'll feel that he is somehow responsible. Out of shame or fear, he may refuse to talk about what happened. Finding out that he has been bullied may take an alertness to subtle changes in his attitudes toward himself, so never minimize his concerns. If he is victimized, he needs your reassurance to know that he isn't a coward or a failure. To stop him from being bullied, you probably will need to seek help from his teachers at school or other adult authorities. He also might try an escalating series of responses to the bully:

- First, ignore the bully.
- Next, stand up to the bully and order him to stop, then walk away.
- Finally—as a last resort—strike back in self-defense; an unexpected show of strength just might stop the bully.

A victimized child needs help to understand that she isn't responsible for the bully's behavior.

BOYS AND GIRLS TOGETHER

During your child's preadolescence, he'll develop mostly same-sex friendships. At some time in his preteens, though, he may start to show an interest in the opposite sex. Learning how to be comfortable with the opposite sex is important, and will help build his capacity for intimacy as he gets older.

A preteen with a budding interest in a member of the opposite sex often ties up the telephone for hours.

Romance and Intimacy

While your child figures out his gender identity, he probably will associate mostly with friends of the same sex. But he also will benefit from opportunities to interact with boys and girls together. Closer contact between the sexes during the predating years lays vital groundwork for the development of healthy relationships later on in life. Mutual respect fostered between the sexes in the preteens also helps provide a smooth transition into adolescence.

Support your child's efforts to develop friendships with both sexes. Make your home a place where he feels comfortable entertaining boys and girls. Encourage him to participate in activities that allow both sexes to interact socially—such as after-school projects, recreational sports, and community clubs. If the emphasis is on activities—not on relationships—you shouldn't worry that such group encounters will lead to early dating or premature sexual activity. On the contrary, too many restrictions on group get-togethers can backfire and result in feelings of social ineptness or even in rebelliousness.

Be careful not to misread your child's early efforts to get to know members of the opposite sex as "romantic." He may take his cue from your misinterpreting and be inadvertently steered into relationships he isn't ready for. Romantic involvements too early can interfere with his learning how to establish trusting and flexible relationships, so be

A child's changing attitude toward the opposite sex is often marked by small courtesies, such as stopping to picking up a dropped book.

Afterthoughts...

"Our son moped around the house for days and wasn't interested in doing anything with anybody. I couldn't get him to open up and talk, and started worrying that something was terribly wrong. But the next day, he came home from school on cloud nine and was his normal, cheerful self. I found out later he had been told by one of his friends that a girl he didn't think liked him actually did."

"My preteen daughter broke the news that an older, high-school boy had asked her out. I could tell she was flattered, but didn't really want to go. She was so relieved when I told her I didn't approve of her dating someone so much older than her: I was the scapegoat and she didn't have to hurt the boy's feelings."

sensitive and watch what you say; don't tease him or attach more significance to a relationship than he does.

Because of the preteen urge to grow up fast, your child may feel pressured to start dating. There's no "normal" age for dating to begin, but he isn't likely to be mature enough for the intense mutual dependency that can develop in an exclusive relationship until well into his teens. If he feels ready to date, you shouldn't be afraid to voice your objections. But while you may try to discourage dating, forbidding a relationship altogether won't be productive. Your opposition may simply push him into a romance that might otherwise end spontaneously; and fighting your disapproval may distract him from noticing the unsuitability of a relationship for himself. Instead, suggest alternatives to dating that are healthy for a relationship—for example, doing homework together, attending each other's family dinners, or signing up for the same dance class.

Preteens flirting with new and powerful sexual feelings may pass each other notes and exchange keepsakes.

Innocent kissing games such as spin the bottle can add a precocious sense of daring to children's early sexual feelings.

PEER PRESSURE

As your child approaches adolescence, few things will matter more to him than the acceptance and approval of his peers. Being in with the right crowd may become the chief focus of his life and his most important reason for going to school. Not all peer pressure is bad, so don't be alarmed if he starts showing a certain amount of conformity. You'll need to intervene, though, if his being included requires behavior that's socially unacceptable.

Conformity and Acceptance

Unlike your child's relationships within the family, his outside interactions with peers provide him with the opportunity to socialize among chosen equals. From the dynamics of group interaction, he gains a lot of interpersonal experience and insight: Not only is he exposed to the perspectives of others, but he has an important forum for learning how to make his own viewpoints understood.

To be accepted by a group of peers, your child will need to practice some conformity—pressure that will build into his adolescence. He'll want to fit in with his friends, so be sensitive and don't overreact to his interest in being like them. You may not approve of his group's dress code, for instance, but there's no harm in letting him wear a certain type of jeans or running shoe. Such conformity helps him feel secure and isn't a risk to his independence.

Contributing to your child's sense of belonging doesn't mean that you can't help him to understand there's more to being friends than dressing alike. But he'll most likely develop friendships that reinforce his familiar patterns if you don't force values on him without recognition of his needs. Relax; if you aren't too strict or permissive and he can communicate openly with you, he won't get into much trouble.

Risk-taking can be tempting to children if it's seen as a way of winning peer acceptance.

DRUG WARNINGS	
✓	Health: Does he have bloodshot eyes, dilated pupils, a runny nose, and a hacking cough? Is he getting more colds and infections than usual? Is he lethargic, less hungry than usual, constipated, and severely distressed or anxious?
✓	Money: Does he suddenly need or have a lot more money than usual?
✓	Schoolwork: Have his grades suddenly dropped? Is he disinterested in or missing school?
✓	Conversation: Does he seem to tell a lot of drug-related stories or jokes, or get defensive when the subject of drugs is mentioned?

Conformity in clothing, hairstyle, and makeup helps children to feel they fit in with their peers.

FAMILY MEMBERS

The intensifying self-awareness that characterizes your child's search for an independent identity brings inevitable changes to his relations with family members. Seeking to influence his own and others' lives, he needs to test himself against more than just the yardsticks provided by his parents. Try to be supportive; if he is encouraged to take responsibility for his own actions, he'll develop a realistic sense of his powers and limitations.

Distancing and Criticism

For your child to establish his own identity, he needs to gain some measure of distance from you. Relationships and experience outside the family help him to develop a better sense of who he is, so don't think there's something wrong if he doesn't seem interested in spending much time with you; he isn't trying to hurt you, simply seeking to prove himself with others. You're still a powerful influence in his life and an important role model for him—just no longer the only one.

Being critical, however, is one way that your child may express his need to feel separate from you. He may start to constantly find fault with everything you do and blame you for all his troubles. He probably will seem ungrateful to you at times, but you shouldn't take his disparaging remarks personally. By permitting him to speak out, you're helping him to feel a sense of power, which makes him less likely to rebel in other ways that may be harmful. And when you acknowledge his right to his own views, you open the door to healthy discussion about the types of criticism that are appropriate statements of opinion.

Your goal is to encourage your child to express himself, but also to know when enough is enough. Although you don't want to discourage him from stating his views, you may have to set limits on how and when he does it. You'll want him to learn how to criticize without being insensitive to others, so respond to his remarks accordingly. Let him know if he hurts your feelings and teach him not to make comments at inopportune times—such as in public places or when guests are present. Also be sure that you set a good example by not being overly critical of him.

As a child gains a sense of her own identity, recognizing that she is looked up to by a younger sibling can encourage her to be a responsible role model.

A child's awkwardness at displays of parental affection often reflects his struggle to find identity as an individual outside his own family.

5

THE SICK CHILD

CARE BASICS

No one knows or cares for your child as well as you do. Your intimate knowledge and day-to-day nurturing will help to keep him healthy. Immunize him against the standard infectious childhood diseases and teach him sensible safety procedures. While your pediatrician is there to advise you when your child falls sick or hurts himself, it's your special touch that will make him feel better and provide the comfort he needs.

Simple remedies are often the best. A cold pack works wonders on bruised flesh; a warm hot-water bottle soothes a sore muscle.

Her implicit trust in your ability to make her feel better will keep you on your toes. From you, she will learn how to cope with the discomforts of being ill, just as she will learn the best ways to stay healthy.

Finding ways to get your sick child to take it easy may test your imagination. Keep her entertained with a generous supply of books and toys and take the time to visit with her; your moments together will help offset her boredom.

A cheerful and matter-of-fact approach to treating your child's ailments will reassure her flagging spirits.

Match her diet to her physical condition: When she has diarrhea or has been vomiting, for example, avoid milk products; give her mostly liquids and a bland diet that won't irritate her digestive system further.

Your knowing touch and keen eyes will pick up on the subtle clues that alert you to the need for special care.

ILLNESSES AND AILMENTS

Every child gets sick from time to time, so don't think that you've failed if your child suffers an illness or ailment. Despite your best efforts to make sure she eats properly and gets enough sleep and exercise, she will develop occasional irritations and infections. When she's not feeling well, you'll naturally be concerned about her health; stay calm and be reassuring, though, so she doesn't worry. Try not to let her fussing and irritability get the best of you; she doesn't mean to aggravate you and she'll stop once she starts feeling better. Refer to this section for guidance on common illnesses and ailments; the more you know about them, the more confident you'll feel in being able to handle them. Never hesitate to discuss concerns about your child's health with your pediatrician; that's what a medical professional is there for.

SICKNESS WARNINGS

A child who's listless and unusually quiet may be on the verge of developing other illness symptoms.

Sudden loss of appetite by your child can alert you to possible sickness.

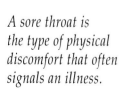

A sore throat is the type of physical discomfort that often signals an illness.

Detecting the Signals
The early signs of illness vary from child to child; one may whine incessantly, another may not eat, and a third may simply vomit. Be alert to changes in your child's behavior and appearance that may signal all is not well. When she's too young to tell you how she feels, you'll need to be especially attentive to her body's cues. Watch for abrupt changes in her patterns; insomnia or lack of urination, for example, may precede other symptoms of sickness. Note the appearance and progress of any rash. Look for changes in her breathing; until her respiratory system develops fully, it's more easily compromised by illness.

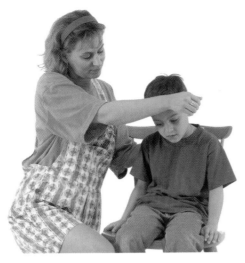

A clue to your child's illness may be a skin rash that appears on his stomach.

If your child's forehead feels warm against the inside of your wrist, he may have a fever; check his temperature using a thermometer.

Calling the Doctor

While each symptom on its own may be relatively benign, use your judgment; if she looks sick and you feel uneasy, call your pediatrician. As a rule of thumb, the younger the child the more quickly she should be seen when she seems sick. With infants, in particular, time can be of the essence; they can get very ill, very fast.

The information on illnesses and ailments that is presented in any book can never do more than provide guidance and reassurance. When your child is sick, there's simply no substitute for the diagnosis and prescribed treatment of your pediatrician. Before calling for medical advice, though, make sure that you're as prepared as possible:

• Take your child's temperature, noting whether the reading is oral or rectal.

• Write down your child's specific symptoms such as fever, headache, cough, earache, or sore throat. Also note changes in her patterns of sleeping, eating, and urinating.

• Try to remember when your child's symptoms started, the order in which they appeared, and—if they're no longer present—how long they lasted.

• Give a reminder of your child's age and any medication she may be taking.

• Stay calm and be careful to neither exaggerate nor downplay your child's symptoms. Your accuracy and reliability can be helpful to your pediatrician in deciding if and when you should bring her in for an examination.

Going to the Doctor

Taking a sick child to see the pediatrician can be stressful for both child and parent. You'll have greater peace of mind if you jot down your health concerns beforehand. Without having to worry about forgetting to ask some-

thing, you'll be free to concentrate on being a comfort to your child while she's being examined.

An important part of your pediatrician's job is to make sure that you understand what's ailing your child and what the best treatment for her is. Make sure you get the answers to the following questions:

• What's the diagnosis? If you don't understand, ask for an explanation.

• What's the cause of the illness? How long can it be expected to last?

• Is the illness contagious? If so, for how long? What precautions should be taken to protect other family members?

• Are there changes in symptoms that should be expected as the illness takes its course? Are there potential complications that should be watched for?

• What's the treatment? If medication is prescribed, make sure that you're aware of when and how to administer it. Ask if there's any information you need to have that won't be found on the pharmacy label. Inquire about possible side effects of the medication and whether it could interfere with other medication that your child may be taking.

CALL THE DOCTOR

Symptoms that indicate your pediatrician should be consulted include:

• unusual lethargy or irritability;

• temperature of 101°F or higher— any fever in the first two months;

• unexplained skin rash;

• vomiting or diarrhea;

• soreness or redness of the throat;

• tender, swollen neck glands;

• nausea or loss of appetite.

SKIN IRRITATIONS

ACNE

Whiteheads

Blackheads

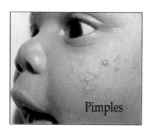

Pimples

What is it?

Acne is caused by hormonally influenced changes in the skin follicles. Babies sometimes develop whiteheads on their foreheads, cheeks, and chins—and occasionally on the scalp and genital area. They usually vanish on their own within a few months. Some children get whiteheads, blackheads, and pimples due to the changes that herald puberty. The face, chest, and back are the most likely sites. This acne usually eases up toward late adolescence.

What can I do?

Don't worry if your baby gets pimples. As his delicate skin grows more resilient, they will disappear. If your older child gets acne, he may find that keeping his skin extra clean helps. Hair oil and friction can aggravate his pimples, so advise him to wash his hair frequently and not scrub his face too hard.

Alcohol wipes, medicated soaps, and abrasive soaps can worsen acne by irritating the skin and blocking pores, so they shouldn't be used. Explain to your child that squeezing or picking at acne will only increase redness and irritation; cosmetic powders and creams, too, are likely to aggravate the condition.

Your child can try controlling his acne with an over-the-counter medication containing benzoyl peroxide. Have him apply it every other day after washing at bedtime. If his skin reddens or peels, he should decrease the amount and frequency of applications. If his acne doesn't get better or if it worsens, ask your pediatrician about prescribing other creams or antibiotics.

1 Encourage your child to wash her face gently at least twice a day using a clean washcloth and warm water.

2 Have your child apply a little anti-acne ointment to her face, avoiding sensitive areas around her eyes and mouth.

3 Suggest that your child keep her hair off her face. She may find that wearing loose-fitting cotton T-shirts helps to reduce skin-irritating friction.

FOOD MYTHS

Junk food has long been blamed for bad skin; but there's little scientific evidence to support this pet theory. Dining on a burger and fries that are washed down with a cola and topped off with a chocolate bar isn't the best example of good nutrition, but it won't worsen your child's acne or trigger a breakout.

COLD SORES

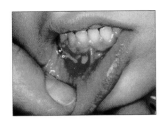

What is it?
A cold sore is a small, painful blister that appears on or around the lips or inside the mouth. Most often caused by the herpes simplex type 1 virus, the sore usually lasts from 7 to 14 days. The virus hibernates in nerve cells and can be reactivated by triggers such as illness, anxiety, or strong sunlight, so sores may reappear from time to time.

What can I do?
There is no real treatment for cold sores. It may help to remove any crusts on the cold sore by using a cold compress and then applying a dab of petroleum jelly. Teach him not to touch the sore and to wash his hands frequently to avoid spreading the infection. If it doesn't get better, consult his pediatrician, who may prescribe an antiherpes ointment. The tingling or burning sensation before a blister surfaces may be alleviated by applying an antiherpes ointment or an ice pack for an hour or so at a time.

Sucking on something cold may bring a child some relief from the sting and ache of a cold sore.

BOILS

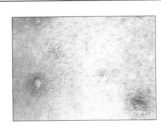

What is it?
A boil is a small, painful, red lump on the skin. It is caused by a bacterial infection of a hair follicle or skin pore that creates a pocket of pus. It may dry up without coming to a head or it may come to a head, rupture, and drain—a process that usually takes about a week.

CALL THE DOCTOR
- if a boil doesn't get better or becomes larger
- if a boil is located in an awkward or difficult-to-treat place
- if a boil is accompanied by fever
- if red streaks branch out from a boil
- if boils occur frequently

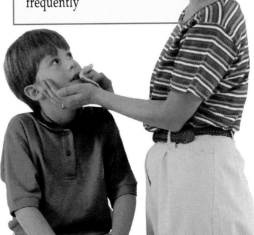

What can I do?
Try to stimulate the resolution of your child's boil by gently pressing a warm washcloth to the affected area for about 15 minutes at a time every few hours. Keep the cloth as warm as possible, but be careful not to scald him. If the boil bursts, clean off the pus and cover the skin with a sterile dressing. Change the dressing frequently and wash the affected area with antibacterial soap.

Keep your child's washcloth and towel separate from the rest of the family's and launder them frequently. Never squeeze or puncture a boil; the infection can spread beneath the skin.

A warm washcloth helps soothe the pain of a boil while encouraging it to resolve and heal more quickly.

Warts

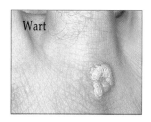

Wart

Plantar wart

What is it?

A wart is a lump of hard skin that is caused by a virus. Mildly contagious, warts are capricious and stubborn, but rarely serious. Warts may occur singly or in a cluster. Their most common sites are the fingers, hands, and soles of the feet. Those on the soles of the feet—called plantar warts—can be quite painful because of the pressure that is placed on them by standing and walking.

What can I do?

Warts are often difficult to get rid of, but some will resolve spontaneously over several months. Discourage picking or chewing at a wart. If your child feels self-conscious, try covering it with adhesive tape for a week, then expose it for a day. Repeat over several weeks. A wart that's itchy and red is healing. If there's no progress, ask your pharmacist about medication and follow directions. If the wart grows fast, is disfiguring, or hurts, see your pediatrician.

1 Soak the affected area in warm water for about five minutes.

2 Apply a topical anti-wart medication according to the instructions on the label. You probably will be directed to cover the wart with adhesive tape and repeat the treatment every day until the root of the wart falls out, leaving a cavity.

Ringworm

What is it?

Despite the name, ringworm has nothing to do with worms; it is a contagious fungal infection. One type causes scaling of the scalp and patchy hair loss. Another type appears as small, round, red spots on the skin and sometimes the nails; as the spots develop, they form circular, ringlike lesions—the rings for which the ailment is called.

What can I do?

If you think your child might have ringworm of the scalp, take her to see her pediatrician, who will prescribe an oral antifungal medication. For ringworm on the body, wash the affected skin thoroughly using antiseptic soap, then follow up with a nonprescription antifungal medication. It may take three or four weeks until the ringworm is gone. To stop the spread of infection, wash brushes, combs, clothing, and bed linens frequently using very hot water.

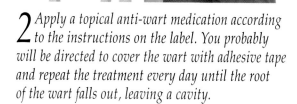

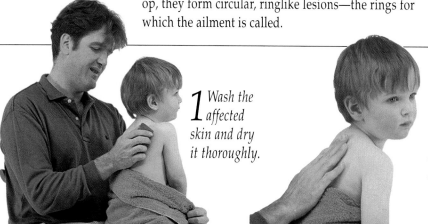

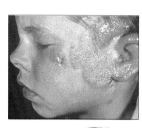

1 Wash the affected skin and dry it thoroughly.

2 Apply an antifungal medication to the skin twice a day until a week after the ringworm has disappeared.

IMPETIGO

What is it?
Impetigo first appears as small red spots or bumps that develop into tiny blisters; the blisters burst and form sticky, yellow-brown crusts. It is a contagious superficial infection of the skin that often begins with a scratched insect bite. Further scratching spreads the infection.

What can I do?
If you think your child has impetigo, have her seen by your pediatrician. Usually, if you regularly clean the area and apply antibiotic ointment, it clears up within a week to 10 days. For more serious cases, oral antibiotics may be recommended. Launder her clothing, bedding, and towels using very hot water, adding chlorine bleach if possible. There's no need to keep her at home after 24 hours of antibiotic treatment; just keep affected patches of skin covered with a sterile dressing.

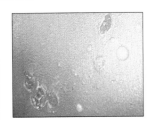

Soak your child's skin in a solution of antibacterial soap and warm water to soften and loosen the crusts, then apply antibiotic ointment.

CALL THE DOCTOR
- if rash spreads quickly
- if rash doesn't respond to treatment
- if child seems sick and has a fever
- if red streaks branch out from a blister
- if skin becomes bright red and tender

Keep your child's nails trimmed short and have him use antibacterial soap when he washes his hands.

THRUSH

What is it?
Thrush is an infection caused by a yeast-like fungus that normally lives in the body. Babies and children on antibiotics are susceptible because the bacteria that usually keep the fungus under control are eliminated. Other causes of infection include poorly sterilized bottle nipples or contaminated hands.

What can I do?
Thrush often disappears by itself, but you should call your pediatrician when you notice any white spots or patches. Ask about prescribing an antifungal medication. If she is bottle fed, inspect all nipples, discarding any that are cracked or old. Sterilize all nipples. Keep your hands clean and pay special attention to cleaning and changing your baby often. If she develops a rash, air her bottom after cleaning. If she's not in diapers, dress her in cotton underwear and encourage her to take showers instead of baths. If soreness or redness persists, take her to your pediatrician.

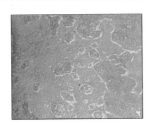

What should I look for?
If your child develops thrush, she'll have white flecks inside her mouth that don't come off easily when gently rubbed; attempts to remove the spots reveal inflamed sores that may bleed.

She may have trouble eating or drinking; a baby will sometimes be irritable and unable to nurse adequately. If she's still in diapers, the fungus may also appear as a diaper rash of reddened, raised skin bordered with red spots.

SEBORRHEA

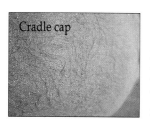
Cradle cap

What is it?
Seborrhea that occurs on a baby's scalp alone is known as cradle cap: yellowish, scaly patches on the head. On an older child, it's dandruff: skin flakes in the hair. Both conditions are harmless, but they can increase the skin's vulnerability to infection.

You can help control your baby's cradle cap by gently rubbing off scales with a soft toothbrush.

What can I do?
Wash your baby's scalp every other day using a mild baby shampoo. If there's a thick buildup of scales, gently massage warm baby oil into his scalp to help soften and loosen them. Cover his head with a warm towel for about 15 minutes, then use a fine-tooth comb or soft toothbrush to gently remove the scales.

If your child has dandruff, brush his hair well and wash it using regular shampoo every day. Discourage him from using hair gels, tonics, or creams. If his scalp looks red and irritated, or if the scales are very greasy, ask your pediatrician for advice on a topical cream or medicated shampoo.

ECZEMA

After your child's bath, seal in the moisture by applying baby oil to her damp skin.

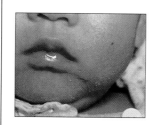

What is it?
Eczema, or atopic dermatitis, may be caused by a genetic hypersensitivity to things such as foods, fibers, and soaps. It may first appear at three or four months as itchy, red, and scaly skin, usually on the face, the inside of the elbows, and behind the knees; the condition is sometimes outgrown by puberty.

What can I do?
Try to break your child's itch-scratch-itch cycle by cutting down on baths and the use of soaps and adding baby oil to the bathwater. Lubricate his rash with moisturizing skin cream twice a day, use a humidifier in his bedroom, and dress him in light, cotton clothes. Consult your pediatrician about corti-sone creams, anti-itch medications, and possible allergies.

CALL THE DOCTOR
- if rash doesn't respond to treatment or gets worse
- if rash is accompanied by fever
- if rash bleeds or becomes infected
- if rash flares up within 24 hours after contact with someone who has a cold sore or chicken pox

HIVES

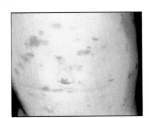

What is it?

Hives are crops of itchy, pink-red, raised bumps—called wheals—that appear and disappear in several different locations on the skin. Hives may develop because of an allergic reaction to food, drugs, or insect bites. Or, they may arise in response to extreme heat or cold, or to a viral infection. Sometimes they even arise spontaneously with no known cause. The wheals vary in shape and can range in size from half an inch to a few inches across. Larger wheals may have pale, whitish centers. An outbreak of hives usually is over within several days.

What can I do?

You can help soothe the itchiness of hives by giving your child a cool bath and then gently smoothing calamine lotion over the rash. Adding a cup of oatmeal to his bathwater will give him extra itch relief.

Talk with your pediatrician about whether you should be using an antihistamine lotion or medication. You'll also want to try to figure out what caused your child's outbreak so that he can learn to avoid the trigger in future.

Alleviate the itchiness of hives by pressing an ice-water compress firmly against the wheals.

CALL THE DOCTOR
• if accompanied by wheezing, dizziness, or difficulty swallowing
• if outbreak triggered by an insect sting or bite
• if swelling of the tongue occurs
• if followed by abdominal pain
• if new medication has been recently started
• if a wheal persists at any location for more than 18 hours

A child with a severe food allergy should always carry a special epinephrine kit. Inform your child's teachers and other caregivers of his food allergy and make sure that they know how to administer the epinephrine in the event that it's needed.

FOOD ALLERGIES

Children with allergies have an immune system that's hypersensitive to certain substances. They react to exposure by producing histamines—one of the body's weapons for defending itself. The flooding of histamines irritates body tissues, which is why children with food allergies suffer such a variety of gastrointestinal, respiratory, and skin symptoms when they eat foods their systems can't handle. Children who experience mild reactions to foods such as milk, wheat, or eggs usually outgrow their allergies by the age of six. A severe allergy to nuts or shellfish is more likely to be lifelong.

INSECT BITES

What is it?		What can I do?
Bee	A bee sting brings on an immediate, sharp pain and rapid swelling. A small black dot at the center of the sting indicates that the bee's stinger is present.	Remove the stinger with gentle, horizontal scraping to avoid squeezing more toxin under the skin. Apply a cold compress to ease pain and swelling. Consult your pediatrician if itching is severe; cortisone ointment or oral antihistamines may be prescribed. Get emergency help for acute swelling or breathing difficulty.
Spider	A spider bite usually is experienced as a sharp sting that develops into an itchy, sometimes painful bump. Hours after the bite, there may be a large, hard bump.	Apply a cold compress to ease pain and swelling. Relieve itching using calamine lotion; discourage scratching by trimming fingernails. Get emergency help for acute swelling or breathing difficulty. Consult your pediatrician if infection develops—bite becomes redder, larger, more swollen, or emits fluid.
Mosquito	The bite of a mosquito causes a stinging sensation; later, a small, red, itchy mound with a punctured center appears. Bright colors and perspiration attract mosquitoes.	Relieve itching using calamine lotion; discourage scratching by trimming fingernails. Consult your pediatrician if infection develops—bite becomes redder, larger, more swollen, or emits fluid.
Red ant	A red ant bite may cause an immediate stinging or burning sensation; a red, itchy bump follows. Watch out for sandy mounds in grassy areas; they may be anthills.	Apply a cold compress to ease discomfort. Relieve itching using calamine lotion; discourage scratching by trimming fingernails. Get emergency help for fever, nausea, or breathing difficulty. Consult your pediatrician if infection develops—bite becomes redder, larger, more swollen, or emits fluid.
Tick	The bite of a tick causes an itchy, painful bump that may develop into a small blister. Ticks hide in hair and on skin, and their presence can be difficult to detect.	Gently pull out the tick with tweezers; if the head and pincers remain, remove them using a sterilized needle. Wash the skin thoroughly and relieve itching using calamine lotion; discourage scratching by trimming fingernails. Get emergency help if symptoms of Lyme's disease develop—skin reddening or rash, fever, headache, or general aching.
Flea	A flea bite leaves a small bump that looks similar to a hive. Bites usually are found in clusters at the waist, neck, and other parts of the body where clothing fits tightly.	Grasp the flea near the head with tweezers and pull it out. Wash the skin thoroughly and relieve itching using calamine lotion; discourage scratching by trimming fingernails. Treat household pets for fleas.

HEAD LICE

What is it?

A child with head lice may complain of an itchy scalp; an examination will reveal nits—tiny, whitish lice eggs attached to the base of hair shafts. The microscopic head lice lay their eggs on hair and feed on blood. Although not disease carriers, they are highly contagious and require prompt treatment.

What can I do?

Don't feel embarrassed if your child gets lice; they are very common and do not reflect on your parenting. Buy anti-lice shampoo and wash her hair thoroughly. Disinfect clothing and bedding by washing them in very hot water and ironing them. Soak all combs, hairbrushes, and barrettes in hot water and anti-lice shampoo. Examine the scalps of all other family members for nits and inform her teacher so her schoolmates can be checked and treated.

1 Wash your child's hair using an anti-lice shampoo to help keep nits under control.

2 Use a fine-toothed comb dipped in vinegar to remove dead nits from your child's head.

SCABIES

Your child's pediatrician probably will prescribe an anti-scabies ointment. Apply the treatment to the affected areas following the instructions.

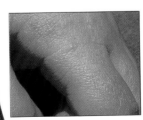

What is it?

Scabies is a red, blistered, itchy rash. Highly contagious, it is caused by small parasites that burrow into the skin to lay eggs. A burrow may be visible as a raised red line on the skin. In infants, scabies can appear anywhere on the body. In young children, they tend to be on the palms and the soles of feet.

What can I do?

Take your child to your pediatrician who may prescribe anti-scabies ointment if scabies are diagnosed. Bathe her in cool water and use antiseptic soap. Dry her with a clean towel and apply the anti-scabies ointment to her entire body. Try to discourage her from scratching. Trim her nails and encourage her to keep her hands clean. Disinfect her clothing, towels, and bedding by washing in very hot water. Inform her teacher so that her schoolmates can be examined and treated if necessary.

PINWORMS

What is it?

Pinworms are tiny, white worms that can enter the body through the mouth or through inhalations. They are common and do not indicate poor hygiene. At night the pinworms travel through the bowel and out of the rectum where they lay their eggs around the anus. The egg-laying causes severe itching.

What can I do?

If your child complains of an itchy anus, check for worms at night with a small flashlight. Or, first thing in the morning, get a sample of eggs by pressing a piece of cellophane tape onto the itchy area and pulling it off. Any eggs will stick to the tape. Place the tape in a jar and take it for medical analysis.

Your pediatrician probably will prescribe medication for the entire family if worms or eggs are found. Insist that everyone wash their hands often, especially before meals and after using the toilet. Keep fingernails clean and short, and discourage nail-biting and thumb-sucking.

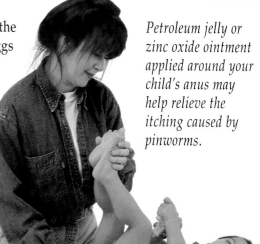

Petroleum jelly or zinc oxide ointment applied around your child's anus may help relieve the itching caused by pinworms.

SUNBURN

What can I do?

If your child's skin seems to be reddening, take him out of the sun immediately; the effects of a sunburn are delayed for a few hours after overexposure. The symptoms of sunburn—redness, pain, swelling, and a sensation of heat—will appear within two to four hours after damage to the skin has been inflicted. His discomfort will be most intense for the next 24 hours. In most cases, the injured layers of skin will peel off after three days. Bathe him in cool water. Add two to three tablespoons of baking soda to the water and don't use any soap. Encourage him to drink lots of fluids. For pain and swelling, lubricate his sunburn with skin cream three times a day. A children's analgesic, such as acetaminophen, will help relieve the soreness of a bad sunburn. Avoid using petroleum jelly or butter, which can worsen the discomfort of a sunburn by trapping in heat and sweat.

SUN FACTS

Every sunburn increases the risk of your child's developing skin cancer later in life. Prevention is extremely important. Be vigilant about using sunscreen and about the amount of exposure. Sun rays are most intense between 10 a.m. and 3 p.m. Even on a cloudy day, over 70 percent of the rays come through. If the skin reddens, decrease the time she spends in the sun. Keep in mind that the skin of fair-haired children and of babies can be burned very easily—never let your child fall asleep in the sun.

Along with a sunhat, a child should wear a sunscreen with an SPF (sun protection factor) of at least 15. Reapply sunscreen after swimming and every few hours in the sun.

CALL THE DOCTOR

• if your child's eyes become highly sensitive to sunlight
• if your child develops a sudden, unexplained fever over 102°F
• if your child feels dizzy or faints
• if your child's sunburn erupts into fluid-filled blisters

POISONOUS PLANTS

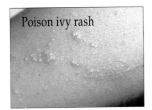
Poison ivy rash

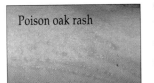
Poison oak rash

What is it?
An oily substance in plants such as poison ivy and poison oak produces an intensely itchy, burning, red rash that swells the skin and produces blisters. Once the blisters burst, weeping sores form and then crust over. In most cases, symptoms appear a day or two after contact and disappear within a week or two. Direct contact with the plants themselves isn't necessary; the allergic reaction can occur after contact with oil that has gathered on clothing or a pet's fur.

Try soothing the itch and swelling with a cold compress that has first been soaked in water with a tablespoon of baking soda. Apply it for 15 minutes to an hour, four times a day.

What can I do?
You may be able to diminish or avert an allergic reaction by washing your child's skin with ordinary dish soap and water within five minutes of exposure. One way to relieve the itching is to bath inflamed areas for 10 minutes in a solution of one tablespoon vinegar to one cup water. Then, cover the rash with calamine lotion, hydrocortisone cream, or a paste of baking soda and water. Repeat the procedure every two to three hours.

Periodic baths containing a cup of oatmeal or hot showers may help to provide relief. Your pediatrician may prescribe medication to reduce severe itching and inflammation. Discourage your child from scratching and keep his fingernails cut short. Clothing exposed to the plants should be washed thoroughly or dry-cleaned. Wipe contaminated shoes with cleaning fluid. Contrary to popular belief, contact with fluid from the blisters will not spread the rash to other parts of the body.

CALL THE DOCTOR
• if the rash covers more than a quarter of the body
• if the rash causes redness or swelling around the eyes, mouth, nose, or genitals
• if the rash is accompanied by severe inflammation, fever, or swollen neck glands

WHAT TO LOOK FOR
If plants such as poison ivy, poison oak, or poison sumac grow in the vicinity of your home, teach your child to recognize—and avoid—them; he may well get an allergic reaction to them. Poison ivy has a reddish stem with three shiny, smooth-edged green leaves that are notched at the edge. The leaves of Eastern poison oak have pointed tips and rippled edges; with Pacific poison oak, the leaves have rounded, slightly rippled edges. The poison sumac bush has long stems with opposing rows of paired leaflets and a single leaflet at the tip; each stem may hold seven to 13 smooth-edged leaflets.

Poison ivy is common throughout most areas of the U.S.; Nevada and California are the biggest exceptions.

Eastern poison oak prevails in the southeastern U.S.; Pacific poison oak is found on the West Coast.

Poison sumac is most common in the low-lying, swampy areas of the Mississippi River region.

CHAPPING

What is it?

Chapped skin can be painful. The tiny cracks often occur on the lips after exposure to the sun, wind, or cold. Deeper cracks, which may even bleed, also can develop on the soles of your child's feet from wearing wet socks and shoes, or on her thumb from sucking. Swimmers may develop cracks in the skin between their toes.

What can I do?

Combat your child's dry skin by reducing her weekly number of baths and by using only mild soap. Lubricate her skin frequently with lotion. Keep deeper cracks on the feet and hands covered with petroleum jelly for at least two weeks; a bandage, socks, or gloves will prevent it from rubbing off. Replace leaky shoes and remind your child to dry her feet carefully after swimming—especially between the toes. If pimples or pus appear in a crack, the skin may be infected; consult your pediatrician.

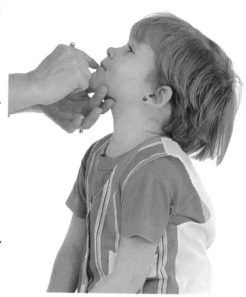

Apply lip balm regularly to chapped lips and discourage your child from licking them, especially in cold weather.

INGROWN TOENAIL

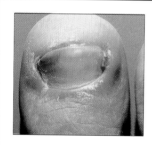

What is it?

An ingrown toenail occurs when the upper corner of a nail—usually on one of the big toes—grows into the skin alongside the nail. Tight shoes or improper nail clipping are most often the cause. An ingrown nail hurts; the toe turns red and the skin may swell or harden. Untreated, it can become a chronic condition.

The pain of an ingrown toenail comes from the rubbing of the nail's corner against the skin. Cut off the corner of the nail to let the raw, tender skin heal.

CALL THE DOCTOR
- if your child also develops a fever or chills
- if pus develops or a red streak spreads beyond your child's toenail

What can I do?

Make sure your child wears comfortable shoes that fit her feet well. Show her how to cut her toenails properly: straight across the top. If she develops an ingrown nail, soak her foot in a solution of one tablespoon bleach or salt and two quarts warm water for five to 10 minutes. As she soaks her foot, gently massage the swollen skin. Repeat the procedure twice daily until the toe gets better. Protect a sensitive toe from rubbing against its neighbor or the side of the shoe by taping cotton between the toes or on the ball of the sore toe. Until the toe heals, encourage her to go barefoot whenever possible.

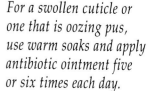

For a swollen cuticle or one that is oozing pus, use warm soaks and apply antibiotic ointment five or six times each day.

ATHLETE'S FOOT

What is it?

Athlete's foot is a common fungal infection that causes a red, scaly rash between the toes or on the instep of the foot. The rash may itch and burn, and often makes the feet smell. Scratching the rash can make it raw and weepy. It is only moderately contagious and usually will not develop on skin that is normal and dry. Your child may contract it during her preteen years as she starts to perspire more profusely. It usually clears up within two to three weeks with proper treatment, but has a tendency to recur.

What can I do?

Have your child wash her feet thoroughly in plain water or in water with a little white vinegar added. Make sure she dries her feet well, especially between the toes. Then, give her a nonprescription antifungal cream to apply to the rash and surrounding area. She should repeat these steps twice a day for several weeks or until a week after the rash disappears. Let her go barefoot as much as possible. In warmer weather, wearing sandals or thongs will keep her feet aired and dry. The rest of the time she should wear cotton socks; they will help keep her feet dry by absorbing sweat. Encourage her to change socks twice a day and shoes every other day. Make sure her footwear isn't too tight; avoid shoes that have plastic or synthetic linings.

If your child is prone to athlete's foot, sprinkling a little antifungal powder into his socks is a worthwhile preventive measure.

JOCK ITCH

The rubbing of briefs can irritate a rash, so encourage your child to wear loose-fitting boxer shorts. Choose cotton, which absorbs moisture, over nylon or synthetic fabrics.

What is it?

Jock itch is a fungal infection that boys may get; it produces a pink, scaly rash on the inner thighs, the groin, and occasionally the scrotum—it doesn't affect the penis. Moisture and friction aggravate the condition, which usually takes up to two weeks of treatment before eventually disappearing.

What can I do?

Explain to your son that he must keep the rash and surrounding area clean using only water and dry himself thoroughly. Get him a nonprescription antifungal medication and show him how to apply it. He should work it meticulously into his skin creases. Encourage him to apply the medication twice daily for several weeks or until a week after the rash disappears. Since jock itch often recurs, be sure that he changes his underwear daily and has his athletic supporter laundered after each use. Remind him always to dry his groin area well after bathing.

EYE, EAR, NOSE, AND THROAT ILLS

COLDS

What should I look for?

Colds are caused by many different viruses; most children get six to 10 colds a year. Watch for a runny or stuffy nose, a sore throat, which may last a week, and a cough, which sometimes lasts three weeks. The cold virus may also cause his temperature to rise slightly for several days and he may develop swollen lymph nodes in the neck. When your child catches a cold, he will be contagious from a couple of days prior to the onset of his symptoms until a day or two after they're gone.

What can I do?

You can make your child feel less miserable by treating the symptoms and comforting him until the infection runs its course. For a fever, give him acetaminophen; because of the risk of

Reye's syndrome, don't give him aspirin. If he's over four and has a sore throat, show him how to gargle with salt water. Most cold and cough medicines have been found not to help and should be avoided for young children. If he's between one and four, try corn syrup for a cough. A cool-mist vaporizer or humidifier may ease his breathing and loosen nasal secretions. Do your best to get him to rest and drink fluids.

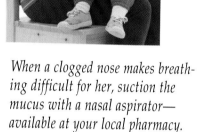

When a clogged nose makes breathing difficult for her, suction the mucus with a nasal aspirator—available at your local pharmacy.

Your baby will sleep better if you clear his stuffy nose before bed. Use warm tap water or saline nose drops to loosen dried mucus, then suction.

BLOWING THE NOSE

Blowing a runny nose doesn't come naturally; infants will need you to clear their noses for them. Teach an older child how to blow by having him exhale through his nose to blow a feather off his hand. Or, let him breathe out through his nose on a mirror; when it fogs up, he'll know he's got the knack.

By exhaling through his nose, he gets a feather to float away.

CALL THE DOCTOR
• if your child's temperature suddenly surges higher after he has run a fever above 101°F for five hours or of 100°F for three days
• if your child breathes fast or has difficulty even after clearing his nose
• if your child discharges yellowish fluid from his nose for 24 hours
• if your child complains that his throat hurts when he swallows
• if your child develops an earache
• if your child acts sick and shows no improvement after three days

CONJUNCTIVITIS

What is it?
Conjunctivitis, or pinkeye, as it is often called, is an inflammation of the membrane that lines the inner eyelids and the whites of eyes. It is caused by a contagious bacterial or viral infection—the bacterial kind can be treated with antibiotics.

What should I look for?
Watch for red, watery eyes that itch. The eyelids may also be swollen and caked with pus in the morning.

What can I do?
Remove dried and liquid pus from his eyes with cotton balls that have been soaked in boiled water and cooled to a lukewarm temperature. Consult your pediatrician, who may prescribe antibiotic eyedrops or ointment. If allergies are suspected as the cause, you may want to have your child tested to pinpoint the allergens in his environment.

Apply eye ointment by gently pulling down the lower eyelid and squeezing a thin line of ointment between the eyeball and lid.

When giving your child eyedrops, make sure the drops fall into the crease between the lower lid and eyeball. Afterward, have him close his eye for half a minute.

STYES

To bring a stye to a head, apply a warm compress to the affected eye several times a day.

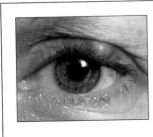

What is it?
Caused by a bacterial infection or inflammation near the root of an eyelash, a stye appears as a small pimple that grows larger, redder, and more painful. After a week or so, it will subside, usually after bursting and releasing pus. Never squeeze or puncture styes.

What can I do?
Make a warm compress by dipping a clean washcloth into boiled water that has been allowed to cool to a warm temperature. Apply the compress to the affected area for 10 minutes or so.

Repeat the procedure several times a day. The warmth should thin the skin at the top of the swelling until the stye erupts. If your child's stye doesn't drain after two days of home treatment, call your pediatrician for advice.

EAR INFECTIONS

What is it?

Most ear infections are the result of a mild inflammation of the middle ear that often accompanies a cold or other upper respiratory tract infections. Because the tube that drains liquid secretions from the middle ear into the back of the nose is short in children, it is easier for germs and bacteria to reach the middle ear. It's not uncommon for some youngsters to get a lot of ear infections. Fortunately, they usually outgrow this kind of recurring problem.

CALL THE DOCTOR

• if your child's earache persists or worsens after treatment

• if your child's ear emits pus or a watery discharge

• if your child's neck is stiff

• if your child has trouble walking

• if your child develops an earache after an injury to the ear

---

What should I look for?

Watch for ear pain or stuffiness—a baby or toddler may rub or pull at her ears; fever and crying in babies; a mild fever in older children; and in both, irritability and loss of appetite.

What can I do?

If you suspect your child has an ear infection, take her to your pediatrician, who may prescribe antibiotics and suggest acetaminophen to lower an accompanying fever or soothe the pain. You can also help relieve her pain by giving her a hot-water bottle filled with warm water or a heating pad set on low to hold against the ear. Alternatively, cool the ear for 20 minutes with an ice pack or ice cubes wrapped in a wet washcloth. If pus or watery fluid drains from the ear, wipe it away as it appears. Never use cotton to plug the ear canal. Check with your pediatrician before giving any over-the-counter eardrops.

When giving your child eardrops, ask him to tilt his head to the side, with the infected ear up. Use one hand to hold his head steady while you deposit the drops in the ear canal. Hold his head still for a full minute after putting the drops in his ear.

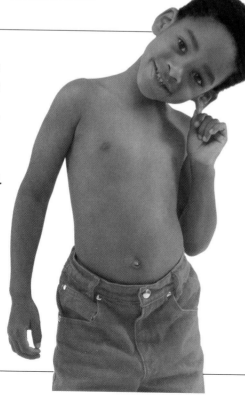

If your child is prone to getting swimmer's ear, encourage him to shake his head and tug on his earlobe after swimming to free trapped moisture. If this is an ongoing problem, your pediatrician may prescribe acetic acid ear drops as a preventive measure.

SWIMMER'S EAR

Swimmer's ear is an infection of the ear canal or outer ear that occurs in children who swim a lot. It develops when the moist skin that lines the external ear flap and the ear canal is invaded by bacteria. Signs that your child may have swimmer's ear are an itchy ear that feels plugged, dull ear pain, and a white discharge that has the consistency of cottage cheese. An untreated infection can cause severe pain and a fever. If you suspect your child may have swimmer's ear, have him examined by your pediatrician. While antibacterial ear drops are commonly prescribed to treat swimmer's ear, in mild cases the pediatrician may need only to clean the ear of pus and debris. Your child shouldn't go swimming until an infection has cleared up.

HAY FEVER

What is it?

Hay fever is caused by an allergen in the air that irritates the nasal passages and upper respiratory tract, producing swelling, inflammation, and fluid secretions. It is often confused with the common cold. If your child has cold symptoms along with itchy, watery eyes for more than two weeks, she may have hay fever. Children with hay fever are usually allergic to tree and grass pollens, mold spores, animal dander, and house dust. Other allergens include cigarette smoke and air pollution. Most children with hay fever have a family history of allergies. Hay fever is a chronic condition that may even last throughout your child's lifetime.

What should I look for?

Look for sneezing and sniffing; nasal congestion and clear, watery discharge; coughing; itchy nose, ears, palate, and upper throat; red, teary, itchy eyes. Her ears also may be congested.

What can I do?

If you suspect your child has hay fever, you may want to take her to an allergist for help in pinpointing the allergens in her environment. While there is no cure for hay fever, you can help manage your child's condition, with the advice of her doctor, by using medication and by teaching her to avoid the substances or environments that trigger an allergic reaction.

There are a variety of medicines to treat hay fever, including antihistamines and anti-inflammatory nose sprays. They should be given at the first sneeze or when exposure to an allergen is expected. If she has a serious allergy to pollen, you may need to give her medicine throughout the entire pollen season. She may prefer to spend more time indoors during these months; to help reduce the need for open windows, use air conditioning.

Encourage your child to shower regularly, particularly when symptoms are severe; showering will rinse away pollen that has collected on the skin and hair. If you have an outdoor pet, explain to your child that she should avoid stroking it during the pollen season—fur frequently traps pollen. If your child is allergic to mold spores, teach her to stay away from damp places such as basements and areas with decaying vegetation such as gardens and vacant lots. Clean your shower stall often to avoid mold buildup.

DUSTPROOFING

Children with hay fever tend to be extremely sensitive to house dust. This is because thousands of microscopic, allergy-causing mites live in each ball of dust. If your child has hay fever or asthma, take the following steps to help eliminate dust mites:

• Begin by emptying her room and closets completely. Thoroughly clean all surfaces with a damp cloth or mop, or a vacuum cleaner. Wash her clothes and dust all her possessions before returning them to her room. Make sure the room is kept vacuumed and dusted, paying extra attention to areas such as shelves where dust can collect.

• Furnish her room with a bed that features a wooden or metal frame, open, metal springs instead of box springs, and a mattress and pillows that contain foam rubber or another synthetic material. Cover mattresses and pillows with special dustproof covers that are available at specialty linen shops. Use cotton sheets and bedspreads or synthetics with a smooth finish. Avoid comforters and quilts. Hang washable curtains on the windows.

• Rugless floors are best. However, if you feel she must have a carpet in her room, give her one made of synthetic fibers with a short pile.

• Air your child's bedding daily. When washing her bedclothes, use the hottest water possible.

• Close heating registers or cover them with fiberglass filters. Change heating and air-conditioner filters regularly. You may wish to install a dehumidifier or air purifier in her room; if so, wash it regularly to keep it dust-free.

A child with hay fever will exhibit symptoms similar to a cold.

SINUSITIS

What should I look for?

Sinusitis is a bacterial infection of the sinuses—the air-filled cavities tucked among the bones of the cheek and forehead—that usually develops in the wake of a cold. If your child develops sinusitis, he will probably cough a lot and have profuse, thick nasal discharge and a headache. He might complain of pressure around the eyes that worsens when he bends over. He may also have a fever.

What can I do?

Consult your pediatrician, who may prescribe antibiotics. If there is discomfort around your child's eyes and forehead, try alleviating it by using a warm compress. Treat a fever by giving him the recommended dose of acetaminophen. Encourage him to drink lots of juice or water and use steam inhalation to help thin his mucus secretions. A cool-mist vaporizer also may help to ease breathing difficulties.

CALL THE DOCTOR
- if the condition recurs frequently
- if swelling around the eyes and cheeks lasts all day
- if a headache is severe or persists
- if vision is blurred or the eyes are sensitive to light
- if a fever doesn't subside after the taking of acetaminophen

STREP THROAT

1 To help relieve her sore throat, mix a teaspoon of salt in a glass of warm water and show her how to gargle.

2 If she finds swallowing painful, offer her lots of soft, cold foods such as milkshakes and applesauce.

What is it?

Throat infections can be caused by viruses or bacteria. Strep throat is one type of bacterial infection, caused by the streptococcus bacteria. Strep throat is sometimes manifest as scarlet fever—a fine, rough, red rash on the chest and abdomen. Strep throat is uncommon in children under three years of age.

What should I look for?

Strep throat often passes unnoticed at first because some children have either mild symptoms or none at all. Watch for mild fever accompanied by a thick nasal discharge; in toddlers, look for a mildly painful throat, mild fever, crankiness, and swollen glands. Older children may get a fever over 102°F, a severe sore throat, and a headache. Decreased appetite, fatigue, and a rash on the chest and groin area are also common symptoms.

What can I do?

If you think your child might have strep throat, take him to your pediatrician, who will prescribe antibiotics if a throat culture confirms the diagnosis. Make sure that your child takes the full course of antibiotics even after the symptoms go away, because a small percentage of children with untreated strep throat will develop rheumatic fever. Give him the recommended dose of acetaminophen for a fever and lots of fluids to drink. After 24 hours on medication, your child will no longer be contagious; as long as he's feeling better, there's no harm in letting him resume his normal activities.

CALL THE DOCTOR
- if your child's fever returns after several days of treatment
- if your child develops the following symptoms: vomiting, earache, skin rash, chest pain, shortness of breath, and a severe headache
- if your child starts coughing a lot, especially if the sputum is green, yellow-brown, or blood-streaked
- if your child develops sore, swollen joints

LARYNGITIS

What is it?
Laryngitis is an infection that causes an inflammation of the mucous membranes lining the voice box or larynx. Most cases of laryngitis without other symptoms are viral in origin and therefore cannot be treated with antibiotics. Often seen in conjunction with the flu, tonsillitis, or an inflammation of the throat, they tend to occur in the winter or spring. Boys appear to be most susceptible. Some children between three months and five years of age are prone to experiencing recurring bouts of laryngitislike hoarseness that can last up to two weeks. Fortunately, complications are rare.

What should I look for?
A child with laryngitis will have a hoarse voice or lose his voice completely. He may cough and complain of a sore throat. Watch for a temperature that rises to about 101°F.

What can I do?
Provide your child with warm drinks to help soothe his sore, scratchy throat. Have him stay quiet and discourage him from doing a lot of talking. Steam inhalation or a cool-mist vaporizer also will help to relieve his symptoms.

In the rare case when the infection causing the laryngitis is bacterial in origin, your pediatrician may prescribe antibiotics. A cough suppressant also may be suggested for nighttime relief.

TONSILLITIS

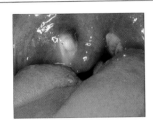

What is it?
Tonsillitis is an inflammation of the tonsils that is characterized by a very sore throat. The tonsils are the reddish, oval-shaped masses on each side of the throat near the base of the tongue. They serve to trap infection and prevent it from spreading. When battling infection, they swell up. Check out your child's tonsils when he's well so that you can tell the difference if they become swollen or infected.

Soft, cooling foods such as ice cream and frozen yogurt are welcome relief for the child with the sore throat of tonsillitis.

SURGERY OR NOT?
Swollen tonsils can be surgically removed in a tonsillectomy. Once practically a ritual of childhood, the operation was frequently recommended as a means of preventing or lessening the severity of other illnesses. Nowadays, it is usually recommended only when the tonsils interfere with normal breathing, or when a child has recurrent episodes of strep throat. Be sure to get at least two medical opinions before deciding on surgery for your child.

CALL THE DOCTOR
• if your child's tonsils are red or covered with white spots
• if your child frequently complains of a sore throat and swollen glands

What should I look for?
Watch for signs that your child has pain when swallowing, a fever above 100°F, and swollen neck glands.

What can I do?
Examine your child's tonsils under a bright light. If they're red or swollen, or covered in creamy spots, they have become infected. Take him to see your pediatrician, who will do a throat culture. If the tonsils are simply swollen and sore, encourage your child to gargle with warm, salty water; this may reduce pain. For a fever, give him the recommended dose of acetaminophen.

CHEST AND RESPIRATORY ILLS

COUGHS

What is it?

Coughing is a reflex to an irritation in the respiratory tract. A cough that sounds like the barking of a dog or a seal may signal an irritation in the larynx (voice box). A deep, raspy cough that is worse in the morning suggests an irritation in the larger airways such as the trachea (windpipe) or bronchi. A persistant cough without a fever may indicate that your child has inhaled a small object into her lungs. A chronic, dry cough that is worse during the night may be caused by allergies, or if she only coughs at night, she may have asthma.

What can I do?

If your child's cough is accompanied by a fever or she has difficulty breathing, she may have a lower respiratory infection; take her to your pediatrician to be sure. For infections that are bacterial in origin, you probably will be prescribed antibiotics. If you suspect your child is coughing because of allergies or asthma, a visit to the pediatrician is also in order. Depending on the cause of the cough, you may be advised to treat it using a cough medicine containing an antihistamine or with a decongestant that loosens the mucus so it's easier to bring up. If her cough keeps her from sleeping at night, ask about a cough suppressant. For most coughs, adding moisture to the air with a humidifier or vaporizer is helpful. But don't give an over-the-counter cough medicine to your child without your pediatrician's approval.

To quiet a dry, hacking cough and help her sleep, try giving her a glass of warm apple cider.

After she's a year old, corn syrup or honey may be used as a homemade cough remedy—but don't give her honey if she's any younger; she may get botulism from it.

CALL THE DOCTOR

- if your child develops a cough before she's three months old
- if your child's cough is sudden and violent or painful
- if your child's breathing becomes rapid, labored, or noisy
- if your child runs a fever for more than four days
- if your child's cough persists for more than 10 days
- if your child's cough is accompanied by whooping, vomiting, or turning blue
- if your child's cough appears with a fever and breathing difficulty

COUGH MEDICINES

- Expectorants thin out mucus that is secreted in the breathing passages, making it easier for a child to cough up mucus.
- Decongestants temporarily shrink the blood vessels in the walls of the breathing passages, thereby decreasing the amount of mucus produced.
- Suppressants repress the cough reflex. Used mainly at night, they should be given only when recommended by your pediatrician.
- Antihistamines soothe a cough caused by an allergy by reducing swelling of the mucus membranes and the production of secretions.

FLU

What is it?
Flu, or influenza, is a highly contagious viral infection of the respiratory tract. Most strains of the flu last from three days—when they're most contagious—to a week, but an accompanying cough may persist for another week.

What should I look for?
Watch for a sudden fever between 101°F and 106°F, accompanied by chills and shakes, dry coughing, stuffy nose, sore throat, headache, muscle pain, fatigue, and possibly diarrhea.

A flu-stricken child won't feel like doing much, so give him acetaminophen to ease his discomfort and encourage him to rest in bed.

What can I do?
Follow the progress of the flu closely because it can make your child more vulnerable to other illnesses, especially pneumonia. You can help her feel better by giving her the recommended dose of acetaminophen to reduce her fever, aches, and pains.

Encourage your child to rest in bed, drink plenty of fluids, and eat light meals. If she has difficulty breathing, moisturize the air in her room with a cool-mist

vaporizer or humidifier. To avoid catching the flu yourself, don't kiss her on or around the mouth. Wash her hands and your own frequently, and make sure that any utensils she uses are washed in very hot, soapy water.

CALL THE DOCTOR
- if your child's breathing is labored
- if your child's temperature rises and falls repeatedly for more than three days
- if your child's cough worsens
- if your child has chest pain or coughs up bloody or greenish mucus
- if your child has ear or sinus pain, or emits a thick, yellowish or greenish discharge from the nose or ears
- if your child begins vomiting or has diarrhea
- if your child has a chronic medical condition such as asthma

CROUP

What is it?
Croup is an inflammation of the larynx and trachea that narrows the breathing passages and makes breathing difficult. You'll recognize croup by its barking-type cough, which sounds like a dog or seal, as well as by its stridor—the harsh, shrill sound heard on inhaling.

What can I do?
A croup attack can be frightening for parent and child. Your child may panic as she struggles for breath. Stay calm and take her into the bathroom immediately. Turn on the hot water in the sink and the shower and close the door. The moist, warm air should help to ease her breathing, but don't use the treatment for more than 10 minutes at a time. Alternatively, wrap her up warmly and take her into the cool, night air. Lower the temperature in her room until it's cool and humidify the air with a cool-mist vaporizer or humidifier. Get her to sip juice or water, but don't use cough medicine; coughing helps breathing.

CALL THE DOCTOR
- if this is your child's first attack of croup
- if your child doesn't improve after half an hour of home treatment
- if your child's temperature rises above 103°F
- if your child's struggle to breathe intensifies or there is stridor at rest
- if your child is drooling or has difficulty swallowing

BRONCHITIS

What is it?
Bronchitis is an infection of the larger central airways leading to the lungs; along with inflammation of the airways' lining, fluids collect in the lungs. Usually viral in origin, bronchitis develops from a cold or flu infection and may last a week to 10 days.

What should I look for?
If your child develops bronchitis, he probably will have a slight fever accompanied by a loss of appetite and a dry, hacking cough that gradually turns into a deep, wet one. His breathing may be raspy and he may cough up yellowish-green sputum. His chest also may burn when he breathes deeply. If he's too young to cough up mucus, he may vomit instead.

What can I do?
Treat your child's fever by giving him the recommended dose of acetaminophen and encourage him to rest. To prevent dehydration and help loosen the mucus in his lungs, provide him with plenty of fluids to drink. Moisten the air in his room with a humidifier or cool-mist vaporizer. He needs to cough up the sputum in his lungs, so don't give him cough medicine unless your pediatrician recommends it. An infant with bronchitis should be moved to different positions to help mucus drain out of the respiratory tract.

PNEUMONIA

What is it?
Pneumonia is an infection of the lungs that can be either bacterial or viral in origin. Viral pneumonias sometimes appear following a respiratory tract infection such as the flu. Bacterial pneumonias may develop if the immune system has been weakened by a viral illness such as measles. Even healthy children can get pneumonia. Occasionally, it results after inhaling a bit of food or other foreign object into the lungs.

What should I look for?
Watch for a fever, possibly with chills, sweating, and flushed skin, accompanied by a cough. Your child's chest may pain him. Be alert to shortness of breath or rapid, labored, noisy breathing. If he's a baby or toddler, he may be pale and limp, and cry more than usual.

Encourage her to drink juice or water and moisten the air in her room. A hot-water bottle or a heating pad set on low will help relieve her chest pain.

What can I do?
If you suspect pneumonia, take your child to see your pediatrician immediately. Antibiotics are commonly prescribed if there is any suspicion that the pneumonia may be bacterial in origin. If the cause of the pneumonia is found to be a foreign object inhaled into the lungs, the object will have to be removed.

Keep your child in bed while he's feeling sick and feverish. Give him the recommended dose of acetaminophen to help reduce his fever. Moisten the air in his room using a humidifer or cool-mist vaporizer. He needs to cough in order to clear mucus from his lungs, so don't give him a cough suppressant.

CALL THE DOCTOR
• if your child's breathing becomes labored or rapid
• if your child's fever rises suddenly or lasts more than two days after starting antibiotics
• if your child's chest pain continues after starting antibiotics
• if your child's coughing brings up bloody mucus
• if your child is nauseated, vomits, or has diarrhea
• if your child develops swollen, reddened joints or a stiff neck

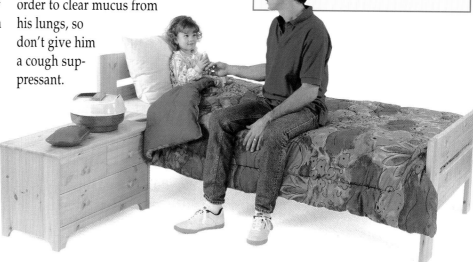

ASTHMA

What is it?

Asthma is a lung disorder affecting the bronchial tubes that makes it difficult to breath. It occurs when the muscles of the bronchial tubes—the small airways that connect the trachea to the lungs—go into spasm. At the same time, the lining of the airways becomes inflamed and produces mucus. The resulting narrowing of the air passages makes it difficult for air to pass through.

Asthma can be triggered by air pollutants such as cigarette smoke or chemical fumes and allergens such as animal dander, mold spores, or pollen. An attack may also be triggered by a cold, vigorous exercise, emotional stress, or food allergies. In children under five an asthma attack most commonly occurs after a viral respiratory infection. A child is more susceptible to asthma if someone else in the family has it. He may outgrow it completely by his middle teens or have milder and less frequent attacks.

What should I look for?

Watch for shortness of breath that may be accompanied by a high-pitched wheezing or whistling sound as the air is forced from your child's lungs when he exhales. Also watch for a persistent or recurring cough unaccompanied by fever, or a cough that increases at night or when exercising. If your child has a severe asthma attack, his breathing and heart rate will become very rapid. He may vomit and his fingernails and lips may turn blue.

What can I do?

If you think that your child has asthma, take him to your pediatrician for a diagnosis; if asthma is confirmed, medication likely will be prescribed. Together you will be able to figure out what kinds of situations trigger an attack. As soon as your child is old enough, discuss how he can avoid these triggers and teach him how to cope when an attack does happen. During an acute attack, administer the prescribed medication, stay calm, and provide your child with the reassurance he needs. Allow five to 10 minutes for the attack to pass. Offer sips of a warm liquid. If respiratory distress is significant, take him to his doctor or a hospital.

CALL THE DOCTOR
- if your child's rapid, labored breathing intensifies—especially if his chest wall pulls when he inhales and he grunts when exhaling
- if your child's eyes or fingertips turn blue or his skin darkens
- if your child becomes extremely agitated or lethargic, or is confused
- if your child experiences pain in the chest, throat, or neck
- if your child doesn't respond to his prescribed medication
- if your child is vomiting and can't take his prescribed medication

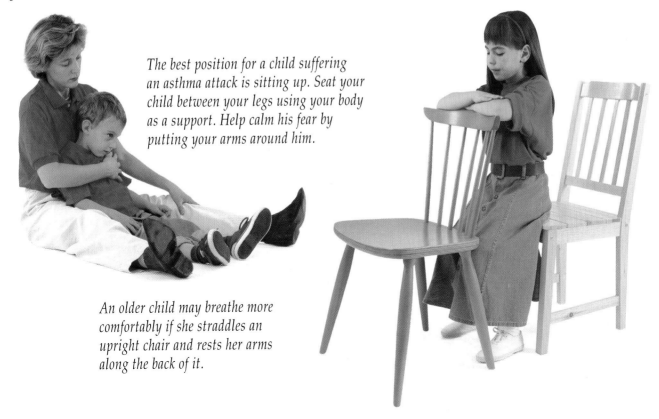

The best position for a child suffering an asthma attack is sitting up. Seat your child between your legs using your body as a support. Help calm his fear by putting your arms around him.

An older child may breathe more comfortably if she straddles an upright chair and rests her arms along the back of it.

STOMACH, DIGESTIVE, AND URINARY ILLS

DIARRHEA

What should I look for?
Breast-fed infants have softer, more frequent bowel movements than bottle-fed infants; they can have up to a dozen or so small bowel movements a day. Within a few months the number will lessen. By the age of two, most children have one or two bowel movements a day, although if their diet includes fruit juices and foods containing fiber, such as bran and prunes, they may have several smaller bowel movements each day and still be healthy.

Watch for sudden changes in bowel movement; a general rule of thumb is the more frequent the passage of unusually soft, runny stool the more serious the condition. Look for changes in stool odor and an increasingly green color. While most diarrhea in children is caused by viruses, it may also be produced by bacteria, parasites, antibiotics, food and milk allergies, or a formula that is too sugary. Even overeating or rich foods can give a child diarrhea.

What can I do?
If your child has watery stool every hour or two—or more frequently—call your pediatrician. If she has mild diarrhea but continues to appear active and hungry and exhibits no signs of dehydration or fever, you can give her oral electrolyte solution, available at your pharmacy, and bland food. Don't use over-the-counter medication without first consulting your pediatrician. For bottle-fed infants, you can continue feeding as long as your baby is able to drink. You can supplement with the oral electrolyte solution. For breast-fed babies, continue regular feedings as long as she can keep up with her stool losses. For children, give the solution, but hold back on solids and milk. After 12 to 24 hours, and if there is no vomiting, resume solid foods slowly, beginning with soups, applesauce, bananas, carrots, rice, and mashed potatoes and then lean meats, soft-boiled eggs, noodles, cooked fruits and vegetables, and active culture yogurt. Milk and dairy products should be given only when the system is back to normal.

DEHYDRATION DANGER
Diarrhea and vomiting can dangerously dehydrate a child. Call your pediatrician if your child develops any of the following symptoms:
• sharply decreased urine output and no tears
• dry mouth and tongue
• sunken eyes
• doughy-textured skin
• sunken fontanelle
• lethargy or drowsiness

CALL THE DOCTOR
• if your baby has diarrhea and is less than six months old
• if your child has diarrhea and is taking antibiotics
• if diarrhea doesn't respond to home treatment
• if diarrhea is accompanied by vomiting or high fever
• if stool contains blood or mucus
• if diarrhea is accompanied by dizziness or abdominal pain

The BRAT diet—bananas, rice, applesauce, and toast—is recommended for children with diarrhea because these foods have a slightly constipating effect.

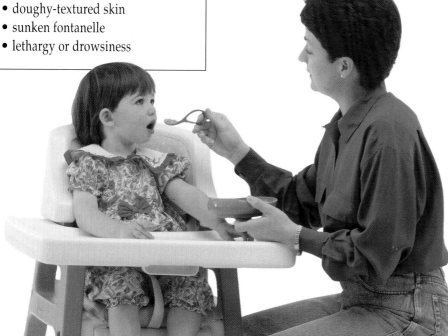

VOMITING

What is it?

Vomiting is a reflex action that causes the abdominal muscles and diaphragm to contract vigorously while the stomach is relaxed. It occurs when the "vomiting center" of the brain is stimulated: Your child may vomit because her gastrointestinal tract is irritated or swollen by infection; because of chemicals such as those in a medication in her blood; because of an inner ear disturbance, as in motion sickness; or because of psychological stimuli from unpleasant sights or smells.

Don't confuse vomiting with regurgitation; vomiting is the forceful throwing up of the stomach's contents, whereas regurgitation is the easy flow of the stomach's contents out of the mouth and is frequently accompanied by a burp. Sometimes infants regurgitate after swallowing air when feeding, overfeeding, or being fed too quickly. If your baby is otherwise in good health, this is nothing to worry about; the tendency to spit up after feeding will cease by the time she is walking.

What can I do?

If your child repeatedly vomits or her vomiting is accompanied by other troubling symptoms, call your pediatrician. Fortunately, most episodes of vomiting run their course within a day or two without complications. In those cases, giving your child plenty of reassurance and replacing her lost fluids with electrolyte solution are your best responses. Don't give her any medication unless you're advised to by the pediatrician. Your child may continue to be breastfed, but don't let her feed for as long as you usually do. If she is on a bottle, substitute small amounts of water or an electrolyte solution for the next eight hours. Start with a teaspoon every 10 minutes, then double the amount after each hour. After eight hours, if her vomiting has stopped, you can resume feeding her formula, but give her one to two ounces less than usual. For an older child, stop solid foods for eight hours and offer small amounts of clear fluids: one teaspoon to one tablespoon every 10 minutes, then double the amount after every hour. If she vomits again, don't give her anything for an hour in order to rest her stomach. Then, start the clear liquids over again. After your child has gone for eight hours without vomiting, she can begin to eat bland foods. Within a day, she is likely to be able to eat normally again.

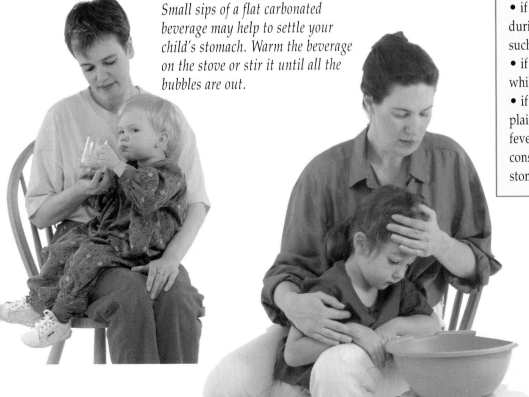

Small sips of a flat carbonated beverage may help to settle your child's stomach. Warm the beverage on the stove or stir it until all the bubbles are out.

> **CALL THE DOCTOR**
> • if your baby vomits repeatedly or vomits and has diarrhea
> • if your child is unable to keep anything down for six hours
> • if your child doesn't urinate for eight hours
> • if your child's vomit is bloody
> • if your child vomits after an injury
> • if your child's vomiting occurs during recovery from a viral illness such as chicken pox
> • if your child vomits repeatedly while taking medication
> • if your child vomits and complains of drowsiness, headache, high fever, breathing difficulties, sharp or constant abdominal pain, bloated stomach, or painful urination

Throwing up can be a frightening experience for a young child. Reassure her that she'll feel better soon and you'll keep her company until she does.

CONSTIPATION

What should I look for?

If your child is constipated, he'll have fewer bowel movements than he normally does. His stools will be unusually hard and dry; they'll be difficult to pass and may cause him pain. A child who feels pressured to be toilet-trained or worries about having accidents may develop constipation in response. In many instances, constipation may be the result of stress or a change in routine—for example, anxiety about using a public washroom or the introduction of a new food in the diet.

What can I do?

Become familiar with your child's normal pattern of bowel movements. Toilet habits vary widely; while some children pass stools two or three times daily, others have bowel movements every other day or once every five or six days. If he strains to pass bowel movements that are larger than normal, consult your pediatrician about altering his diet. For a baby under four months, a half ounce or so of prune juice may help the situation. If he's older, you may be advised to eliminate cooked carrots, bananas, apples, white rice, or milk products from his diet for a while and substitute high-fiber foods such as whole wheat cereal, bran, strained peas, beans, cauliflower, broccoli, and spinach. Fruits such as apricots, pears, peaches, and plums also are good sources of fiber. While your child is constipated, make sure he drinks lots of fluids—especially water and fruit juices. Don't be tempted to use oral laxatives; they may cause cramps and their overuse can lead to dependency. Enemas and suppositories can irritate the anus and cause tears; avoid them as well, unless your pediatrician advises you to use them.

REGULARITY TIPS

- Encourage your child to drink plenty of water.
- Include foods high in fiber in your child's diet. For example, serve bran muffins or cereal at breakfast, sandwiches of whole wheat bread at lunch, or brown rice at dinner. For snacks, provide graham crackers, popcorn, raw vegetables, or fresh fruit.
- Be sure your child understands that he may go to the toilet whenever he feels the need to and may stay there for as long as he wants.
- Don't start toilet-training your child before he's ready; avoid being insistent or overly enthusiastic so he doesn't feel pressured.
- Encourage your child to be physically active.

CALL THE DOCTOR

- if your child is in extreme pain
- if your child is in constant pain for more than two hours
- if your child has infrequent bowel movements of large, dry stools
- if your child frequently passes hard stools
- if your child strains but cannot pass a stool
- if your child soils involuntarily between passes of hard stools
- if your child's stool is bloody

If your child complains of discomfort when having a bowel movement, give her a warm bath. Holding her knees against her chest will help relax the anus so she can more easily push stool out.

GASTROENTERITIS

What should I look for?
Nausea, vomiting, diarrhea, and possibly a fever are signs of gastroenteritis. An inflammation of the lining of the stomach and intestines, gastroenteritis is usually caused by a viral infection, but can result from a bacterial infection. Spoiled food may be the source of a bacterial infection; go over what your child has eaten to pinpoint the source.

What can I do?
Keep him at home until all the symptoms are gone; encourage him to rest and drink plenty of fluids—including an oral electrolyte solution. If he's under two, be aware that he is particularly vulnerable to dehydration from vomiting or diarrhea. Make sure that he drinks at least two pints of liquid a day. When he's ready to eat again, serve him bland foods. Strained bananas, applesauce, and rice cereal are appropriate for babies. Older children also may eat mashed potatoes, bread and honey, and saltine crackers. If he cannot drink enough to keep up with his diarrheal or vomiting losses, if you are concerned that he may be dehydrated, or if his symptoms persist for more than two days, consult your pediatrician.

URINARY TRACT INFECTIONS

What is it?
Urinary tract infections, a not uncommon ailment in children, are usually bacterial in origin. More girls get them than boys because the female urethra is not only closer to the anus but is also shorter allowing bacteria to move more easily into the bladder. In children, the bacteria infecting the tract tends to come from fecal matter.

What should I look for?
In newborns, watch for listlessness, fever, a reluctance to feed, and jaundice; in infants, frequent or dribbling urination, fever, squirming, and irritability; and in children over the age of one year, watch for frequent or painful urination, dribbling, or urine that is bloody or foul-smelling. There also may be a recurrence of bed-wetting, a pus-like discharge in the urine, and fever.

What can I do?
If you think your child has a urinary infection, take him to your pediatrician for a urine analysis. If a bacterial urinary tract infection is confirmed, antibiotics will be prescribed. Make sure that you give your child the full course of medication. Depending on his age, your child may need radiologic studies of their urinary system. If he's still in diapers, change him frequently.

Encourage an older child to empty his bladder completely each time he urinates; it may help him to try a second time after waiting a few minutes. Teach your daughter to wipe herself from front to back to help prevent a recurrence. For fever or painful urination, give the recommended dose of acetaminophen. Make sure he drinks lots of fluids; water and cranberry juice are both good.

Cranberry juice is recommended for urinary tract infections because the high acid content will neutralize the alkaline environment in which the bacteria thrive.

CALL THE DOCTOR
• if your child is taking antibiotics for a urinary tract infection and develops a fever higher than 101°F

MOTION SICKNESS

What should I look for?
Sometimes the movement from riding in a car, boat, or plane or from going on an amusement park ride disturbs the balance of fluids in the canals of the inner ear and makes a child feel sick. During and after a trip, watch your child for symptoms such as sweating, dizziness, nausea, and vomiting. Watching passing scenery tends to exacerbate the nausea, as do strong odors such as tobacco smoke and engine fumes. Fortunately, most children outgrow motion sickness as their nervous system matures and is better able to cope with the effects of movement.

What can I do?
Ask your doctor about an over-the-counter medication to give your child an hour before traveling. During the trip, repeat the dosage according to the instructions. Be aware that the medication may induce drowsiness. Take along tissues and a resealable plastic bag in case of vomiting. If she starts to look queasy, help calm her stomach by giving her small sips of a clear liquid—flat carbonated beverages are best. Chewing gum and soda crackers or other mildly salty foods also may stave off the nausea. Some children are helped by distractions such as songs or word games.

TRAVEL TIPS
• In cars, open a window—at least a crack. Sit her in the middle of the back seat or in the front seat to help keep her from looking out the side windows. Don't let her read.
• On planes, request seats over the wings and in the center of the aircraft where the ride is a little smoother and more stable.
• On boats, keep her on the deck level. In a motor boat, seat her at the center, toward the bow and away from exhaust fumes.

APPENDICITIS

What is it?
Appendicitis is the severe inflammation of the appendix, the small, hollow, finger-shaped branch that extends out from the beginning of the large intestine. Sometimes the channel inside the appendix becomes blocked, trapping hardened feces inside. Inflammation and infection result. If untreated, a diseased appendix may rupture, puncturing the intestine and spreading feces and bacterial infection into the abdominal cavity.

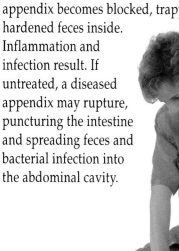

What should I look for?
If your child complains of lower right abdominal pain or pain around her navel that next shifts to the lower right side of the abdomen and has a fever of 100°F or higher, she may have appendicitis; in some cases, the pain is not localized, so don't take chances. Other signs include loss of appetite; nausea and vomiting that come on after the

A child with appendicitis will usually complain of pain that is felt first in her stomach around the navel.

pain begins; diarrhea; an accelerated heartbeat; and more frequent urination or a burning sensation while urinating.

What can I do?
If you think your child may have appendicitis, call your pediatrician; for acute appendicitis, emergency surgery may be required to remove the appendix. In the meantime, don't give her any food and make sure that she drinks only small amounts of clear fluids. Monitor her temperature every two hours but avoid giving her any medication unless you're instructed to do so by her pediatrician.

CALL THE DOCTOR
• if your child complains of lower abdominal pain for more than two hours, develops nausea or vomits, and runs a fever of 100°F or higher

Hernias

What should I look for?

A lump around your child's navel or groin region may indicate a hernia. Hernias occur when part of one of the internal organs protrudes through an opening in the abdominal muscles or the lining of the abdominal cavity, called the peritoneum.

Umbilical hernias are usually diagnosed at birth from a small round bulge in the center of the child's navel that becomes more evident when she cries or tenses her body. It normally feels soft to the touch and causes the baby no pain. An umbilical hernia develops when the gap in the stomach muscle below the navel does not close completely after birth. It also may develop because of a weakness in the abdominal wall or because there is an abnormal separation in the wall's muscle layers. In any case, the result is that part of the infant's intestine pushes up under the navel, creating a lump.

If your child has an inguinal hernia, you will notice a round bulge, usually in the groin by the right leg crease. It too will increase in size when she cries or strains. In older children, inguinal hernias may appear suddenly after strenuous exercise or develop gradually throughout the day. Inguinal hernias occur in boys more than girls and are likely to appear as an enlargement of the scrotum. They arise when the peritoneum does not develop properly in utero and leaves a small sac protruding into the inguinal canal—the small, muscle-lined corridor that runs from the abdomen to the groin. As a result, part of the intestines may poke into the sac, producing a bulge—usually on the right side of the groin. The bulge may be small or large. In most cases, it will cause little discomfort. Never try to reduce or cure a hernia of any kind by strapping on a support, band, belt, or truss.

What can I do?

Don't worry too much if your baby is diagnosed with an umbilical hernia; the chances are it will disappear gradually over the next few years as the gap in the muscle wall closes. As long as a temporary reduction in the swelling can be accomplished by gently pushing the hernia back through the abdominal wall, there is no problem. If the hernia lasts beyond her fifth birthday or if it begins to cause her pain, your pediatrician may advise surgical correction.

If you notice a lump in your child's groin or scrotum, report it immediately to your pediatrician. Inguinal hernias require surgical correction, but the operation is fairly routine and most children are treated as outpatients.

CALL THE DOCTOR
- if you detect a bulge in your child's groin or abdomen
- if your child has a hernia and develops pain or redness on the lower abdomen, and becomes constipated or vomits
- if your child has an umbilical or an inguinal hernia that hardens or becomes painful, seek emergency medical treatment immediately

---

If you suspect an inguinal hernia, check by gently pressing his stomach while he's crying. If a round bulge appears in the groin area, consult your pediatrician.

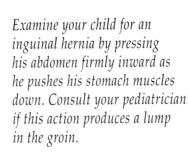

Examine your child for an inguinal hernia by pressing his abdomen firmly inward as he pushes his stomach muscles down. Consult your pediatrician if this action produces a lump in the groin.

INFECTIOUS DISEASES

MEASLES

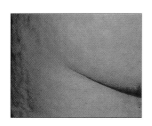

What is it?
Measles is a highly contagious viral illness that is contagious for up to six days before and four days after the rash appears. Immunity is granted by the MMR vaccine, usually given to children at around 12 to 15 months. Make sure immunizations are up-to-date.

Soothe her itchy, sensitive eyes by dabbing them with a clean, wet cotton ball, and dim the lighting in her room.

What should I look for?
The first symptoms of measles develop a week or so after exposure to the virus and are likely to be red, itchy eyes that are sensitive to light, fever, a brassy cough, and a runny nose. Several days later, white specks will appear in his mouth followed by a blotchy, angry-looking, red rash at the hairline and behind the ears. The rash then moves to the face and trunk.

What can I do?
There's not much you can do except help your child feel less miserable—and watch carefully for any sign of complications. He'll probably want to stay in bed while the fever is high. Give him plenty of liquids along with the recommended dose of acetaminophen. The rash will last about a week or so, but after four days he's likely to start feeling better.

CALL THE DOCTOR
- if you think your child has measles
- if your child has any breathing difficulties or is dehydrated
- if your child exhibits symptoms of encephalitis—lethargy, stiff neck, severe headache, and convulsions

RUBELLA

What is it?
Also known as German measles, rubella can cause serious birth defects in an unborn child. A child with rubella is contagious for several days before and about seven days after the appearance of the rash. Immunity to the virus is granted by the MMR vaccine, which is usually given to children at around 12 to 15 months.

CALL THE DOCTOR
- if your child's rash bleeds openly or into the skin
- if your child exhibits symptoms of encephalitis, which include extreme lethargy, stiffness of the neck, severe headache, and convulsions

What should I look for?
Symptoms of rubella appear some 16 days after exposure to the virus. Watch for swollen, tender lymph nodes at the back of the neck and base of the skull, and slightly raised, pink-red spots that merge into large patches. The rash, which varies from child to child, first appears on the face and then spreads to the rest of the body over the next 24 hours. He probably will suffer a fever for less than two days.

What can I do?
Keep him at home to rest and don't let him near any woman who might be pregnant. Give him plenty of fluids and, for a fever over 102°F, the recommended dose of acetaminophen.

ROSEOLA

What is it?
Roseola is a viral infection that usually affects children between the ages of six months and three years. The symptoms of roseola appear within seven to 17 days of exposure to the virus and your child will be mildly contagious until after the fever is gone.

CALL THE DOCTOR
- if your child's fever persists for more than four days
- if your child complains of an earache, develops a cough, or becomes lethargic

What should I look for?
Roseola is rarely serious. The main thing to watch for is fever, which comes on suddenly and lasts three to five days; it may go as high as 105°F. A small percentage of patients will have a seizure or convulsion associated with the fever. Your child also may have a poor appetite and be sleepy. When his temperature returns to normal, a patchy, rosy red, slightly bumpy rash may emerge on his trunk and spread to his arms and neck; if you press on the patches, they will turn white. After a day or two, the rash will start to fade. Occasionally, a child also may develop redness in the throat, a runny nose, or swollen glands in the neck.

What can I do?
Treat your child's fever by giving him the recommended dose of acetaminophen and provide him with plenty of fluids to drink. Dress him in cool, light-weight cotton clothing. If his fever goes above 104°F and acetaminophen isn't alleviating it, give him a sponge bath in lukewarm water.

FIFTH DISEASE

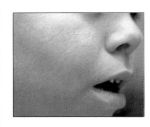

What is it?
Fifth disease is a moderately contagious viral infection. Symptoms appear from four to 14 days after exposure to the virus and it is most contagious in the week before the rash appears. By the time the rash is evident, your child will no longer be contagious.

What should I look for?
If you think your child has been exposed to the virus, watch for a bright red rash on both cheeks that is raised and warm to the touch; a slightly raised, lacy, pink rash on the upper arms that spreads to the trunk, buttocks, and thighs; and mild cold symptoms such as a sore throat, runny nose, pink eyes, headache, and fatigue. The rash will fade after five or 10 days.

Keep him at home until he's feeling better. Once the fever is gone, he needn't stay in bed.

What can I do?
If you think your child has fifth disease, call your pediatrician, who may want to examine him to be certain that's what he has. Alleviate his cold symptoms as you would those of an ordinary cold. The rash may reappear and vanish again over a period of three to five weeks, triggered by warm baths, exercise, and sunlight.

CALL THE DOCTOR
- if your child's fever rises higher than 101°F
- if your child's rash becomes extremely itchy

What is it?
The symptoms of chicken pox appear 10 to 21 days after exposure to the varicella virus. Children are contagious from 24 hours before the rash appears until after all the sores are crusted over—about a week later. The rash begins as flat, red lesions that become pimplelike and then develop into small blisters—called vesicles—that break and become crusted and scabby.

What should I look for?
The first signs of chicken pox are usually a mild fever, headache, fatigue, and loss of appetite. A day later, a very itchy rash will appear on your child's torso before spreading to her face and the rest of her body. Every day for four or five days, new crops of pox will erupt. The sores also may occur on the mouth, the eyelids, and around the genital area. Her fever is likely to be highest on the third or fourth day, but will subside after most of the sores have crusted over.

CALL THE DOCTOR
- if there is pus in the scabs
- if there is bleeding into the pox
- if breathing becomes rapid, labored, or otherwise difficult
- if fever lasts more than four days
- if vomiting occurs
- if your child has a chronic medical condition or a serious illness
- if your child is now on or recently has taken steroids medication
- if your child exhibits symptoms of encephalitis, which include lethargy, stiffness of the neck, severe headache, and convulsions

What can I do?
As soon as you think that your child is coming down with chicken pox, consider your home under quarantine. Be prepared for the virus to spread to vulnerable siblings. Fortunately, one bout of chicken pox provides lifelong immunity against a recurrence.

When the rash emerges, soothe your child's itchiness by bathing her several times a day in a tub of tepid water with one-half cup baking soda or one-quarter cup cornstarch added. Use a clean towel each time to pat her dry; don't rub her skin as this will irritate the sores. Dab calamine lotion on the rash to ease minor itching. Severe itching that disturbs her sleep may require treatment with antihistamines. Treat any fever with acetaminophen—never aspirin. If she develops sores in her mouth, keep her away from salty foods and citrus fruits; give her soft, bland foods such as mashed potatoes, eggs, and jello. Get her to gargle with a cup of water that contains a half teaspoon of salt.

Although chicken pox looks terrible, for most children it is a mild disease. The marks usually fade within six to 12 months and scarring only occurs if the pox become infected with impetigo or if a child repeatedly picks off the vesicle crusts.

Dab your child's itchy skin with cotton balls dipped in calamine lotion. Soft, cotton clothing is best; change his clothes and bedsheets daily.

Discourage scratching by trimming your child's nails short, and wash her hands frequently with antibacterial soap. Put clean cotton socks over the hands of young children and babies to prevent them from scratching the sores in their sleep.

MUMPS

What should I look for?

Immunity to the mumps virus is granted by the MMR vaccine that children receive at around 15 months. If your child hasn't been immunized and complains of swollen glands, she may have caught mumps—especially if she's been exposed to them in the past two to three weeks. Gently feel her glands below the ears; the mumps virus causes swelling of the salivary glands, making it difficult to discern the jawbone with the fingertips. Before you notice the swelling, she may have had a fever and complained of a headache and possibly an earache. The swelling may make it uncomfortable to chew or swallow. Fortunately, mumps is a fairly mild disease for children; many who catch the illness do not even show signs of swelling. Children with mumps are contagious for two days before the first symptoms appear until about five days after the onset. Complications include neck stiffness and occasionally a boy entering puberty may develop an inflammation in the testicles; in such an instance, you should notify your pediatrician right away.

Make a cold compress by wrapping ice in a damp towel, then place it around her neck to help ease the pain and swelling of her glands.

What can I do?

Ice cream and jello are the kinds of smooth, soft foods your child will find soothing. Avoid sour foods and citrus foods or juices. You will want her to rest as much as possible and drink lots of clear liquids like apple juice or ginger ale. Give her the recommended dose of acetaminophen to ease her discomfort and help reduce any fever.

CALL THE DOCTOR
- if swelling continues for more than seven days
- if skin over swelling turns red
- if fever lasts more than five days
- if there is repeated vomiting or acute abdominal pain
- if your child experiences dizziness or difficulty hearing
- if your child exhibits symptoms of encephalitis, which include lethargy, stiffness of the neck, severe headache, and convulsions

WHOOPING COUGH

What should I look for?

Although the DTP vaccine greatly diminishes the chance of a child ever contracting whooping cough—also called pertussis—some of those vaccinated are still susceptible. Watch for cold symptoms and then the development of intense coughing spasms, followed by a whooplike sound as the child struggles to inhale. In whooping cough, the pertussis bacteria inflames the lining of the airways and causes the accumulation of mucous secretions, bringing on violent coughing fits.

What can I do?

If you suspect that your child has whooping cough, take her to your pediatrician immediately; if your suspicion is confirmed, antibiotics probably will be prescribed. Don't try to suppress her coughing spasms with cough medicine. Instead, comfort her during her coughing spells; their intensity can be frightening. If she vomits after coughing, make sure that you increase her fluid intake so she doesn't become dehydrated. The symptoms may continue on and off for three months or more.

CALL THE DOCTOR
- if your child is not immunized against whooping cough and is exposed to someone who has it
- if your child experiences severe difficulty breathing
- if your child turns blue, suffers a seizure, or loses consciousness during a coughing spell
- if your child shows symptoms of pneumonia—such as a wet cough with rusty or pinkish sputum

EMERGENCIES AND FIRST AID

Cuts, bruises, splinters, and sprains are all part of the normal legacy of growing up. A child's insatiable curiosity and immature understanding of danger are a volatile combination; there's no getting around the likelihood of at least a few mishaps. Fortunately, most of the injuries that may occur in the rough-and-tumble of daily life will require little more than a first-aid kit and your own common sense.

But all parents also should be familiar with a few basic emergency procedures, so that they can respond quickly and calmly if the need ever arises. Take the time now to familiarize yourself thoroughly with lifesaving procedures and techniques; you never know when you might be called on to handle an emergency. For information on family first-aid courses, contact your local community center or ask your pediatrician.

EMERGENCY READINESS

Household Preparedness
To prepare yourself and your home for an emergency:
• Take a certified first-aid course that includes hands-on training in mouth-to-mouth resuscitation and cardiopulmonary resuscitation (CPR).
• Equip your home with a well-stocked first-aid kit.

• Talk to your child's pediatrician about situations you should handle as emergencies and ask about emergency facilities available in your community.
• Post a list of emergency numbers by your telephones. Note all numbers that might be useful—such as your local hospital emergency room, your child's pediatrician, the police, the fire depart-

ment, and the regional poison-control center. Program emergency numbers into your speed-dial telephones.
• Display your home telephone number and address prominently. Include the nearest cross street.
• Learn the quickest route to the nearest hospital emergency room by making a few trial runs.

HOME FIRST-AID KIT
Every household should have at least one first-aid kit reserved for only emergency use. A well-stocked kit will contain the items displayed here. Label your kit clearly and store it well out of the reach of small children.

When traveling, take a first-aid kit with you. Keep duplicate kits in your car and at any place that you and your family spend a lot of time.

Never raid your first-aid kit for everyday medical supplies. If you use something, replace it as soon as possible. Check the expiration dates on perishable items regularly. Syrup of ipecac, for example, should be replaced annually.

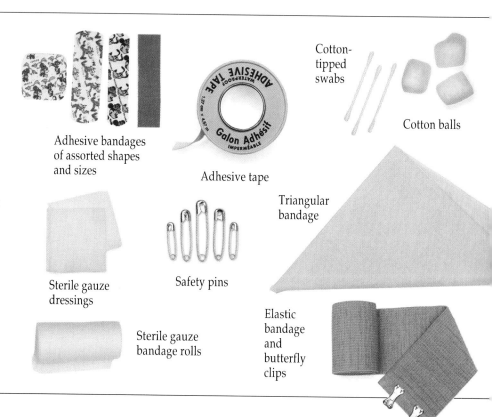

Adhesive bandages of assorted shapes and sizes

Adhesive tape

Cotton-tipped swabs

Cotton balls

Triangular bandage

Sterile gauze dressings

Safety pins

Sterile gauze bandage rolls

Elastic bandage and butterfly clips

Caregiver Preparedness

Whenever you leave your child in the care of someone else—whether a relative, friend, or hired baby-sitter—be sure to provide the following:

• a list of your child's allergies;
• details on any medication that your child is taking—including full instructions on how much and how often it should be given;
• a telephone number where you can be reached, as well as the numbers of two neighbors or relatives who can be contacted for help;
• the location of medical supplies and your household first-aid kit;
• a medical release form in which you authorize the provision of any essential emergency medical care that may be required at the request of the bearer.

Self Preparedness

In the event of a medical emergency, the correct actions taken quickly can sustain a life until medical help arrives. Stay calm; your child needs you to stay in control. The first step in providing assistance is always clear thinking and an unpanicked response. Attend to your child immediately, then telephone for medical assistance; if possible, instruct someone to make the call for you. Reassure your child that medical help is on the way.

CALLING 911

When you dial 911—or any other emergency number—immediately tell the person who answers that you're making an emergency call and give your name and address. Be prepared to provide information on the nature of the emergency and to describe actions that have been taken. In most areas of the U.S., 911 is linked to a computer system that tracks the address of the caller in the event that the caller cannot speak or the call is interrupted. Teach your child to call 911 in an emergency.

The following are among the medical emergencies that are life-threatening and require your immediate action:

• loss of consciousness (page 228);
• no breathing (page 230);
• no pulse (page 232);
• choking (page 235);
• uncontrollable bleeding (page 236);
• shock (page 247).

Familiarize yourself with the symptoms of medical emergencies and the procedures for handling them. Practice monitoring the body's vital life signs (page 228) and using the recovery position (page 234) so you're prepared in advance to cope with a potentially life-threatening situation.

GOING TO THE HOSPITAL

If you have to take your child to the hospital for emergency treatment, be sure to bring along:

• your pediatrician's phone number;
• your child's immunization record;
• any medication that your child currently is taking;
• your health insurance card.

Once you arrive at the hospital, tell the staff as much as you can about your child's condition. As well as a description of the signs and symptoms that worry you, they also need to know the time of the accident or onset of the illness and any first-aid procedures you may have tried.

Be aware that your child will be looking to you for support; try to appear calm and give him the comfort he needs. Even though he's sick or hurting, you may have to wait a while before he's attended to; emergency room staff give priority to the sickest or most seriously injured patients. However, if you feel your child's condition is getting worse, don't hesitate to speak up.

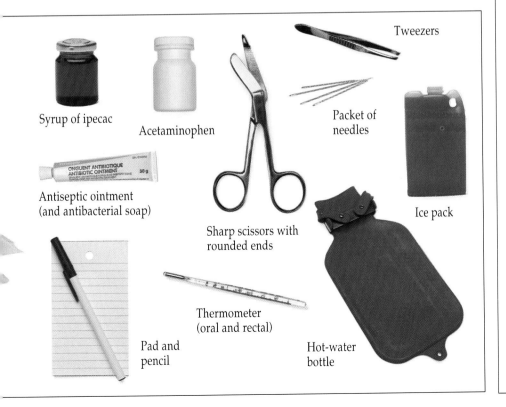

Syrup of ipecac

Acetaminophen

Tweezers

Packet of needles

Antiseptic ointment (and antibacterial soap)

Sharp scissors with rounded ends

Ice pack

Pad and pencil

Thermometer (oral and rectal)

Hot-water bottle

VITAL LIFE SIGNS

Monitoring Vital Signs

If your child falls seriously ill or suffers a severe injury, you'll need to monitor her vital signs carefully. This involves checking that she's conscious, she's breathing, and she has a pulse. Take immediate action to stabilize her condition at any absence of these signs.

Checking for Consciousness

Loss of consciousness results from a disturbance of the nervous or circulatory system. An unconscious child won't respond when spoken to or will be very confused; she'll have no muscle response or muscle response only to pain; and she won't open her eyes or will open them only when in pain or spoken to. If your child loses consciousness, check her breathing and pulse.

Checking for Breathing

Illness, injury, or an airway that is blocked by a foreign object can interfere with a child's ability to breathe. If your child stops breathing, you must immediately take over her breathing (page 230) to prevent brain damage.

Checking for Pulse

If your child has no pulse, an interference with her cardiovascular system has caused her heart to stop pumping blood throughout the body. A normal pulse is strong and regular. A weak or irregular pulse is an indication of a rapidly deteriorating physical condition that requires professional medical help. Only if there is no pulse at all should external compression on the chest (page 232) be attempted to start the heart beating again.

Checking for Fever

Fever is the body's normal response to infection. By activating the body's immune system, a fever increases the release and activity of disease-fighting white blood cells and other germ-killing substances. During a fever, excess heat is released by the body automatically in

1 To test your child's responsiveness, alert him with your voice and lightly pinch his earlobe; don't shake him—you may worsen an injury. If he doesn't respond, gently rub your knuckles on his breastbone. If you still don't get a response, he may have lost consciousness; check his breathing and pulse.

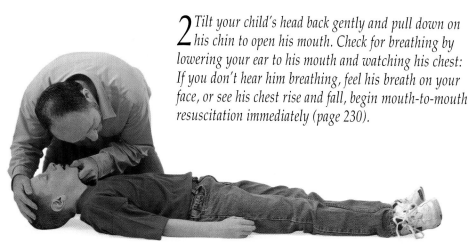

2 Tilt your child's head back gently and pull down on his chin to open his mouth. Check for breathing by lowering your ear to his mouth and watching his chest: If you don't hear him breathing, feel his breath on your face, or see his chest rise and fall, begin mouth-to-mouth resuscitation immediately (page 230).

3 Gently press the tips of your index and middle fingers into the hollow between your child's windpipe and neck muscles to feel for his pulse. If there isn't a pulse, begin CPR (page 232). If his pulse is weak or erratic, place him in the recovery position (page 234) and seek emergency medical help.

several ways—such as by flushing, sweating, and rapid breathing. A fever is a positive sign that the body is protecting itself, but the higher the body temperature, the more likely your child has an infection. Therefore, you should monitor a fever above 100°F every half hour to be sure that it doesn't get higher or last too long.

A fever below 102°F does not require treatment unless it is interfering with your child's normal eating, drinking, or sleeping habits, or causing discomfort. Treat a fever of 102°F or higher using only the recommended dose of acetaminophen. Never give aspirin for fever; it has been linked to a rare and serious illness called Reye's syndrome.

ASSESSING AN INFANT
(Up to 18 Months)

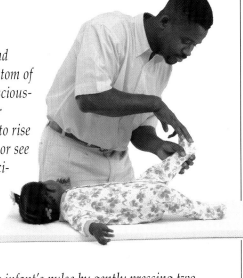

1 If your infant doesn't respond when you lightly tap the bottom of her foot, she may have lost consciousness. Put your head close to her mouth and watch for her chest to rise and fall. If you don't hear, feel, or see signs of breathing, begin resuscitation (page 231).

2 Take your infant's pulse by gently pressing two fingers on the inside of the upper arm, midway between her elbow and armpit. If there isn't a pulse, begin CPR (page 233).

HIGH FEVER

In most cases, you'll be able to reduce your child's fever by giving him regular doses of acetaminophen. Don't give him acetaminophen more than once every four hours or for more than three days in a row.

Consult your pediatrician before giving acetaminophen to a baby under the age of four months. For a child under two years of age, the correct dosage is determined by his weight:

• 6 to 12 pounds: 40 milligrams
• 12 to 18 pounds: 80 milligrams
• 18 to 24 pounds: 120 milligrams

For a child over two years old, the correct dosage can be estimated by age:

• 2 to 4 years: 160 milligrams
• 4 to 6 years: 240 milligrams
• 6 to 9 years: 320 milligrams
• 9 to 11 years: 400 milligrams
• after 11 years: 480 milligrams

When your child's fever rises above 104°F, however, don't wait for acetaminophen to take effect. Sit him in a bath of cool water or, if he's still a baby, just place him on a towel to sponge him down. Don't use cold water; it will only increase his fever and make him feel even more uncomfortable. Wet a sponge or washcloth and briskly rub his face, neck, stomach, and the inside creases of his knees and elbows where the blood vessels are most highly concentrated. Continue sponging for 20 minutes. If he begins to shiver, raise the water temperature. Pat him dry and dress him in thin cotton clothing.

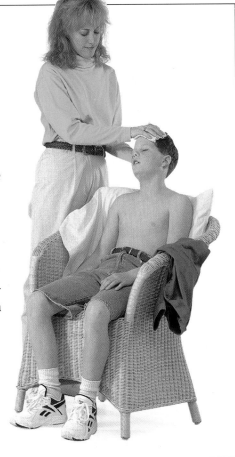

If he runs a high fever and thrashes around, don't try to get him into the bathtub. Sit or lie him down and sponge him on the spot.

MOUTH-TO-MOUTH RESUSCITATION

The Breath of Life

If your child stops breathing, you will need to breathe for him until he can breathe on his own. Restarting his breathing should take priority over any other emergency first-aid procedure. Check first to see if he's breathing (page 228). If he isn't breathing, lay him gently on his back on a flat surface, loosen his clothing at the neck and waist, and begin artificial respiration. (See the box on page 231 if the child is less than 18 months old.) Children have been known to be resuscitated after several hours, so don't give up.

WARNING

If your child may have injured his neck or spine, don't move him unless it's absolutely necessary. Check his breathing without repositioning him. If you must resuscitate him and he's lying on his stomach, get help to turn him onto his back without twisting his spine. Working with someone, you can support his neck and shoulders while at the same time carefully turning him over.

2 Inhale deeply. Place your open mouth over her mouth to form a tight seal. Give two one-second breaths, two seconds apart. Break contact with her mouth in between to let air flow out and to take a breath. If she has injured her mouth, close her mouth and breathe through her nostrils.

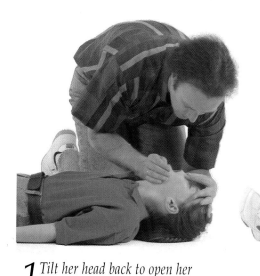

1 Tilt her head back to open her airway, pushing down gently on her forehead and lifting her chin; this action will move her tongue away from the back of the throat. Pinch her nostrils closed.

3 Watch her chest as you deliver each breath to see if it rises. If her chest rises, check her pulse (page 228). If she has a pulse, deliver one breath slowly every three seconds: Count "one one-thousand," take a breath yourself on "two one-thousand," and breathe into her on "three one-thousand." Check her pulse again after 20 breaths. Continue the cycle until she begins to breathe on her own or emergency help arrives.

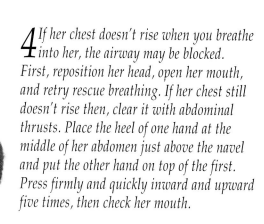

4 If her chest doesn't rise when you breathe into her, the airway may be blocked. First, reposition her head, open her mouth, and retry rescue breathing. If her chest still doesn't rise then, clear it with abdominal thrusts. Place the heel of one hand at the middle of her abdomen just above the navel and put the other hand on top of the first. Press firmly and quickly inward and upward five times, then check her mouth.

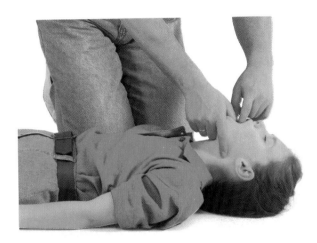

6 Tilt her head back again and deliver two more breaths, watching to see if her chest rises. If the airway remains blocked, repeat the cycle of abdominal thrusts, finger sweep, and two breaths until any obstruction is removed.

5 If there's an object visible in her mouth, remove it with a finger sweep. Place your thumb on her tongue to hold her mouth open, then slide your finger along the inside of one cheek, across the throat, and back along the other cheek to "hook" and pull out the object.

7 Once the airway is clear, keep delivering one breath slowly every three seconds until she starts breathing on her own or emergency help arrives. When she begins to breathe on her own, place her in the recovery position (page 234).

HELPING AN INFANT
(Up to 18 Months)

1 Place your baby on his back. Tilt his head back by gently lifting his chin and pushing down on his forehead. This will open the airway by drawing his tongue away from the back of the throat.

2 Place your open mouth over your baby's mouth and nose, making a tight seal. Deliver a light, one-second breath, watching his chest to see if it rises. Don't deliver a full, deep breath; you may force air into his stomach and make him vomit. Take a breath and give another breath, then remove your mouth to let air flow out.

3 Check the pulse (page 229). If he has one, give one light breath every three seconds for one minute. After these 20 breaths, check his pulse again. Repeat the cycle until he starts to breath on his own or help arrives. If the chest doesn't rise when you breathe into him, reposition his head and repeat step 2. If his chest still doesn't rise, the airway may be blocked; treat for choking (page 235).

CARDIOPULMONARY RESUSCITATION

Restarting the Heart

Cardiopulmonary resuscitation—or CPR—is a lifesaving technique used to start a heart that has stopped beating. CPR allows you both to breathe for the child and to manually pump her heart with external compressions to the chest to start it beating on its own again. When a heart stops beating, it's usually the result of a breathing emergency that has deprived the blood of oxygen and starved the heart.

An emergency requiring the use of CPR may be caused by choking, smoke inhalation, a severe respiratory infection, near drowning, or suffocation. Reading about CPR is not enough. In order to be certified in CPR, you must receive formal training in a course certified by the American Red Cross. All parents of young children are advised to take a CPR course; the information presented here is not a substitute for proper training and practice.

WARNING
- Do not perform CPR on a child whose heart is beating.
- Don't move a child who may have a back or neck injury unless it's absolutely necessary. If you must do CPR, get help to hold her head, neck, and shoulders in position so that she can be turned onto her back with no twisting of her spine.
- Call for emergency help if your child loses consciousness, stops breathing, or doesn't have a pulse.

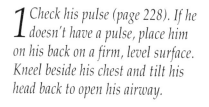

1 Check his pulse (page 228). If he doesn't have a pulse, place him on his back on a firm, level surface. Kneel beside his chest and tilt his head back to open his airway.

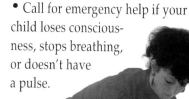

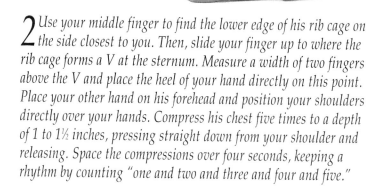

2 Use your middle finger to find the lower edge of his rib cage on the side closest to you. Then, slide your finger up to where the rib cage forms a V at the sternum. Measure a width of two fingers above the V and place the heel of your hand directly on this point. Place your other hand on his forehead and position your shoulders directly over your hands. Compress his chest five times to a depth of 1 to 1½ inches, pressing straight down from your shoulder and releasing. Space the compressions over four seconds, keeping a rhythm by counting "one and two and three and four and five."

3 Keeping his head tilted back, lift his chin and pinch his nostrils. Seal your mouth on his and give one slow breath until his chest rises. Repeat the cycle of five compressions and one breath 10 times—this should take about one minute.

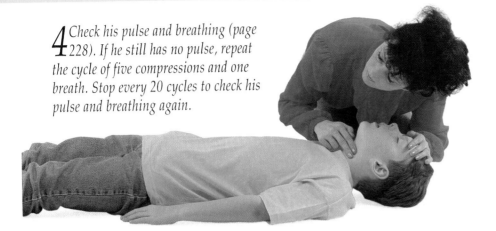

4 Check his pulse and breathing (page 228). If he still has no pulse, repeat the cycle of five compressions and one breath. Stop every 20 cycles to check his pulse and breathing again.

5 As soon as he has a pulse, stop delivering chest compressions and check his breathing. If he isn't breathing, give him mouth-to-mouth resuscitation (page 230) until he breathes on his own or emergency help arrives. When he starts breathing on his own, place him in the recovery position (page 234).

HELPING AN INFANT
(Up to 18 Months)

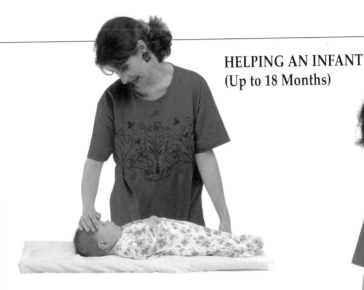

2 Compress your baby's chest five times to a depth of ½ to 1 inch, pressing straight down with your fingers and releasing. Space the five compressions over three seconds, keeping a rhythm by counting "one and two and three and four and five."

1 If your baby doesn't have a pulse, place her on her back on a firm surface. Gently tilt her head back to open her airway. Locate the center of her breastbone by drawing an imaginary line between her nipples, then place the tips of your middle and ring fingers one finger's width below the center of this line.

3 Keeping your fingers in position on your baby's chest, seal her mouth and nose with your mouth. Deliver one light breath slowly until her chest rises. Repeat the cycle of five compressions and one breath 20 times—this should take about one minute. Then, check her pulse and breathing (page 229). If she still has no pulse, repeat the cycle of five compressions and one breath. Stop every 20 cycles to check her pulse and breathing again.

4 As soon as your baby has a pulse, stop giving chest compressions and check her breathing. If she isn't breathing, give her artificial respiration (page 231) until she breathes on her own or emergency help arrives.

RECOVERY POSITION

Keeping the Airway Clear

Place your child in the recovery position if he is unconscious but breathing and has no evidence of trauma—unless you think he might have injured his neck or back (for example, in a fall or a car accident). When he is in the recovery position, his tongue cannot fall back into the throat to obstruct his breathing and he won't choke on any blood or vomit. Cover him with a blanket or coat, call for help, and stay with him until emergency help arrives. Monitor his vital signs (page 228) every three minutes.

(page 228)

> **WARNING**
> Don't move your child into the recovery position if you suspect that he may have suffered an injury to his neck or spine.

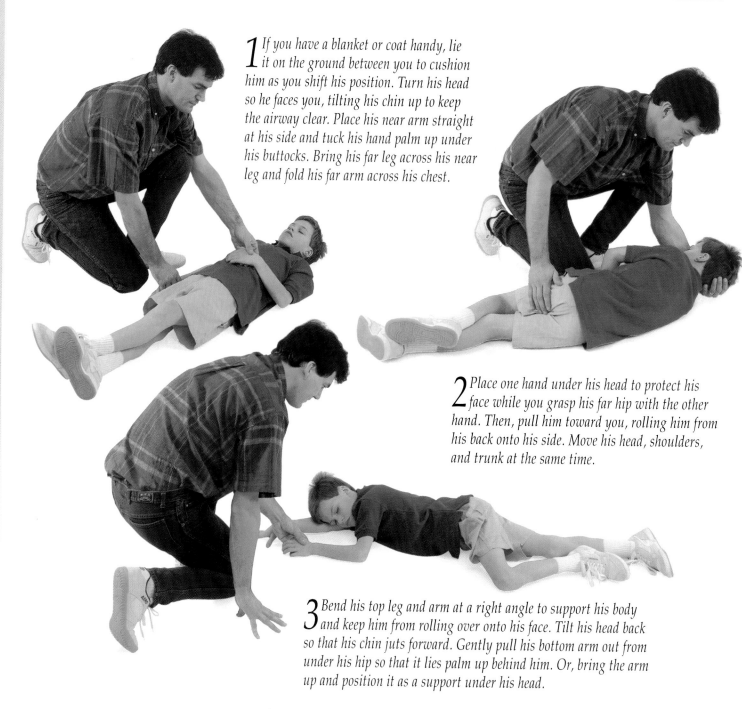

1 *If you have a blanket or coat handy, lie it on the ground between you to cushion him as you shift his position. Turn his head so he faces you, tilting his chin up to keep the airway clear. Place his near arm straight at his side and tuck his hand palm up under his buttocks. Bring his far leg across his near leg and fold his far arm across his chest.*

2 *Place one hand under his head to protect his face while you grasp his far hip with the other hand. Then, pull him toward you, rolling him from his back onto his side. Move his head, shoulders, and trunk at the same time.*

3 *Bend his top leg and arm at a right angle to support his body and keep him from rolling over onto his face. Tilt his head back so that his chin juts forward. Gently pull his bottom arm out from under his hip so that it lies palm up behind him. Or, bring the arm up and position it as a support under his head.*

CHOKING

What can I do?

Peanuts, buttons, and marbles are just a few of the things a young child may try to swallow. If your child begins to choke, your first step is to clear his windpipe. Usually, he'll try to cough up the object, but sometimes it can become lodged as he gasps for breath. Several firm blows with the heel of your hand to his back between the shoulders may be enough to dislodge the object. But if he still has breathing difficulty, you will need to perform the steps shown below.

> **EMERGENCY**
> Seek medical help immediately if:
> - your child stops breathing
> - your child continues choking after the object is removed
> - you cannot dislodge the object

1 Position yourself behind your child; if possible, sit her on your lap. Wrap your arms around her waist. Bend your thumb so you can grip it with your fingers to make a fist. Place the fist against her stomach, slightly above the navel.

2 Hold your fist with your other hand and press quickly six to 10 times in a rolling, inward-and-upward direction against her stomach. Once she expels the object, check her breathing (page 228).

HELPING AN INFANT (Up to 18 Months)

Your baby may flail as he gasps for air, so be careful not to drop him. Turn him facedown, resting him on your forearm with his head lower than his body. Deliver five sharp blows between his shoulder blades using the heel of your hand. Then, turn him over and support his head below his body. Place two fingers just below the center of his breastbone and press to a depth of 1 inch five times in quick succession.

3 If she doesn't expel the object and if you can see it, use your finger to sweep along the inside of one cheek and across the throat to "hook" and extract it. Be careful not to push it farther down.

BLEEDING

What can I do?

For heavy bleeding—particularly if the wound is bleeding in spurts—your priority is to stem the flow of blood long enough to give the blood a chance to clot. Lie your child down with her feet elevated about a foot. Place several sterile dressings over the wound and use the palm of your hand to apply forceful and continuous pressure to stop the bleeding. If the dressing becomes soaked through with blood, place another dressing on top of the first. Continue to apply pressure with your hand or with an elastic bandage over the dressing until the bleeding stops or your child can be treated by emergency medical personnel. If you do not have a clean dressing available, use your fingers to draw the edges of the wound together and press firmly with your hand. Raise a bleeding limb that isn't broken above the level of the heart.

If your child receives a hard blow to her torso, stomach, or chest, watch for signs of internal bleeding, which will require immediate medical help. Signs of internal bleeding may include: reddish vomit that may have what looks like coffee grounds; coughing up red, foamy blood; stools containing blood or a tarlike substance; and abdominal pain. If your child exhibits these signs, lie her down and call for emergency help. While you wait, keep her warm and as comfortable as possible, but don't give her anything to eat or drink.

Your comforting words and calm voice will soothe your child, who may well be frightened by the sight of blood.

CUTS AND ABRASIONS

Your child's cuts and scrapes usually will be treatable at home using your first-aid kit; most won't need more than soap and water. As an added precaution, use a three-percent hydrogen peroxide solution—not iodine—as an antiseptic. If you think a cut may scar or that it has damaged a nerve or tendon, take your child to see your pediatrician. Watch for signs of infection; a cut that oozes pus, is extensively red or swollen, or causes a fever may need to be treated with antibiotics. Keep your child's tetanus shots up to date and consult your pediatrician if he gets punctured by a rusty nail or his cut is contaminated by street dirt or manure.

1 Rinse the wound under running water to get rid of loose dirt, then wash it thoroughly with water and a mild soap. Rinse again and pat dry with a clean towel.

2 Draw the edges of a cut together with an adhesive bandage and keep the area dry. Leave large, shallow scrapes uncovered. For a deep scrape, apply a dressing of sterile gauze and hold it in place with adhesive tape.

BRUISING

What can I do?
A bruise is a purplish black-and-blue mark indicating that tiny blood vessels have ruptured and are bleeding into the skin. As the blood coagulates and the body absorbs the clot, the bruise will fade to a yellow-green color.

You can help to soothe your child's pain and reduce the swelling by applying a cold pack—ice or an ice bag wrapped in a soft, damp cloth—to the bruise.

Encourage her to rest the injured limb while she holds an ice pack wrapped in a soft cloth against it. Don't put ice directly on the bruise.

If no ice is available, use a soft cloth soaked in very cold water. If she bruises her eye, apply the cold pack and call your pediatrician. If she bumps her head, check the skin under the cold pack every minute—if a red patch with a waxy white center forms, remove the pack. Watch for signs of a possible internal head injury.

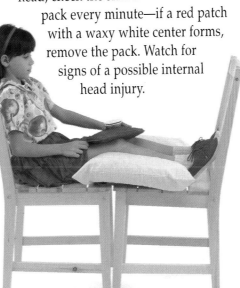

EMERGENCY
Seek medical help immediately if:
• your child is in acute pain or bruising is extensive
• your child's bruise is near an eye—especially if vision is affected
• your child has difficulty moving a severely bruised limb or joint
• your child has a pinched and bruised fingernail or toenail
• your child's bruise is out of proportion to the strength of the blow or your child develops bruises for no apparent reason
• your child may have suffered a concussion or skull fracture
• your child develops a fever

HEAD INJURIES

If you can't rouse him, call your pediatrician or take him to a hospital emergency department immediately.

can't rouse her, check her vital signs (page 228) and call for emergency help.

If your child cuts her head, place a clean dressing over the wound and apply pressure to control the bleeding; even a superficial cut to the head may bleed a lot. Clean minor cuts or scrapes, but don't clean a deep scalp wound. Instead, secure a dressing over the wound with bandages and take her to the nearest hospital. If the blow breaks a tooth, put it in milk and take it to the hospital with you.

What can I do?
If your child receives a blow to the head, monitor her carefully for 24 hours in case she has suffered a skull fracture or a concussion—where the brain is shaken in the skull. When she sleeps, wake her up every three hours; if you

EMERGENCY
Seek medical help immediately if any of the following symptoms develop after a head injury:
• loss of consciousness
• drowsiness and confusion
• convulsions
• repeated vomiting
• difficulty breathing or speaking
• severe and persistent headache
• unequal pupil size or painful sensitivity to light
• bruised appearance around the eyes or behind the ears
• clear or bloody discharge from the nose or ears

FRACTURES

What should I look for?

After an accident, examine your child for painful, swollen, discolored, or visibly crooked limbs. If he's unable or reluctant to use an injured limb or he experiences intense pain, numbness, tingling, or a low pulse in the injured area, suspect a fracture. Also, a snapping sound may have been heard at the time of the accident. Wrists, elbows, and collarbones are common sites for broken bones. Fortunately, since the bones of young children are still soft and pliable, they usually heal fairly quickly.

What can I do?

To prevent further damage to your child's nerves and blood vessels, immobilize the injured limb in the same position that you find it. If there's heavy bleeding, apply immediate pressure to control it. If a bone protrudes from a wound, carefully cover it with a sterile cloth. Don't give your child anything to eat or drink, and get him to the hospital as quickly as you can.

EMERGENCY

Call for medical help or take your child to the hospital immediately after you have given first aid for a suspected fracture.

Immobilize a leg by splinting it to the uninjured leg. Place a rolled up towel or sweater between the legs to provide padding. Use strips of cloth to tie the legs together above and below the injury from hip to ankle.

3 To fully immobilize the injured arm, bind it to his chest. Wrap swathes of cloth around him and knot them under his uninjured arm.

IMMOBILIZING AN ARM

1 Make a splint with a rolled up magazine or another stiff material. Tie the splint above and below the injury with cloth strips, making sure it isn't too tight. Make a sling by draping a large cloth or shirt around his neck and down the front behind the injured arm.

2 Fasten the sling by tying the ends of the cloth or the sleeves of the shirt together at his shoulder or behind his neck. Tuck away excess fabric at the elbow and fasten it with a safety pin.

SPRAINS AND STRAINS

What should I look for?

Sprained joints swell and look bruised. Wrists and ankles are the most vulnerable joints, but knees get damaged, too, especially on young athletes. A strained muscle, although painful, will probably neither swell nor bruise.

What can I do?

Treat a sprained wrist, ankle, or knee with RICE—rest, ice, compression, and

Apply an ice pack to a sprained joint to help ease the swelling, then wrap it in an elastic bandage. Make sure your child rests the joint until the swelling and pain subsides. As the joint heals, encourage him to move the limb gently in all directions to help ease stiffness.

elevation. To make sure that the injury is a sprain and not a fracture, consult your pediatrician.

If your child strains a muscle, have him rest the injury. Provide him with a hot-water bottle or a warm compress to soothe the aching muscle.

> **EMERGENCY**
> Seek medical help immediately if:
> • a broken bone is suspected
> • a sprained knee moves from side to side or cannot be straightened

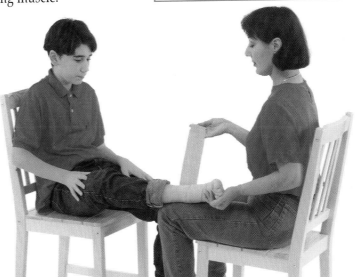

ANIMAL BITES

What can I do?

Wash the bite thoroughly with mild soap and water. If the skin is broken or the wound is bleeding, cover the bite with a sterile dressing and apply pressure. Then, apply a clean dressing over the wound and secure it with adhesive tape. Watch the wound carefully for signs of infection—such as swelling or reddening of the skin. Make sure that your child is seen by your pediatrician for any bite that breaks the skin.

Rabies is the greatest danger from an animal bite. If it's at all possible, trap the animal so it can be taken for rabies testing. If you can't capture and contain the animal safely yourself, call your local animal authorities or the police.

> **EMERGENCY**
> Seek medical help immediately if the wound of a bite bleeds profusely or you suspect the animal has rabies.

Most bites are minor, but the experience can be terrifying to a young child. He may need a lot of reassurance before he gets his confidence back.

> **TETANUS**
> Immunity to the disease tetanus is provided by the Diptheria Tetanus Pertussis (DTP) vaccination that most children get during their early years. Make sure your child receives his DTP vaccination and follow-up boosters. If he gets a puncture wound from an animal bite or a rusty nail, or gets street dirt or manure trapped under the skin, your pediatrician may recommend that he be given a booster.

EMBEDDED OBJECTS

What can I do?

If your child gets bits of dirt or gravel in a cut, a careful wash in warm, soapy water will probably get rid of the debris. Apply gentle pressure to the skin around the cut to encourage further bleeding to clean the wound. Once you're sure all the bits have been removed, disinfect the cut with three-percent hydrogen peroxide solution and cover it with a sterile bandage. Check it several times a day to make sure it stays clean. Wash the wound again, if necessary, and watch for signs of infection. If pus, swelling, tenderness, reddening, or red streaks develop, consult your pediatrician.

If your child happens to get something such as a shard of glass or piece of sharp metal lodged deeply in her skin, don't try to pull it out. Instead, immobilize the object as best you can by wrapping sterile gauze around—but not on top—of it. Control any bleeding by applying gentle pressure to the area around the object. If you can, keep the injured limb elevated higher than the level of your child's heart while you take her immediately to the hospital for treatment.

Don't remove anything embedded in your child's eye. Protect the eye by taping a sterile gauze pad loosely in place and seek emergency treatment immediately.

EMERGENCY

Seek medical help immediately if:
- your child gets a foreign object embedded in the eye
- your child gets a puncture wound to the chest, abdomen, or a joint—such as the knee or elbow
- your child gets a deep puncture wound

FISHHOOKS AND SPLINTERS

If your child gets a fishhook embedded in his skin, the best thing to do is gently push the hook farther in the same direction it went in until the barb pokes out from the skin. Then, use wire cutters or pliers to snip off the barb and carefully pull the shaft of the hook back out. Wash the injured area thoroughly in warm, soapy water and cover the punctured skin with a sterile bandage. Consult your pediatrician if the wound looks deep, infection appears, or if tetanus vaccinations are not up to date.

Superficial splinters often work their way out of the skin on their own. But to speed up the process, soak the affected area in warm water and Epsom salts for half an hour several times every day. You can try removing a splinter following the steps shown below. However, if it is large, deep, or dirty, or if the splinter is a metal or glass fragment, consult your pediatrician.

1 Before removing a splinter of wood, numb the area by rubbing the skin with an ice cube.

2 Sterilize a needle with rubbing alcohol, then slip it under the skin above the splinter. Gently pull the needle up to make a slight tear in the skin. Then, slide the needle under the splinter and raise it up.

3 Use tweezers to grasp the splinter and pull it back and out along the line of entry.

4 Wash the area thoroughly with soap and water.

FOREIGN OBJECTS

What can I do?

If you suspect your child has something stuck in her eye, ear, or nose, look for the object carefully and remove it only if the procedure can be done easily. Otherwise, take her to your pediatrician to have the object removed.

In the eye

If your child has a stray eyelash or speck of sand in the eye, get her to blink several times to produce tears. If the tears don't wash it away, pull the upper eyelid down over the lower eyelid and hold it in place for a few minutes. If this doesn't work, examine her eye under a good light. Gently lift the upper eyelid to expose the particle against the white part of her eye and dab at it carefully with the corner of a clean handkerchief. Alternatively, rinse the object out of the eye with water from an eyecup or eyedropper.

In the ear

Children sometimes get things stuck in their ears. Whether it's an object such as a button or an insect, don't let your child try to dislodge it herself by thumping on her head. You should not try to remove anything unless it's in plain sight and you can grasp it with your fingertips. If this isn't possible, take her to your pediatrician or the hospital right away to have it removed.

Don't try to flush an object from your child's ear. If the trapped item can absorb water, it may swell up and become even more difficult to remove. Flushing also increases the risk of infection, especially if the eardrum has been perforated. However, if your child has a buzzing insect in the ear, you may put in a few drops of mineral or baby oil to help ease her discomfort.

SWALLOWED OBJECTS

Infants and toddlers do a great deal of exploring with their mouths; many will swallow any small item that strikes their fancy—including coins, marbles, safety pins, needles, and eyes that can be pulled off stuffed toys. Youngsters need constant monitoring during early years. Frequent vacuuming and sweeping of areas where she crawls and plays will pick up most of the hazardous items that might catch her eye.

Most of the little things your child may pick up and swallow will pass through her system without difficulty and reappear in her stools within a few days. There is danger, though, if an object lodges in her windpipe; treat her for choking (page 235). Otherwise, call your pediatrician if:

- she has any pain or discomfort
- she experiences difficulty breathing or swallowing, or she drools after having swallowed an object
- she swallows a large object or one with sharp edges
- an object she swallows doesn't reappear in her stools within a week

In the nose

A foreign object in your child's nose may go undetected for several days. The first sign may be a foul-smelling, possibly blood-tinged discharge that signals a nasal infection. Or, your child may have difficulty breathing through the affected nostril. Ask her to blow her nose several times to try to dislodge the object. Then, examine her nostril under a bright light. If you can see the object clearly and can grasp it easily with your fingers, try to remove it; otherwise, take her to your pediatrician to have it removed. Avoid trying to remove the object with a tool that may accidentally push the object further into the nose.

If your child's eye seems irritated, examine it carefully under a bright light. If you can't see anything that may be causing irritation, he may have an eye infection and should go to see your pediatrician.

BURNS IN THE EYE

Take your child for emergency treatment if she burns her eye with ash, chemicals, or any corrosive material. Unless it's a deep burn, flush the eye with cool running water for a few minutes and cover it with sterile gauze before you go. For a deep burn on the eye, just cover the wound with gauze and take her immediately to the hospital.

POISONING

What should I look for?

Poisoning symptoms vary according to the type of poison ingested or inhaled. Suspect poisoning if you find your child playing with any medicine container, or if he exhibits abdominal pain, vomiting or diarrhea, burns or discoloration on the lips, mouth, and tongue, unusual drowsiness, convulsions, loss of consciousness, or the symptoms of shock (page 247). He may appear agitated and have hallucinations, or his eyes may flicker or dart.

What can I do?

If you think your child has been poisoned, act swiftly. Check his mouth for pills or other evidence of an ingested poison. Remove him from the source of poisonous fumes; if necessary, cover your mouth with a cloth before moving him to fresh air. If he has stopped breathing, begin mouth-to-mouth resuscitation (page 230).

Before calling your emergency poison control number, try to establish the identity of the poison, how much was ingested, and when the poisoning took place. Look for the source of the poison; the container that held an ingested substance is likely to be nearby. When you call the emergency line, the instructions on the container label will help emergency personnel tell you what first aid to give before taking your child for treatment. If your child swallowed an acid, alkali, or petroleum product, or if he is not awake and alert, don't make him vomit. Keep him upright to prevent the poison from reentering his esophagus and have him drink one to two glasses of milk or water. But if your child swallowed a prescription drug or household product that doesn't contain acid, alkali, or petroleum, you may be told to induce vomiting with syrup of ipecac—¾ tablespoon for a baby, 1 for a toddler or older child. Take a sample of vomit and the poison container with you for analysis when you go for emergency treatment.

POISONING PREVENTION

Protect your child against accidental poisoning by observing the following commonsense guidelines:

• Buy all medications and household products in child-resistant containers and never transfer them to containers that were once used for food.
• Throw out leftover medicines.
• Never refer to medicine as candy.
• Never take medication in front of very young children whose curiosity might lead them to copy you.
• Read the labels on household products before buying them and find the least toxic one for the job. Buy only what you need for immediate use.

• Don't underestimate your child's agility or curiosity; keep potential poisons—including medicine, vitamins, mouthwash, alcohol, and household cleaning products—locked away.
• Don't keep cleaning products under the kitchen sink unless the cabinet is equipped with a secure safety lock.
• Use stickers to identify poison containers. Teach your child what the stickers mean.
• Don't leave a poisonous substance unattended; even for a short interruption, cap it and take it with you.
• Post your poison control number by the phone.

EMERGENCY

Get medical help immediately if you think your child has been poisoned.

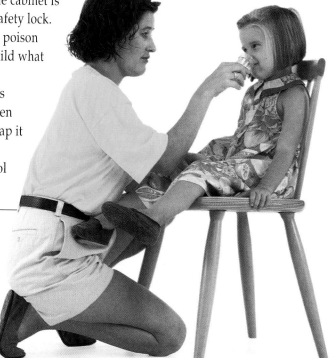

If you think your child may have swallowed a chemical product, wash off her lips, give her a glass of milk or water, and call your poison control center or hospital emergency room for further instructions.

BURNS

What can I do?

If your child burns himself, immediately lower the temperature of the burn by placing the affected skin under slowly running cool—not ice cold—water. Or, soak the area in a basin of cool water or apply cool, damp cloths. Keep the burn cooled until the pain subsides. If water isn't available, use a cool liquid that is. Remove any part of his clothing that has been touched by the burning substance unless it sticks to the burned area. In this case, cut away the fabric. Don't apply antiseptic sprays or ointments to burns. Elevate a burned limb higher than the heart. Give acetaminophen for pain and make sure your child drinks plenty of fluids. Watch for signs of shock (page 247). If blisters form, be careful not to break them and don't peel off any skin that comes loose as the burn begins to heal.

If your child's clothes catch on fire, grab the nearest blanket, towel, or coat and wrap him up in it to smother the flames.

Apply a cool, wet compress to the burn to ease discomfort and keep it moist. Then, bandage it with a loose dressing of sterile gauze.

> **EMERGENCY**
> Seek medical help immediately if:
> • a burn covers an area that is larger than the child's hand
> • a burn occurs to the face, hands, feet, or pelvic area
> • a burn leaves the skin looking charred; it may be red, white, or black in color
> • a burn is due to electrical shock

CHEMICAL SPLASHES

What can I do?

If your child splashes a liquid chemical such as drain or oven cleaner, paint stripper, or battery acid on his skin, immediately flush the area with cool running water. Be careful not to let the water spread the chemical to unaffected areas of the skin or to his eyes; don't rub the burned skin. As the water runs over the affected area, remove any clothing that has been splashed. For powdered lime or other dry chemicals, brush the chemicals off first and then put the affected area under cool running water. After flushing all traces of the chemical from the skin, blot the area dry with a clean cloth. Cover the burn loosely with a sterile bandage. If it is severe, keep it moistened. In all cases of a serious chemical burn, take your child to the nearest hospital. Chemical burns to the eye need immediate medical care.

> **EMERGENCY**
> If your child gets splashed by a potentially dangerous chemical, give him first aid immediately and then get him to the hospital for emergency treatment. Don't try to neutralize a chemical without specific instructions from a doctor or your local poison control center.

HEATSTROKE

What can I do?

Heatstroke is a medical emergency that requires an immediate response. It can occur when a child is in a very hot place, such as a beach. Never leave a child alone in a closed car. Symptoms include hot, dry, red, or pale skin; a body temperature over 104°F; an absence of sweating; and a strong, rapid pulse. Your child may have a headache, dizziness, confusion, or even lose consciousness. Your priority is to lower her temperature and give her plenty of liquids. Remove her clothing and place her in a tub of cool water. Alternatively, sponge her down with cool water or spray her with a garden hose until her temperature drops to at least 102°F. Call an ambulance or take her right away to the hospital, keeping her as cool as possible on the way. Give her a cool drink—but not anything that contains alcohol or caffeine.

EMERGENCY
If your child suffers heatstroke, give first aid immediately and get her to a hospital for treatment.

One way to quickly lower the temperature of a young heatstroke victim is to soak a sheet in cold water and wrap her up in it. Then, take her right away to the hospital.

FROSTBITE

What can I do?

Your child is more vulnerable to frost-bite than you are because her circulatory system isn't fully developed yet. If her skin gets so cold that it turns red and stings a lot, goes grey and mottled, or blisters, it must be thawed gradually in warm water. Since frostbitten areas become numb, keep her from sitting too close to a radiator or fire as she may burn herself without realizing it. If you can't go indoors, warm frozen extremities in your hands or tuck them in your armpits. After giving her first aid, call your pediatrician as soon as possible for advice. If her skin is waxy, white, and feels hard to the touch, she has third-degree frostbite; quickly get her to the hospital for treatment.

EMERGENCY
Seek medical help immediately if your child shows signs of third-degree frost-bite—numbness and waxy, white skin that is hard to the touch.

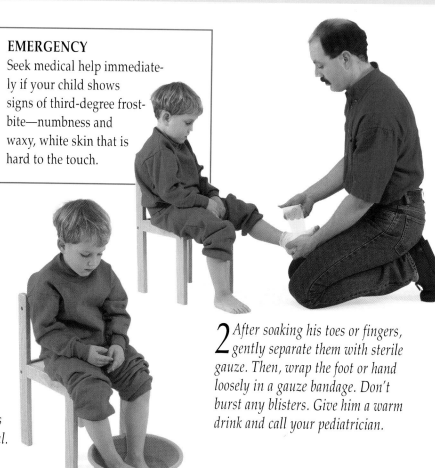

1 Get him to soak frostbitten extremities in warm water that doesn't exceed 110°F. As they thaw, they will swell and be very painful.

2 After soaking his toes or fingers, gently separate them with sterile gauze. Then, wrap the foot or hand loosely in a gauze bandage. Don't burst any blisters. Give him a warm drink and call your pediatrician.

ELECTRICAL SHOCK

What can I do?

Electrical burns may look small, but can be quite deep. If your child is still conscious after receiving an electrical shock, comfort her and watch for signs of shock (page 247). Treat any burn by wrapping it lightly in sterile gauze. Don't put the burn in water. Call your pediatrician and monitor your child's vital signs (page 228); be ready to begin mouth-to-mouth resuscitation (page 230) or cardiopulmonary resuscitation (page 232). Once your child's condition is stable, place her in the recovery position (page 234).

1 If your child is frozen by a live current, shut off the power at the main electrical service panel. Alternatively, stand on a dry rubber mat, towel, or pile of newspapers and separate your child from the source of the current using a broom handle or other wooden tool. If you have a wood-handled axe or insulated wire cutters nearby, cut any live wires.

2 If there is no wooden tool nearby, wrap your hand in a dry cloth for protection and grab hold of your child's clothes—not his skin—to drag him away from the source of the current.

EMERGENCY
Seek medical help immediately if:
- your child loses consciousness
- your child stops breathing or her heart stops beating

DROWNING

What should I know?

Infants and young children are especially vulnerable to drowning, even in the shallow water of a wading pool or bathtub. When their faces become submerged in water, their automatic response is to open their mouths in an attempt to scream.

What can I do?

Once your child has been removed from the water, your first priority is to check her vital signs (page 228). If she's gasping for air or unconscious but still breathing, lie her in the recovery position (page 234) to let the water drain from her mouth. Remove her wet cloth-ing and wrap her in a warm blanket or coat. Call for emergency medical help.

If she has stopped breathing, clear any debris such as mud or seaweed from her mouth and immediately begin mouth-to-mouth resuscitation (page 230)—even as she is carried from the water. Continue giving her artificial respiration until she begins to breathe on her own or emergency help arrives.

EMERGENCY
If your child almost drowns, give first aid immediately and get her to the hospital for treatment.

GETTING TO SAFETY
A drowning child is a lot stronger than she may seem; when rescuing her, be careful not to let her struggles pull you under the water. If she's conscious and close to land, extend a pole or safety ring for her to grab, being sure to keep your own body low and away from the water's edge. If she's further away, you may need to wade into the water until you can give her something to grab on to. If she's unconscious, pull her to safety while keeping her nose and mouth above the water.

SUFFOCATION

What should I know?

Babies between birth and three months are most at risk for suffocation because they lack the strength to lift their heads and turn their faces away from the suffocating material. Place your newborn on his side or back for sleeping, and keep feather pillows and comforters out of his crib. And never let your child play with plastic bags; children have been known to suffocate in them.

What can I do?

Quickly remove your child from whatever is causing him to suffocate and check his vital signs (page 228). If he's conscious, comfort and reassure him. If he's unconscious but breathing, place him in the recovery position (page 234) and call for emergency help. If he stops breathing, give him mouth-to-mouth resuscitation (page 230). If he has no pulse, start cardiopulmonary resuscitation (page 232). Continue your first-aid measures until emergency help arrives.

SUDDEN INFANT DEATH

Sudden infant death syndrome (SIDS)—also known as crib death—is the sudden, unexplained death of an infant who showed no previous signs of illness. In the U.S., one or two newborns out of every one thousand die of SIDS each year. Infants between four and 16 weeks are most at risk. SIDS occurs more often in winter among low-birthweight male infants and appears to recur in families. Risk factors include premature birth and mothers who smoked during pregnancy. Children who sleep lying on their backs or sides appear to have a reduced risk.

EMERGENCY

Get medical help immediately if your child loses consciousness or displays any other symptoms that cause you to worry.

CONVULSIONS

What should I know?

A convulsion, or seizure, is produced by a disturbance in the normal electrical brain activity. Among the possible triggers are things such as a high fever, brain injury, or electrical shock. Most convulsions last less than five minutes and are rarely life-threatening.

What do I look for?

If your child has a convulsion, he may lose consciousness, wet his pants or lose bowel control, and display involuntary muscle spasms, clench his teeth, and roll his eyes back in his head.

What can I do?

To keep your child from hurting himself during the convulsion, clear the area around him. Don't try to restrain his movements unless it is absolutely necessary in order to prevent him from injuring himself. Stay calm; he won't swallow his tongue as he convulses. If he has a fever, reduce it with sponging and give him the recommended dose of acetaminophen after he has become alert. Call your pediatrician immediately for advice.

EMERGENCY

If your child happens to stop breathing during a convulsion, give first aid immediately and get him to the hospital for treatment.

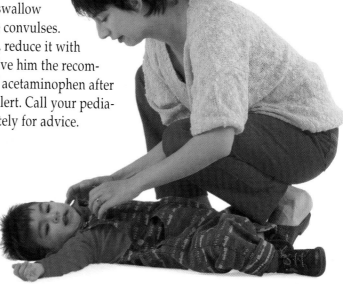

Protect a convulsing child from injury by clearing the area, and loosen any tight clothing at his neck and waist.

FAINTING

What should I look for?

Fainting is a temporary loss of consciousness that occurs when there is an insufficient supply of blood to the brain. If your child is about to faint, he is likely to feel dizzy and nauseous and look pale and sweaty. His vision also may blur, and his hands and feet may feel tingly or numb.

EMERGENCY

If your child faints and does not regain consciousness within a few minutes, get him to the hospital immediately for medical treatment.

What can I do?

If your child faints, position him on his back and elevate his legs eight to 12 inches off the ground. Keep him warm with a coat or blanket while you wipe his forehead and face with a cool, damp cloth. If he starts to vomit, turn his head to one side. Afterwards, clear his mouth of anything like mucus or vomit that may block his breathing. Report his fainting spell to your pediatrician right away.

If your child is about to faint, get her to sit on a chair and bend her head down between her knees. Wiggling her toes will help to stimulate her blood circulation.

SHOCK

What should I look for?

If your child suffers a severe injury—such as a burn or heavy bleeding—or if he has had prolonged diarrhea or vomiting, watch him closely for symptoms of shock. These include pale, clammy skin; bluish lips; a weak, rapid pulse; shallow breathing; sunken eyes; and lethargy.

If your child develops an extreme allergic reaction to a drug, or an insect or animal bite, he may go into anaphylactic shock. Symptoms include breathing difficulties, a tingling sensation around the face, swelling, hives, itchy eyes, and cramps.

Shock is a life-threatening condition. Elevate his feet about eight inches to help the blood circulate to his vital organs.

What can I do?

Call for emergency help immediately. If your child is having an anaphylactic reaction, give him antihistamines. Lie him down and elevate his feet above the level of the heart—unless his leg is fractured or he has received a poisonous bite. If he is having difficulty breathing and there is no possibility of a head injury, you may prop up his head and neck with a pillow. Loosen tight clothing and cover him with a blanket or coat. If he complains of thirst, just moisten his lips with a wet cloth. If he has been burned, you may give him tiny sips of water.

EMERGENCY

Call an ambulance or immediately take your child to the hospital if he displays the symptoms of shock.

ADOLESCENCE AND TOMORROW'S ADULT

*S*ynonymous for many parents with rebellion and alienation, adolescence is often considered a stage to be endured. But the reality of adolescence bears little resemblance to its myth, so you needn't fear the worst or wish that your child could bypass the period altogether.

Celebrate your child's adolescence; an invigorating stage, it's loaded with promise and charged with excitement for both of you. As she shapes her identity and takes her place in the world, the pace and intensity of her experimentation with roles, ideas, and relationships may astound you. Make the most of this special opportunity to reflect on your own life and reexperience for yourself some of the unbridled exuberance and passion that you carried into adulthood.

Without question, there will be some trying times. As your child struggles to secure his identity, find his place among his peers and in the community, and move toward financial independence, he's bound to take a few missteps. Conflict over issues such as drug-taking or sexual activity may be unavoidable as you strive to reconcile his right to decide with your worry about his choices. Finding a comfortable equilibrium may be your biggest challenge as a parent. But there's no agenda to follow in arriving at adulthood, so try not to feel too pressured; there will be plenty of time to work things out.

Respect your adolescent's increasing maturity, but don't interpret signs of her independence too literally. While she may not ask you as often for help with her homework and may seem more reticent about confiding in you, she still needs you to be a parent. Don't let the psychological and physical changes of puberty overshadow the importance of your continuing emotional support. In loosening your strings so she can learn about life's realities, you'll want her to know that your bond of love is just as tight as ever—and will be, no matter what.

Although there's no recipe for adulthood, knowing how to make decisions is an essential ingredient. Encouraging your child to decide things for himself will be of great benefit to him during adolescence. By letting him make choices about clothing, for instance, you've shown trust in his judgments and helped his self-confidence. In settling disagreements in an open, reasonable, and positive way, you've helped him learn to resolve conflicts through discussion and compromise. By having admitted you were wrong from time to time, you've helped teach him to base his self-esteem on realistic expectations. His adolescence won't be as fraught with turmoil if you simply continue to put your emphasis on helping him to develop ways of coping with stressful challenges. With your unconditional love and appropriate limits on behavior, he'll mature in his capacity to make wise decisions and successfully handle the many competing demands on his life—from friends, school, as well as family.

INDEX

ACKNOWLEDGMENTS

Studio Photographer Christian Lévesque
Studio Coordinator Valery Pigeon-Dumas

Philippe Alarie, Chanel Arbour, Vanessa Arbour, Suzanne Aubut, Gabriel Aubut-Lussier, Jade Aubut-Lussier, Ludovic Aubut-Lussier, Alain Baccanale, Hugo Baccanale, Dominique Bastien, Yan Beauchamp, Marie-Michelle Beaudry, Étienne Beaulieu, Nathalie Bellerose, Félix Belzil-Desrochers, Max Belzil-Desrochers, Philippe Benny, Gilles Benoit, Guillaume Benoit-Martineau, Vincent Benoit-Martineau, Mireille Bessette, Chantal Bilodeau, Danielle Bishop, Estelle Boileau, Lyne Bouchard, Émile Bouchard, Jade Brossard, Alessio A. Brotto, Egidio Brotto, Salina Y. Brotto, Elizabeth Cameron, Emily Cameron, Simon Cantin, Maxime Carisse, Jesse Carmichael, Josée Caron, Richard Carrier, Marc Cassini, Alexander Cassini-Brochu, Eric Cassini-Brochu, Maxime Ceballos, Sonia Ceballos, Denis Chabot, Lucien Chabot, Marie-Esther Chabot, Virgile Chabot, Monique Chamberland, Sylvain Chayer, Jean Coutu, Kevin Coutu, Mathieu Coutu, Zelia Craveiro, Christine Côté, Claudia Daoust, Joe Delaney, Diane Denoncourt, Marc-André Denoncourt, Marie-France Denoncourt, Sophie Denoncourt, Korinne Desmarais, Louis-Olivier Desmarais, Pierre Desmarais, Lili Desrochers, Nathalie Dinh, Lê-anh Dinh-Williams, Hélène Dion, Colin Dion-Martel, Jérémy Dionne, Maryse Doray, Karine Doré, Lorraine Doré, Ronald Doré, Vanessa Doré, Danyelle Drouin, Gabrielle Drouin, Stéphane Dubuc, Donald Dufort, Nicholas Dufort, Laurent Dufresne, Michel Dufresne, Natalie Dugré, Pierre Dussault, Lise Dénomée, Alexis Dénomée-Godin, Antoine Dénomée-Godin, Michel D'Aoust, Jamie D'Souza, Stacey D'Souza, Clifford Erlington, Valérie Favron, Anthony Favron-Kneeshaw, Chantal Filion, Andrée Filion Chabot, Frédéric Fortin, Suzanne Francoeur, David Frankel, Jeffrey Frankel, Alexis Freedman-Gervais, Sylvie Gadbois, Béatrice Gadbois-Filion, Monique Gagnon, Dominique Gagné, France Gagné, Marc-Anthony Gagné, Lise Gaudreault, Anika Gerols, Diane Giguère, Louise Giguère, Marie-Paule Gratton, Thomas Gravel, Catherine Grenier, Laurence Grenier, Andrée-Anne Guesthier, Marc-Antoine Guesthier, Sabrina Guesthier, Vincent Guesthier, Cristelle Henry, Emmanuelle-Fay Henry, Danielle Hervieux, Ariel Home-Douglas, Pierre Home-Douglas, Félix Huard, Jérôme Huard, Guillaume Huot, Céline Hébert, Dominique Janelle, Michelle Janelle, Jean-Sébastien Jodoin, Nicolas Jodoin, Annie Jolicoeur, Mathieu Jolicoeur, Marie Joubert, David Joubert Leclerc, Daniel Kneeshaw, Camille Lachapelle, Denis Lachapelle, Marie-France Lacoste, Samuel Lafontaine, Guillaume Lafortune, Jonathan Lafortune, Suzanne Lagacé, Danielle Lambert, Angélie Langlois, Marie-Alex Langlois, Gaspard Larochelle D'Aoust, Katheryn Larose, Jason Lau, Thierry Lavergne, Maude Lavoie-St-Laurent, Alfred LeMaitre, Maya LeMaitre, Lyne Leclair, Patrick Leclair, Valérie Leclair, Jérémie Leclerc, Justine Leduc, Elizabeth Lewis, Nathaniel Lewis-George, Amélie Loiseau, Gabriel Loiseau, Marilyne Loiseau, Pierre Loiseau, Valérie Luneau, Pierre-André Lussier, Rob Lutes, Anne Léger, Gisèle Lévis, Emanuel L'Espérance, Micheline L'Espérance, Rachel Mantha, Alex Manua Desfontaine, Michelle McRae, Nathalie Meloche, Jenny Meltzer, Karina Mercier, Sarah Mercier Valbrun, Heather Mills, Jonathan Mills, Zachary Mills, Gina Molino, Carol Mordy, Marie-Josée Normandin, Camille Normandin-Corriveau, Ève Normandin-Corriveau, Katryn Oblak, Éric Ouellet, Ariane Paradis, Ashlinn Parsons, Brendan Parsons, Brian Parsons, Caitlin Parsons, Cassandra Patenaude, Claude Patenaude, Martin Pelland, Maude Pelland, France Picard, Louis-Philippe Picard, Félix Picard-Duperré, Laurie Picard-Duperré, Valery Pigeon-Dumas, Gabriel Piotte, Maxime Piotte, Stéphanie Piotte, Charles Plamondon-Dubois, Geneviève Plamondon-Dubois, Isabelle Plamondon-Dubois, Carole Pomerleau, Lise Pomerleau, Thierry Pomerleau Benny, Nicole Poulin, Guy Prévost, Julie Prévost, Mathieu Prévost, Charles Renaud, Blanche Richer, Danielle Richer, Marie-Pier Richer, Jean-François Rivet, Guylaine Robert, Emma Robitaille, Louis-Philippe Robitaille, Marie-Ève Rochon, Danielle Rodrigue, Victoria Roffey, Lana Romandini, Arianne Romby, Pascal Roy, Patrick Roy, Robin Saldahna, Michael Saldanha, Sarah Saldanha, Jérôme Savard Gratton, Ophélie Savard Gratton, Marc-André Senécal, Kim Snyder, Joëlle Sévigny, Laurent Sévigny, Marie-Lou Sévigny, Ève Sévigny, Laurence Tanguay Carrier, Jason Tavares, Coryne Thibault, Sophie Thibault, Gabriel Thibodeau, Sean Kristopher Thomas Erlington, Amélie Thériault, Éric Thériault, Martine Tousignant, Thomas Tousignant, Suzanne Tremblay, Emanuelle Tremblay-Ouellet, Frédérique Tremblay-Ouellet, Marcia Turbide, André Vaillancourt, Marilyne Vaillancourt, Martine Vaillancourt, Roxanne Vaillancourt, Simon Vaillancourt, Antoine Vaillancourt-Larocque, Emmanuel Vaillancourt-Larocque, Christiane Voyer, Anne-Sophie Vézina, Esther Vézina, Jocelyn Wakefield.

Photo Researcher Geneviève Monette
Scanner Operators Martin Francoeur, Sara Grynspan
Systems Coordinator Éric Beaulieu

194 (left) Custom Medical Stock Photo; 194 (middle) J.F. Wilson, Science Source/Photo Researchers; 194 (right), 195 (upper) Courtesy of the American Academy of Dermatology; 195 (lower), 196 (upper) Custom Medical Stock Photo; 196 (lower), 197 (upper) Courtesy of the Centers for Disease Control and Prevention; 197 (lower) Biophoto Associates/Science Source/Photo Researchers; 198 (upper) Custom Medical Stock Photo; 198 (lower) Courtesy of the American Academy of Dermatology; 199 Biophoto Associates/Science Source/Photo Researchers; 200 (from top to bottom) Rick Brady, The Stock Shop, Inc/Medichrome; Custom Medical Stock Photo; Custom Medical Stock Photo; David York, The Stock Shop, Inc/Medichrome; Michael Tamborrino, The Stock Shop, Inc/Medichrome; Biophoto Associates/Science Source/Photo Researchers; 201 (upper) Custom Medical Stock Photo; 201 (lower), 203 (upper top) Courtesy of the American Academy of Dermatology; 203 (upper bottom) Courtesy of the Centers for Disease Control and Prevention; 203 (lower left) Courtesy of the Jardin Botanique de la Ville de Montréal; 203 (lower middle) Courtesy of the Royal Botanical Gardens, Hamilton, Canada; 203 (lower right) Courtesy of the Jardin Botanique de la Ville de Montréal, Photo by Romeo Meloche; 204 Courtesy of the American Academy of Dermatology; 205 Custom Medical Stock Photo; 207 (upper) Biophoto Associates/Science Source/Photo Researchers; 207 (lower) Sue Ford/Science Photo Library/Photo Researchers; 211 St. Bartholomew's Hospital/Science Photo/Photo Researchers; 222 (both) Courtesy of the Centers for Disease Control and Prevention; 223 (upper) Courtesy of Diane Denoncourt; 223 (lower), 224 Courtesy of the Centers for Disease Control and Prevention.

The editors also wish to thank the following persons for their assistance:

Philippe Arnoldi, Elizabeth Cameron, Lorraine Doré, Dominique Gagné, Pascale Hueber, Megan Newman, Jane Pavanel, Maryo Proulx, Edward Renault, Dr. Harold Rich, Dr. Corinne Saunders, Jennifer Thomas, Jennifer Williams, Judy Yelon.